STEP BY STEP:
A PROGRAM FOR CHILDREN
AND FAMILIES

CREATING
CHILD-CENTERED
CLASSROOMS:
3-5 YEAR OLDS

**Pamela A. Coughlin, Kirsten A. Hansen, Dinah Heller,
Roxane K. Kaufmann, Judith Rothschild Stolberg,
Kate Burke Walsh**

Foreword by Pamela A. Coughlin

Children's Resources International, Inc.
Washington, DC

Library of Congress Catalog Card Number: 97-069001

The Step by Step Program is a collaboration project of the Open Society Institute, the network of Soros Foundations and Children's Resources International. The Soros Foundations/Open Society Institute is a network of foundations, programs, and institutions established and supported by philanthropist George Soros to foster the development of Open Societies around the world, particularly in the former communist countries of Central and Eastern Europe and the former Soviet Union. To this end the Soros Foundation cooperates with Children's Resources International to develop and implement the project called Step by Step: A Program for Children and Families.

CRI, a nonprofit organization located in Washington, D.C., promotes the implementation of sound educational practices developed in the United States while maintaining the cultural traditions of the participating countries.

Open Society Institute, New York
888 Seventh Avenue
New York, New York 10106
212.757.2323 *phone*
212.974.0367 *fax*
E-Mail: oshews@sorosny.org

Children's Resources International, Inc.
2262 Hall Place, N.W., Suite 205
Washington, D.C., 20007
202.625.2508 *phone*
202.625.2509*fax*
E-Mail: CRIInc@aol.com

FOREWORD

This is the first of a series of publications developed under the Step by Step Program. Step by Step began in 1994 when George Soros dedicated substantial resources of his Open Society Institute for an early childhood education project in Central and Eastern Europe and countries of the former Soviet Union. The purpose of this compelling education initiative was to develop a new participatory citizenry beginning with the youngest members of society and to draw families into the education of their children for the first time.

The Step by Step Program introduced developmentally appropriate teaching techniques from the United States to the well-established early care and education system in the countries that chose to adopt the program. An essential part of the implementation of the Step by Step Program was the development of a written curriculum, *Creating Child-Centered Classrooms*. It provides teachers with a guide for the establishment of a classroom environment designed around activity centers, involvement of families in classrooms and the larger school community, and individualization of teaching geared to the needs and interests of each child.

The Step by Step Program uses *Creating Child-Centered Classrooms* in combination with on-going training. Each country team, responsible for implementation of the program, is coupled with two or more trainers from the United States who offer on-going assistance. *Creating Child-Centered Classrooms* has been accepted by the Ministries of Education as an alternative curriculum in the participating countries and has been translated into their languages.

In the first year, the program was operational in 250 classrooms, burgeoning in the second year to more than 1500 classrooms serving over 37,500 children. Step by Step grew not only in participation, but in scope. It subsequently developed complementary programs for children from birth to three years, in primary grades, launched a higher education initiative for pedagogic faculties, and published *Education and the Culture of Democracy: Early Childhood Practice*, a text that links early childhood teaching and democracy.

This document attests to the tireless work of our partners who implemented the program in Central and Eastern Europe and countries of the former Soviet Union. It is they who have made the dream we dreamed come true. We hope its application will lead others to the realization of active participation in open societies.

Pam Coughlin
Children's Resources International

TABLE OF CONTENTS

Foreword..iii

Table of Contents..v

Acknowledgements xii

Introduction..xiv

PART ONE: Child-Centered Thinking
I.   Introduction, Philosophy, and Program Rationale 1
           Introduction 1
           Philosophy of the Step by Step Program 2
           Approaches to Early Childhood Education........................2
           Three Major Tenets of the Step by Step Program.................4
           Individualizing the Learning Experience 6
           Activity Centers..7
           Family Participation...11
           What Are Developmentally Appropriate Activities 12
           Making Philosophy Happen 15

II.   Goals and Developmental Guidelines 19
           Goals and Developmental Guidelines 19
           Goals 19
           Age Related Characteristics 21
           Common Characteristics of Three-Year-Old Children 22
           Common Characteristics of Four-Year-Old Children 22
           Common Characteristics of Five-Year-Old Children 23
           Chart of Normal Development 25

PART TWO: Family Participation
III.   Family Participation 35
           Philosophy 35
           The Benefits of Family Participation 36
           Opportunities for Collaboration 38
           Strategies for Communicating with Families 40
           *Tips for Using Bulletin Boards 42
           Families in the Classroom 45

Welcoming Families to the Classroom 46
Instructions for Activities 48
*Explanation of a Preschool Dramatic Play Center 49
Showing Appreciation 50
*Note for a Participating Family Member 51
*General Information for Families in the Classroom 52
*Showing Appreciation to Family Members 53
Getting Men Involved 54
Family Meetings and Gatherings 55
Discover Family Interests 57
*Family Interest Form 58
*Determining Family Interests: Staff Review Sheet 60
Planning Informal Events or Gatherings....................................60
Activities to Promote Family Participation 62
Evaluating Family Meetings 64
*Family Meeting Evaluation Checklist.......................................65
Confidentiality 66
*Suggested Guidelines for Maintaining Confidentiality................68
*Suggested Opportunities for Family Participation 69

IV.   Building Community 73
Setting the Tone...74
*Ways to Show Respect for Children in the Classroom.................75
Teaching about Diversity..76
Teaching Responsibility 78
Decision Making 79
Classroom Rules 80
*Promoting Cultural Diversity and Cultural Competency 84

V.   Observing, Recording, and Reporting Children's Development 91
Observing and Recording 91
What to Observe 96
Reporting Information to Families 104
*Observation Checklist for Teachers..108
*Sample MidYear Narrative Report 113
*Student Progress Report 115

VI.   Planning the Integrated Curriculum 123
Need for Long- and Short-Term Planning...................................123
Importance of a Written Plan 124
Planning the Daily Schedule 124

Preparing Families for Preschool 130
Planning Thematic Projects...132
How to Develop a Thematic Project 133
*Thematic Project Planning Sheet 137
Factors to be Considered in Planning 139
*Example of Individualizing an Activity 141
Documenting and Tracking Individual Progress....................141
*Sample Daily Schedule for Three- and Four-Year-Olds 142
*Sample Daily Schedule for Five- and Six-Year-Olds 143
*Friendship Theme Web 144
*Farm Web..145
*Weekly Schedule 146
*Monthly Schedule 147

PART THREE: Child-Centered Learning
VII.   Designing the Learning Environment 153
*The Classroom Environment Checklist....................................156
Classroom Safety 157
*Safety Checklist....................................157
*Classroom Arrangement Chart 159
*Classroom Arrangement Chart 160

VIII.. Art..163
Children at Play: The Art Activity Center 163
Impact on Developmental Areas 167
Setting Up the Art Activity Center 168
The Teaching Team's Role 169
Stimulating Creative Activity 170
"Do's" and "Don'ts" for Encouraging Children's Interest in Art ..171
Activities and Projects....................................173

IX.   Blocks 183
Children at Play: The Block Activity Center 183
Stages in Block Building....................................183
Impact on Developmental Areas 184
Setting Up the Block Activity Center 186
The Teaching Team's Role 188
Activities and Projects....................................190

X.   Cooking..195
        Children at Play: Cooking and Learning about Food 195
        Impact on Developmental Areas 196
        Setting Up for Cooking 198
        The Teaching Team's Role 200
        Safety Is Most Important...202
        Activities and Projects...204
        Recipes...207

XI.   Dramatic Play 215
        Impact on Developmental Areas 216
        Role of Dramatic Play in the Preschool Curriculum 218
        Integrating Creative Drama and Play with Activity Centers 219
        Setting Up a Dramatic Play Activity Center 220
        The Teaching Team's Role 222
        How to Nurture Dramatic Play 224
        Activities and Projects...225

XII. Literacy 239
        Children at Play: The Literacy Center 239
        The Teaching Team's Role 241
        Activities and Projects...241
        Samples of Children's Work 244
        *Conditions for Natural Language Learning 248

XIII. Mathematics/Manipulatives 251
        Children at Play: Mathematics/Manipulatives 251
        Integrating Mathematics into the Daily Schedule..................253
        Integrating Mathematics with the Other Activity Centers 255
        Setting Up a Mathematics/Manipulatives Are 256
        The Teaching Team's Role 260
        Mathematical Activities and Projects 260

XIV. Music 265
        Children at Play: Music in the Classroom 265
        Impact on Developmental Areas 265
        Integrating Music into the Classroom Schedule 268
        The Teaching Team's Role 269
        Music Activities and Projects 270

XV.   Outdoors 277

      Children at Play: The Outdoors 277

      Impact on Developmental Areas 278

      Setting Up the Outdoor Environment 281

      Playing Areas 282

      The Teaching Team's Role 286

      Special Considerations for Outdoor Activity 287

      Expanding Children's Outdoor Learning 289

      Activities and Projects 291

XVI. Sand and Water 301

      Children at Play: The Sand and Water Activity Center...........301

      Impact on Developmental Areas 301

      Setting Up the Sand and Water Activity Center 303

      The Teaching Team's Role 305

      Activities and Projects 306

      Making Paper - A Project for the Water Table 307

XVII. Science 313

      Children at Play: The Science Activity Center 313

      Setting Up a Science Program...314

      Integrating Science Skills with Activity Centers 316

      The Teaching Team's Role 317

      Science Activities and Projects 319

      References..325

      Publications...331

* Indicates a chart or figure

ACKNOWLEDGMENTS

We want to thank Mr. George Soros for his support of this document and the Step by Step Program. It is remarkable that he has spent his personal time and energy in reviewing the plan and conceptual framework of this project. He has truly demonstrated his belief that the early years of a child's life are important.

We would not have embarked on this adventure without Liz Lorant,who believed in the dream and held our hand every step of the way. We admire her dedication to the families and children of the emerging democracies in Eastern and Central Europe and the countries of the former Soviet Union. Her humor has kept us smiling and her intelligence has clarified the vision.

We appreciate the personal interest of Sarah Klaus. She has kept us on track and has helped support the implementation of this methodology throughout Europe.

Without the humor, guidance, and tenacity of the Children's Resources International (CRI) executive team, under the guidance of Pam Coughlin, this document would not be reality. We thank Julie Empson and Carolyn Rutsch for their reviews.

The efforts of many people went into the development and production of this publication. We want to thank everyone for their support, energy, and dedication to the project. The rich traditions of Eastern and Central Europe and the countries of the former Soviet Union have enhanced and made real the words written in this document. We are truly appreciative of the extremely hard work and dedication of the country directors and master teacher trainers who have made this project more successful than we could have imagined.

Several people contributed to the development of the content. These people include:

Elanor Cato	Liz Kuhlman
Neal Fitzpatrick	Mary Marcoux
Nancye Hesaltine	Steffen Saifer
Adelle Jacobs	Tawara Taylor
Suzana Kirandzikda	Sylvia Thompson
	Jim Welch

A thank you goes to the staffs of Greenacres School in Rockville, Maryland, and

A thank you goes to the staffs of Greenacres School in Rockville, Maryland, and Beauvoir School in Washington, D.C., who contributed many ideas and forms for this document. We are also grateful to Beauvoir School for allowing us to take pictures in their classrooms.

The illustrations have been lovingly created by Jean Iker, the former art teacher at Beauvoir school. We appreciate her ability to turn words into pictures and capture the whimsy of young children. We enjoyed working with The Crosby Group on the cover illustration.

We owe a big thank you to all of the trainers across the United States who have travelled to the nineteen countries in the Step by Step Program and contributed their ideas, stories, and expertise to this document.

We also want to thank Cassie Marshall for her assistance in editing the document under very tight time restrictions.

Pamela A. Coughlin   Kirsten A. Hansen   Dinah Heller
Roxane K. Kaufmann   Judith Rothchild-Stolberg Kate Burke Walsh

INTRODUCTION

This document was created as part of the Step by Step Program. It describes classroom methods for children ages three to five years old that were originally developed as a guide for teachers in nineteen countries in Central and Eastern Europe and the former Soviet countries.

Part I, Child-Centered Thinking, introduces the Step by Step Program described in *Creating Child-Centered Classrooms*. Chapter I presents the philosophical overview and theoretical basis for the content. Chapter II describes the goals for the program and details developmental guidelines for children.

Part II, Child-Centered Teaching, describes the roles of teachers and families in implementing a child-centered classroom. Specific methods for involving families in their children's education are covered in detail in Chapter III. Chapter IV discusses ways to build a feeling of community in the classroom and school. Chapter V specifies methods of observing, recording, and reporting children's development. Chapter VI puts the whole section together by discussing how to plan an integrated curriculum for children.

Part III, Child-Centered Learning, which includes Chapters VIII-XVIII, provides an overview of the learning environment and discusses each of ten activity centers in detail. The activity centers include art, blocks, cooking, dramatic play, literacy, mathematics/manipulatives, music, outdoors, sand and water, and science. The teacher's role, materials needed to set up the center, and specific activities and projects are fully described.

Each chapter offers the reader concrete examples and clear ideas on how to create and implement a child-centered classroom that promotes democratic principles and practices. Sample forms, schedules, and checklists are included for easy use. This book was written by experienced teachers for practical classroom use.

PART 1

CHILD-CENTERED THINKING

I. INTRODUCTION, PHILOSOPHY AND PROGRAM RATIONALE

Introduction

Throughout their lives, regardless of where they live, today's children will have to face change: social, political, and environmental changes; changes in science and technology; and industrial changes that affect job markets. The rapid changes occurring throughout the world today make it important to nourish in children a desire for lifelong learning.

In order to prepare children to be motivated learners, the Step by Step Program builds a foundation for the attitudes, knowledge, and skills that are vital to meet current challenges and those expected in the twenty-first century. The program recognizes, values, and encourages the development of characteristics that will be needed in rapidly changing times. Among these are the ability to

- Meet and effect change

- Be critical thinkers, able to make choices

- Be problem finders and problem solvers

- Be creative, imaginative, and resourceful

- Be concerned with community, country, and environment

The Step by Step Program is a unique program for children ages three through six and their families. The curriculum integrates research based practices of early childhood education with a firm commitment to work with families and communities to individualize experiences for each child. The program is designed to meet each child's specific needs and respects a variety of cultural traditions. Several features are present in all program classrooms. These include an emphasis on:

- Individualizing learning experiences for each child

- Assisting children to make choices through planned activity and activity centers

- Family participation

Philosophy of the Step by Step Program

The Step by Step Program is based on the belief that children grow best when they are intrinsically involved in their own learning. The Step by Step carefully planned environment encourages children to explore, to initiate, and to create. The teaching team uses its sound knowledge of child development to create the environment and provide the materials for learning. The team's role is to set appropriate goals for individual children and for the group as a whole, to respond to the interests of the children, to respect the individual strengths and needs of each child, to keep alive the natural curiosity of the young child, and to foster cooperative learning.

Approaches to Early Childhood Education

In the field of early childhood education there are two basic approaches to teaching children between the ages three through six: the **behavioral approach** and the **developmental approach**.

The behavioral approach assumes that concepts have no point of origin within the child and do not develop spontaneously. All concepts must be imposed on the child and are absorbed by the child. A behavioral classroom is teacher-centered, based on explicit instruction that "fills" the child over time, much as we would fill a container. The teacher presents specific information in a prescribed manner. This information is usually analyzed carefully, broken into discrete tasks, and presented sequentially to the child. The teacher is seen as "owner" of all information; it is his or her job to impart this body of knowledge to the child. The child is expected to master a task through practice and drill before moving on to the next step. The correct response is often reinforced through drill and rewards. The behavioral approach requires that the teacher carefully assess the information the child possesses, and reassessment occurs before moving on to the next step. There are a number of prescriptive, commercially sequential checklists and assessments that teachers can use in their classrooms (Seefeldt, 1994). Influential behaviorists include John Watson, Edward Thorndike and B.F. Skinner.

2

The Step by Step Program uses a **developmental approach**. A developmental perspective provides a framework for understanding and appreciating the natural growth of young children. It assumes that young children

- Are active learners who are constantly acquiring new information about the world through play

- Proceed through predictable stages of development

- Are dependent on others for emotional and cognitive growth through social interactions

- Are unique individuals who grow and develop at different rates

The developmental approach is based primarily on the theories of Jean Piaget, Eric Erikson, and L.S. Vygotsky. Both Piaget and Vygotsky viewed the child as a biological organism. However, they held different theories concerning the influence that nature and society have on development. Glassman (1994) summarizes the philosophy of these two educators as follows:

- Two lines of development — the natural and the social — interact continuously in the development of thinking. Each is essential for cognitive development.

- Cognitive development is initially the result of direct experience in an environment; eventually, children become capable of transforming their experience mentally through internal reflection.

- The pace of an individual's development is influenced by the social milieu.

- Cognitive development involves major, qualitative transformations in thinking.

Piaget believed that growing children move through a series of stages. The first is the sensorimotor period, which occurs between birth and approximately two years of age. Next is the stage of concrete operations, which occurs between the ages of two and eleven years. The third phase, the formal operations stage, generally begins in early adolescence. For Vygotsky, thinking is radically transformed when 1) children become capable of linguistic communication and 2) instruction leads them to become aware of and to master their own thoughts.

Erikson's theory of psychosocial development presents a series of three age related stages that represent the individual's relationship to the social environment. Erikson views healthy development as the resolution of conflicts that are characteristic of particular ages. From birth to three years, growth is characterized by the development of trust; from one to three years, the focus is the development of autonomy; and from three to six years, the healthy individual acquires a sense of initiative.

These educational philosophies enhance our understanding of child development and provide important ideas for translating theory into practical, classroom applications. These philosophies provide a helpful guide for teachers as they plan for young children. When developmental theory is applied within the historical context of progressive education the child becomes the starting point for curriculum development. This defines a *child-centered* classroom.

Program Rationale: The Three Major Tenets of the Step by Step Program

The Step by Step Program encompasses three major early childhood initiatives: constructivism, developmentally appropriate practices, and progressive education.

Constructivism

Constructivists believe that learning occurs as children strive to make sense of the world around them. Learning becomes an interactive process involving children, adults, other children, and the environment. Children construct or build their own understanding of the world. They make sense of what is happening around them by synthesizing new experiences with what they have previously come to understand. Jacqueline and Martin Brooks (1993) describe the process:

> *"Often we encounter an object, an idea, a relationship or a phenomenon that doesn't quite make sense to us. When confronted with such initially discrepant data or perceptions, we either interpret what we see to conform to our present set of rules for explaining and ordering our world or we generate a new set of rules that better accounts for what we perceive to be occurring. Either way, our perceptions and rules are constantly engaged in a grand dance that shapes our understandings."*

The following example illustrates constructivist learning. A young child whose family has a dog is out driving with his parents. They drive past a cow in a field. The child points and says "dog." The parents tell him it is not a dog but a cow

4

and that a cow is different from a dog. The new information will be refigured against what is known and mental accommodations will be made. Although children must construct their own understanding, knowledge, and learning, the role of adult as facilitator and mediator is essential. The teaching team must provide the tools, the materials, the support, the guidance, and interest to maximize the child's opportunities for learning.

Developmental Appropriateness

A **developmentally appropriate** curriculum is one that is based on a knowledge of child development. All children progress through common developmental stages but, at the same time, each child is also a unique and individual being. The teaching team must know about typical child growth and development in order to provide a realistic array of learning materials and activities. The team must also watch and listen for differences between the skills and special interests of same-age children (Seefeldt, 1994; Bredekamp, 1993). A developmentally appropriate curriculum includes activities that are based on children's interest, their cognitive level of functioning, and their social and emotional maturity. Such activities appeal to young children's natural curiosity, enjoyment of sensory experiences, and the desire to explore their own ideas.

A developmentally appropriate program is designed to help children answer their own questions. When children pose the questions, their interest, motivation and attention are automatic. The teacher's role is to find ways to arrive at answers that satisfy the child without oversimplifying the question or overwhelming the child with information. Through developmentally appropriate practices, teachers can find a balance that satisfies and extends a learning situation.

Progressive Education

John Dewey, recognized as the father of **progressive education**, emphasized that education be viewed as a process of living, not a preparation for future life. Dewey (1938) argued that education as preparation for adult life "denied the inherent ebullience and curiosity children brought with them to school and removed the focus from students' present interests and abilities to some more abstract notion of what they might wish to do in future years."

We accept that child-centered education does both; it recognizes that these points of view do not have to be mutually exclusive. Progressive education practices build on developmental and constructivist principles. It fosters a learning environment that enhances the skills and interests of the individual child while acknowledging the importance of peer-to-peer and small-group learning.

Individualizing the Learning Experience

The Step by Step teaching teams set the foundation for children to become fulfilled, achieving, active adults who care about others and are able to make an impact on their world. The teachers are also concerned with the "here and now" of childhood. They implement this focus by valuing play and individualizing. Individualizing is achieved by respecting the present developmental stage of each child and planning a range of appropriate activities to ensure each child's successful experiences. The ability to individualize involves knowledge about child development that encompasses health, physical and emotional growth, and cognition. It is a decision-making process in which a teacher observes a child, assesses the child's developmental level in significant areas, and takes action to provide a particular response to the assessed developmental stage of the child.

Why do we need to individualize? Individualizing matches the developmental stage, strengths, and needs of each child with the learning activity. When this match is made, children gain competence and self-esteem. They are ready to tackle new challenges.

A child-centered classroom supports individualized learning. The equipment, materials, and layout of the classroom enhance the growth of every child, and the activities chosen are relevant to each child. Children individualize for themselves when they choose an activity center or select a five-piece rather than a twelve-piece puzzle. Individualization also requires that the teacher create activities that make each child feel successful and challenged. It is possible to optimize the amount of individualization that occurs in the classroom. By planning flexible and interesting activities and by carefully observing children during activities, the teacher can change and adapt materials and activities as needed. Most group activities are conducted in small groups to maximize the amount of individualization. The daily schedule should accommodate each child's needs for activity and rest. Individualization is an important part of a child-centered curriculum because the more individualization there is, the more effective a teacher will be.

Activity centers allow children to individualize for themselves based on their skills and interests. In the art area, for example, one child tears paper while another uses scissors to cut out a complex shape. In the manipulative area, one child chooses a four-piece wooden puzzle while another chooses a twenty-five piece cardboard puzzle. The teacher observes the children and takes notes on their development. Over time, she provides the children with more challenging materials, or when necessary, more direct help in mastering a challenging skill. When the preschool experience is individualized, children can grow and develop at their own pace. The Step by Step classroom is a dynamic and changing environment filled with materials and experiences designed to correspond to children's individual interests and developmental stages.

The teaching team facilitates and plans the classroom space and activities that are designed to be appropriate to the developmental level of each child. The daily plan includes a variety of work time for children: in small cooperative learning groups, on individual tasks, with a teacher's guidance, or without guidance. There is time for the children to select their own activities; this helps them learn how to make choices and to develop their own interests and skills. Making choices, learning to be problem solvers, communicating with others, and working toward individual goals are emphasized in the Step by Step classroom.

Activity Centers

The Step by Step Program designs opportunities for children to make choices through classroom arrangement. Each classroom has several activity centers that contain many different materials for exploration and play. The activity centers vary from classroom to classroom, but all classrooms include these basic centers:

Art	Mathematics/Manipulatives
Blocks	Music
Cooking	Outdoors
Dramatic Play	Sand and
Water	Science
Literacy	

Art

The **art** activity center encourages children to develop and explore their own creativity and have fun with new materials and tactile experiences.

Materials in this area may include paints, paper, scissors, crayons, chalk, fabric, and scraps of materials for gluing and pasting. Many natural materials can be added to this area, including wood, leaves, and sand. This area encourages creativity, verbal and non-verbal communication, self-esteem, small and large motor development, and intellectual skills.

Blocks

The **block** activity center is filled with blocks of different sizes and shapes for creating imaginary or identifiable structures, such as buildings, towns, farms, and zoos. Children learn many things from building with blocks. They develop math skills, expand thinking skills, increase social and problem-solving skills, and strengthen their power of concentration. Creativity is used and concentration developed. Many items, including cars, trucks, animals, people, airplanes, and fabric, can be added to this area by both children and teachers, .

Cooking

Cooking provides a special time for children to learn science, taste new foods, eat food they make, and understand mathematical concepts such as measuring. Cooking together offers children time to be social, to learn to share and to work in pairs. Many basic concepts are taught through cooking, as teachers discuss colors, numbers, shapes, nutrition and science. Cooking provides real-life experiences for children.

Dramatic Play

The **dramatic play** center has dress-up clothes and other items that encourage the children to act out what they see in their lives, helping them understand their world and practice various roles. The items in this area are selected by the teaching team. They may include objects for a washing activity, the next week, items to play astronaut or circus performer, and objects relating to animal care after that. The choice of objects depends on the children's interests at a particular time.

Literacy

The **literacy** activity center includes books and materials for listening and writing activities. This area is a quiet one where children can look at books, read to one another, or have a teacher or parent volunteer read to them. Literature is used throughout the Step by Step preschool day. Children are invited to create their own books, and invent, dramatize, and listen to stories.

Mathematics/Manipulatives

The area for **mathematics/manipulatives** has materials that children can take apart and put together, such as puzzles and small blocks. This area also has games to assist the children in learning to match, count and categorize, create their own games, and practice their language skills. Activities in this center help children develop their intellectual skills, small muscles, and eye-hand coordination. They also learn social skills like sharing, negotiating, and problem solving.

Music

Music can be used throughout the day to integrate activities. Singing, moving, clapping, dancing, playing instruments or listening quietly all contribute to a full program day. Music enhances the senses, teaches rhythm, counting and language patterns, strengthens small and large muscles, and allows for creativity.

Outdoor Activities

Outdoor activities are a critical part of the daily schedule. Everything that can be learned and taught indoors can be done outdoors. Children can learn social skills, appreciation for nature, and science and math skills. They also increase the use of their small and large muscles. Creativity is enhanced in the outdoor area through dramatic play and group activities. Activities that may seem ordinary indoors become special events when they take place outside: for example, eating, cooking, drawing and painting, and creating theater productions. Other activities like gardening and playing in snow, mud, and puddles, are special because they can only be done outdoors. Field trips to community settings like the market and the fire station provide real learning experiences for children. The outdoors offers a vast array of opportunities for children to learn about their environment and helps them understand how they fit into the world. The outside area is seen as an extension of the classroom, and outside activities are planned as carefully as inside ones.

Sand and Water

The **sand and water** activity center, both indoors at the sand and water table and outdoors in the sandbox and water area, is busy with children playing and learning. These areas offer many opportunities for children to use their senses. Through exploration of these natural materials, children create, think, and communicate. They exercise large and small muscles. Materials used in this center include shovels, sieves, funnels, and buckets. Mathematical concepts, scientific ideas, and creativity are developed.

Science

The **science** activity center directly reflects the children's interests in natural occurrences and found objects. The teacher arranges a place in the room for display and exploration of interesting "treasures." This activity center is one that changes frequently in response to interests, seasonal changes, and thematic studies. Properties of physical science such as magnetism, water, and laws of gravity can be introduced through materials.

Learning occurs through environmental and natural science as children explore the outdoors, plants, trees, and animals. The teacher's role is to emphasize the scientific process.

Materials from different centers are shared with other areas. For example, children move toy animals from the table toy area to the block area when they build a zoo and need the animals to put in cages. The teaching team changes materials in the activity centers throughout the year so that they continue to be appropriate for the children's changing interests and ongoing development. Additional activities (for example, cooking, woodworking, theme-related activities, and special events) may be rotated in the classroom or added as space permits.

The teaching team is responsible for creating the environment, inviting conversation, arousing curiosity, and observing the children so that activities can be adapted to meet their changing needs. Small group and individual learning activities are planned throughout the week to focus on specific learning tasks identified by the teaching team and the family. When families enter the Step by Step classroom, they feel the energy and learning that is taking place as children talk, negotiate, explore, make choices, and learn the skills needed to develop into productive and creative citizens.

Family Participation

The emphasis on family participation is a unique feature of the Step by Step Program. The Step by Step Program believes that families have the greatest influence on their children. They are their primary educators. Families desire the best for their children and want them to be successful and productive citizens. Families must, therefore, be seen as partners who play a critical role in the child's educational process. They must be encouraged to become involved in the learning experience for their children in the program. The Step by Step Program promotes family participation in a variety of ways. Although methods vary from site to site and family to family, depending on individual and community circumstances, the teachers and administrators encourage all families to become involved in all aspects of the program.

Family Room

For example, each program is encouraged to create a family room where family members can meet with teachers, visit with other parents, and read about child development, health issues, discipline, or other topics of interest. Parents may also borrow these materials from the center. This room is available for parent meetings and workshops. Families are welcome to come to the school and work with the children, help with parent activities, and meet with the teaching team. Families are encouraged to join their children in classroom activities and bring their special talents to share with the children. Some family members can be hired as teacher assistants. Others can be encouraged to volunteer in the classroom, build equipment, and assist on field trips and other activities.

Staff and Family Communication

Communication between the teaching team and families is an important component of the Step by Step Program. Such communication takes many forms, including notes, home or school journals, conversations when children are dropped off and picked up at the center, family meetings, workshops, and parent support groups. The teaching team is encouraged to make visits to family homes. Parent conferences are scheduled regularly with family members. At these sessions parents and teachers discuss the child's progress and develop strategies for learning that can be applied at home.

Family Advisory Committee

Another element in the Step by Step Program is the Family Advisory Committee, which meets with the staff to discuss the operations of the center or school. The committee consists of parents of children enrolled in the program; it may also include other members of the community. The Step by Step Program staff works with the families to conduct an assessment of family needs that provides a total profile or picture of each family being served by the program.

In summary, the Step by Step Program's goal is to build a supportive community that holds the family at the center and includes the teaching team and community members. This group of people creates a network that plans, communicates, and discusses issues and concerns in order to build a program that supports the growth and development of children and their families.

What Are Developmentally Appropriate Activities?

The National Association for the Education of Young Children, the major professional early childhood organization in the United States, ascribes two dimensions to the term "developmentally appropriate": age appropriateness and individual appropriateness (Bredekamp, 1987).

Age Appropriateness

Human development research indicates that children undergo universal, predictable sequences of growth and change during the first nine years of life. These predictable changes occur in all domains of development: physical, emotional, social, and cognitive. Knowledge of typical development of children within the age span served by the program provides a framework from which teachers prepare the learning environment and plan appropriate experiences (Bredekamp, 1987).

To implement developmentally appropriate practices, the teaching team must be cognizant of the range of normal development. The teachers should keep in mind that, although there are predictable sequences of growth, they do not take place on the same day, week, or even month. Inevitably, there will be differences among the children in a class.

The Chart of Normal Development (found at the end of Chapter II) describes development of gross motor skills, fine motor skills, communication skills, understanding language, spoken language, cognitive skills, self-help skills, and social skills for children in the United States. Development charts should be reviewed regularly, and integrated into curriculum planning.

When classroom activities are not linked to developmental factors, children experience failure and frustration. The Step by Step Program offers opportunities for success, not frustration. However, the teaching team does not make everything easy for the children; instead teachers tailor challenging activities to each child's developmental level.

Individual Appropriateness

Each child has a unique pattern and timing of growth, as well as an individual personality, learning style, and family background. Both the curriculum and adults' interactions with children should be responsive to individual differences. Learning results from the interaction between the child's thoughts and experiences with materials, ideas, and people. These experiences should match the child's developing abilities while challenging the child's interest and understanding (Bredekamp, 1987, p. 2).

To make classroom activities individually appropriate, the teaching team must observe each child carefully and determine each child's abilities, needs, interests, temperament, and learning style. It also requires a keen knowledge of the potential activities in each of the activity centers.

Children who are challenged at their own level of development will feel good about themselves and will be able and eager to explore new ideas and activities. Children for whom expectations are above or below their level of development may lose interest, and become bored, restless, or frustrated.

Individualizing through Play

Play is the heart of good early childhood programs. The research on play shows that it is an important part of the lives of young children (Johnson, Christie, Yawkey, 1987). Play and development unfold together, so environments for young children allow for ongoing opportunities for free play. Play occurs in a wide variety of ways: solitary play with objects, unstructured, associative play with one other child, interactive and complex dramatic play with props and other children, and more structured play in group games as children get older.

Experts agree that:

> *"Children need to play in order to develop cognitive and motor skills and to learn about the social world and their place in it. Children develop social skills through interaction with their peers. They learn what rules are, how rules are made and what justice and fairness are about. They learn how to cooperate and how to share. They develop self-esteem by successfully challenging themselves, by interacting with other children and by mastering personal, physical, intellectual and social challenges."*
> (Frost and Jacobs, 1995, p.47).

The Step by Step teaching team supports play through an indoor and outdoor environment that has been set up with activity centers. In these centers, an expanding curriculum using real experiences relates to each child's interests, understanding, background and environment, and matches each child's developing abilities. Each center thus becomes a laboratory for children's initiative, creativity, and imagination.

The activity centers influence the design and arrangement of the classroom; however, activities are not restricted to a particular center. Puppets, for example, might be made in the art activity center, but used in the block activity center where children have built a small stage, or in the dramatic play center, where children decided to use a table as a stage. Allowing for a flexible use of materials ensures that the children's interests determine the program content.

The daily schedule affords children time and opportunities for choosing which centers interest them. Initially, children who have not had an opportunity to see such an array of equipment may want to move quickly from center to center. In time, however, they will focus on tasks that interest them in their chosen centers. Play should be self-directed; therefore, children should be able to move among centers at their own pace.

By following the lead of children, adults make possible the kind of play that is cognitively and emotionally necessary for children. Stanley Greenspan, a child psychologist who has been studying the emotional needs of children for years, advocates "floor time" for teachers and parents with their young children (Greenspan, 1989). By getting on the floor with children, teachers and parents can join in mutual give-and-take, allowing the child to lead and guide the play.

The materials in the centers stimulate and challenge children to use all their senses. Through experimentation, investigation, and discovery, children test ideas and gain information in their own individual ways. This is how children begin to develop the habit of finding and solving problems, thinking critically, making choices, and developing concepts.

There is a hum of activity in the centers as children spontaneously interact with their peers. As they communicate with each other and with the adults, they develop social skills. As they play, children also develop their small and large motor skills and eye-hand coordination.

The role of the teaching team is to act as facilitators. They are ready to extend and enhance play by knowing when to ask open-ended questions that encourage thinking. They know when to provide appropriate information, when to clarify misconceptions, when to add materials, and, if feasible, when to arrange new experiences such as short trips, that will further stimulate the children's interests and learning. It is a belief of the Step by Step Program that teachers who model playfulness themselves will better appreciate the importance of an environment that allows for different opportunities and times for play.

Making Philosophy Happen

A child-centered classroom is built around two core principles:

- Children create their own knowledge from their experiences and interactions with the world around them.

- Teachers foster children's growth and development best by building on the interests, needs, and strengths of the children.

The classroom is a laboratory where children experiment with roles as explorers, artists, friends, and scientists. Teachers are responsible for transforming the classroom into this kind of a laboratory. They are responsible for organizing materials to encourage creative and ongoing experimentation, discovery, and problem solving by the children.

Teachers respect children's ideas and use those ideas to mold the curriculum. Teachers interact with children as they work and play: they model supportive, caring behaviors; they observe and listen to children in activity centers; they record and evaluate their observations; and they use their observations in planning and individualizing for children. In an environment where teachers encourage children to pursue their interests, children develop a strong sense of importance and self-initiative.

Teachers set the mood and tone for the classroom. The teacher personifies the qualities that she wants to help develop in the children — empathy, caring, enthusiasm, and intellectual curiosity. Teachers should also remember how to have fun. There are few things more rewarding than the joy expressed by a child who has joined a teacher to write a story or make up a silly joke or take time to discuss a new interest. Teachers who communicate their enthusiasm to children make learning exciting and vital. Teachers who are aloof and authoritarian may frighten children and inhibit their curiosity.

Both children and teachers initiate and direct activities. A delicate balance is achieved between teacher and child, with each taking turns leading, inquiring, and responding. Children are encouraged to initiate much of their own learning. Their creative expression is promoted and valued. Teachers take advantage of the children's interests and play and use them to stimulate further thinking and learning. By providing opportunities for children to have direct contact with people, materials, and real-life experiences, teachers foster children's intellectual growth.

Activity centers provide a choice of learning areas and materials. Themes or projects are encouraged and planned by the teacher, based on the interests of the children, and may be integrated into activity centers. Young children should never be made to pursue a theme or project that is not of interest to them. The classroom is always set up to provide a choice of activity centers and diverse materials from which children may choose.

In the child-centered classroom, children

- Make choices
- Play actively
- Use open-ended materials
- Work together and care for each other
- Take responsibility

The daily schedule provides security and predictability. Materials are developmentally appropriate and open-ended. Teachers observe children as they interact with peers and classroom materials to identify strengths and needs. Rules help children learn that caring for each other is an integral part of the school.

GOALS AND DEVELOPMENTAL GUIDELINES

II. GOALS AND DEVELOPMENTAL GUIDELINES

Goals and Developmental Guidelines

Children of the twenty-first century will face changes that have been unimaginable before now. Rapid change is occurring in every aspect of life. Skills and facts from the pretechnological era will not serve children in tomorrow's world. The rapidity and extent of change calls for continuous, intelligent adaptation. To prepare children for the challenges facing them in the future, we must prepare them to be life-long learners. The Step by Step Program believes that the development of a solid foundation for life-long learning is essential for today's children. The program has been designed to enable each child to become an active citizen in a new world.

Goals

The goals of the Step by Step Program are that each child will develop the ability to:

- Meet and effect change

- Be a critical thinker and be able to make choices

- Be a problem finder and problem solver

- Be creative, imaginative and resourceful

- Be concerned with community, country, and environment

To nurture these abilities, the Step by Step Program aims to create a learning environment that puts the child at the center of curriculum planning. The Step by Step Program helps children construct their understanding of

- The **physical world,** through activities such as measuring, weighing, building with blocks, woodworking, sand and water play, using pulleys and ropes, and mixing paint

19

- **Social and cultural information**, through games, cooking, reading stories, dramatic play, and participation in community events

- **Logic and mathematics**, through measuring, comparing, counting, discovering equivalents, ordering, sequencing, sorting, and classifying

- **The written and spoken word**, through reading, writing, drawing pictures, dictating, listening, and expressing their ideas

Because the program is based on developmental theory, the **whole** child is the focus of the curriculum. All aspects of development — physical, social, emotional, and cognitive — are addressed. The curriculum enhances

- **Physical development**, through movement, climbing, throwing, cutting, sewing, drawing, writing, dressing

- **Social emotional development**, through resolving disputes and differences, expressing feelings, controlling impulses, caring and respecting others, initiating and following, sharing, caring for materials, and working cooperatively

- **Cognitive development,** through problem-solving opportunities, using objects for classification, sorting and logical thinking skills, organizing thinking, and articulating opinions

The Step by Step Program is based on an understanding of developmental theory, a constructivist view of learning, and progressive concepts about education. It assures that children:

- Have ample time to explore their environment

- Have opportunities to learn through multiple avenues: cooking, writing, building, dramatic play, use of the outdoors, reading, woodworking, sand and water, art, math, and science

- Have a safe place to explore their feelings, make mistakes, and solve conflicts

- Have chances to make choices about which activities they will participate in

- Have a place to display their work

The Step by Step approach assures that teaching teams:

- Understand child development

- Take time to observe children at work and play

- Plan group and individual goals that are based upon interest and need

- Provide a changing, flexible environment

- Show respect for children and value their ideas

- Encourage children to solve their own problems and respect each other

- Ask probing questions that stimulate thought

Age Related Characteristics

Although each child grows and develops in a unique way, all children proceed through known sequences of developmental stages. Within those stages, they often share characteristics common to many children of the same age.

Common Characteristics of Three-Year-Old Children

Children between the ages of three and four years can be exuberant, loving, and rude at the same time. They are struggling to make sense of their world. They continue to have difficulty distinguishing between fantasy and reality. They are beginning to understand that their actions have consequences and they are learning to set their own limits. In doing so, this age group is affectionate and cooperative one minute, bossy and demanding the next.

Three-year-olds are rapidly developing language skills, and they easily move between using baby talk and descriptive paragraphs. They often talk out loud to themselves as they work out a problem or complete an activity. These children have very high energy, but short attention spans, typically moving quickly from activity to activity. Their play is both parallel and social. The teacher is often the first adult outside of the family with whom the child forms a strong attachment.

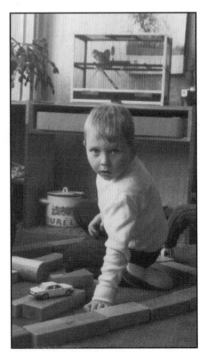

Common Characteristics of Four-Year-Old Children

Children between four and five years old often feel invincible and ready to tackle any new challenge. Unlike their younger peers, this age group engages in elaborate, cooperative social play. They are beginning to show empathy for others and can talk about their own and other's feelings.

These children test limits and rationalize their own behavior. They feel comfortable telling lies, but are outraged if adults stray from the truth.

22

Although four-year-olds still have relatively short attention spans, they are becoming expert problem solvers, and can concentrate for a sustained period of time if a topic is of special interest to them. Moreover, they are able to generalize from one activity or situation to another.

This age group is very interested in their own and others' bodies, and can become preoccupied with cuts or injuries. They have many fears, and may experience terrifying dreams.

These children are developing large motor skills, and show nonstop physical gymnastics. Their energy seems boundless. They have growing vocabularies, and use well-formed sentence structure and more complex grammar.

Common Characteristics of Five-Year-Old Children

The child between five and six years old is often sweet and eager to please adults. They are very social and play with three or four friends at a time. At this age, children prefer playmates of the same sex. They have a sense of humor,

often making up silly jokes that they tell over and over. They love to play games but want to win, and frequently change the rules to their own advantage.

At this age, children exhibit longer attention spans. More complex thinking and problem-solving abilities also develop. The child is able to focus on tasks and strives to meet self-set standards. Five- and six-year-olds love to talk, are articulate, and like to play with words—their language development is advanced. They use more complex sentences and will self-correct incorrect verb tenses.

Physically, children this age are very agile and are becoming interested in gymnastics and organized sports. They are beginning to develop better motor skills. Such activities as dressing, cutting, drawing, and writing are easier to perform.

These children are beginning to have a sense of their own past, and often enjoy recounting events that occurred when they were "little."

Children between five and six years old move between compliance and oppositional behavior. They are literal and concrete, and like structure and consistency.

Chart of Normal Development

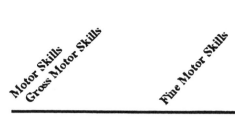

	Motor Skills Gross Motor Skills	Fine Motor Skills	Communication Skills Understanding Language	Spoken Language
24-36 Months	Runs forward well. Jumps in place, two feet together. Walks on tiptoe. Kicks stationary ball forward. Walks up 4-6 stairs alternating feet. Jumps over 15 cm. (6") high object, landing on both feet together. Throws ball overhead.	Strings 4 large beads. Turns pages singly. Snips with scissors. Holds crayon with thumb and fingers, not fist. Uses one hand consistently in most activities. Imitates circle, vertical, horizontal lines. Rolls, pounds, squeezes, and pulls clay. Controls grasp and release (stacks objects, puts small objects in slots).	Points to pictures of common objects when they are named. Can identify objects when told their use. Understands question forms **what** and **where.** Understands negatives **no, not, can't,** and **don't.** Enjoys listening to simple storybooks for 10-15 minutes and requests them again. Places objects in, on, under, beside. Points to pictures of action works (eating, sleeping, running).	Joins vocabulary words together in 2 to 4 word sentences. Asks **what** and **where** questions. Makes negative statements (for example, **Can't open it**). Answers simple yes/no, what is this, what do questions. Requests needs and wants. Uses "s" on nouns to indicate plurals.
36-48 Months	Runs around obstacles. Balances on one foot for 5 to 10 seconds. Hops on one foot. Pushes, pulls, steers wheeled toys. Uses slide without assistance. Catches ball bounced to him or her. Walks down 4-6 stairs alternating feet. Steers and pedals tricycle. Turns somersault/does forward roll.	Builds tower of 9 small blocks. Imitates Cross. Manipulates clay materials (for example, rolls balls, snakes, cookies). Uses 2 hands together for simple activities (unscrew jar lid, hold and turn egg beater drive nails & pegs). Traces template. Cuts across paper.	Understands relationships expressed by **if ... then** or **because** sentences. Carries out a series of 2 to 3 related directions. Understands when told, **Let's pretend.**	Talks in sentences of 4-5 words. Tells about past experiences. Uses simple past tense. Refers to self using pronouns **I** or **me.** Repeats at least one nursery rhyme and can sing a song. Speech is understandable to strangers, but there are still some sound errors. Asks "What", "Who", "Why", questions for information. Answers "Who" & "Why" & "How" questions.

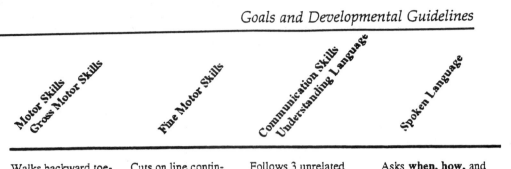

	Motor Skills Gross Motor Skills	Fine Motor Skills	Communication Skills Understanding Language	Spoken Language
48-60 Months	Walks backward toe-heel. Jumps forward 10 times, without falling. Throws hard-sized ball with one hand to person 4-6 ft. away. Catches tennis ball thrown from 3 feet.	Cuts on line continuously. Copies square. Prints a few capital letters. Uses individual finger movements during finger plays. Draws simple recognizable pictures. Pastes and glues appropriately.	Follows 3 unrelated commands in proper order. Understands comparatives like **pretty, prettier,** and **prettiest.** Incorporates verbal directions into play activities. Understands sequencing of events when told them (for example, **First we have to go to the store, then we can make the cake, and tomorrow we will eat it**). Points to between, above, below, top, bottom.	Asks **when, how,** and **why** questions. Joins sentences together (for example, **I like chocolate chip cookies and milk**). Talks about causality by using **because** and **so.** Uses irregular verbs and nouns. Defines familiar nouns. Demonstrates a variety of uses for language (gaining information, giving information, fantasy expressing opinions).
60-72 Months	Walks on balance beam forward, backward, sideways. Can cover 2 meters (6'6") hopping. Jumps rope. Swings independently. Demonstrates 2 complex ball skills (dribble, bounce/catch, hit with bat).	Cuts out simple shapes. Copies triangle. Prints first name legibly. Copies numerals 1to 10. Colors within lines. Has adult grasp of pencil. Has handedness well established (that is, child is left- or right-handed).		There are few obvious differences between child's grammar and adult's grammar. Still needs to learn such things as subject-verb agreement, and some irregular past tense verbs. Can take appropriate turns in a conversation. Communicates well with family, friends, or strangers. Routinely answers one question during a group activity of 10-15 mins. Pretends and acts out a story.

26

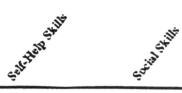

Cognitive Skills   **Self-Help Skills**   **Social Skills**

24-36 Months

Cognitive Skills

Responds to simple directions (for example: **Give me the ball and the block. Get your shoes and socks).**

Selects and looks at picture books, names pictured objects, and identifies several objects within one picture.

Touches and counts 1-3 objects.

Matches 4 colors.

Attempts to play with unfamiliar toy.

Can talk briefly about what he or she is doing.

Imitates adult actions (for example, housekeeping play).

Has limited attention span. Learning is most through exploration.

Uses 5 toys functionly.

Points to big/little objects.

Self-Help Skills

Uses spoon, spilling little.

Drinks from child-sized cup.

Takes off simple unfastened clothing.

Puts on coat, sweater with help with fasteners.

Washes and dries hands with assistance.

Uses toilet with assistance - has day time control.

Helps adult put toys/materials away.

Social Skills

Watches other children, joins briefly in their play.

Makes a choice given 2 alternatives.

Defends own possessions.

Begins to play house, engages in simple role play.

Participates in small group activity (for example, sings, claps, dances) for 5-10 minutes.

Knows gender identity.

Insists on doing things independently.

Consistently takes turns with one reminder.

Independently plays on own initiative for 15 minutes.

Expresses a range of emotions through actions, words or facial expressions.

36-48 Months

Cognitive Skills

Names 4 colors.

Intentionally stacks blocks or rings in order of size.

Recognizes and defines a problem.

Completes a 2-3 part art project.

Asks questions for information (**why** and **how** questions requiring simple answers).

Counts up to 7 objects.

Has increased understanding of concepts of the functions and groupings of objects (for example, can put doll house furniture in correct rooms, puts pictures in categories).

Begins to be aware of past & present (for example: **Yesterday we went to the park. Today we go to the library).**

Self-Help Skills

Pours well from small pitcher.

Buttons and unbuttons on own clothing buttons.

Washes hands unassisted.

Uses toilet independently.

Feeds self a variety of foods using spoon, fork and glass.

Puts on shoes or boots independently.

Social Skills

Initiates soual interaction with another child or adult.

Shares toys, materials or food.

Begins dramatic play, acting out whole scenes (for example, traveling, playing house, pretending to be animals).

Asks permission to use things that belong to others.

Participates in small group activity (teacher directed) for 10 to 15 minutes.

	Cognitive Skills		Self-Help Skills	Social Skills

36-48 Months

Cognitive Skills

Knows own age.

Names 6 body parts when described by function.

Sorts objects into groups that are the same on one attribute (color, shape, size).

Names or pairs objects that go together (what goes with tooth brush?).

Self-Help Skills

Feeds self a variety of foods using spoon, fork and glass.

Puts on shoes or boots independently.

Cleans up spills independently.

Gets drink from sink or fountain independently.

Puts away toys or materials independently.

Social Skills

Plays with 2-3 children with frequent interactions for 15 minutes.

Waits or delays a want for 5 minutes.

Routinely follows 3 classroom rules.

48-60 Months

Cognitive Skills

Supplies rhyming word to complete a set (hat, bat...)

Draws a person with 6 recognizable parts, such as head, trunk, arms, legs. Can name and match drawn parts to own body.

Draws, names, and describes recognizable picture.

Knows own street and town.

Has more extended attention span. Learns through observing and listening to adults as well as through exploration. Is easily distracted.

Self-Help Skills

Cuts and spreads soft substances with a table knife.

Laces shoes.

Dresses self without supervision.

Blows nose with one reminder.

Brushes teeth with supervision.

Puts zipper in catch and zips.

Social Skills

Plays simple table games.

Dramatic play is closer to reality, with attention paid to detail, time, and space.

Resolves problems with peers using substitution, persuasion or negotiation.

Tells about recent experiences/events.

	Cognitive Skills		Self-Help Skills	Social Skills

48-60 Months

Cognitive Skills

Can complete 4 opposite analogies (ice is cold, fire is hot).

Predict a realistic outcome for an event or story.

Names some letters and numerals.

Time concepts are expanding. The child can talk about yesterday or last week (a long time ago), about today, and about what will happen tomorrow.

Give specified number of items (1-5).

Retells 3 main facts from a story.

Self-Help Skills

Carries out one daily classroom chore with one reminder.

Independently obtains/returns materials needed for a task.

Social Skills

States reasons for peer's feelings.

Consistently attempts developmentally appropriate tasks independently.

Carefully uses items belonging to others.

Terminates inappropriate behavior with one reminder.

60-72 Months

Cognitive Skills

Retells story from picture book with reasonable accuracy.

Names all numerals (1-10) and most alphabet letters.

Counts out quantities up to 12.

Uses classroom tools (such as scissors and paints) meaningfully and purposefully.

Answers questions to add and substract numbers to 5 given objects.

Points to some, most, all, first, middle, last.

Begins to relate clock time to daily schedule.

Reads 10 common words.

Attention span increases noticeably. Learns through adult instruction and play. When interested, can ignore distractions.

Time concepts are expanding into an understanding of the past and future in terms of major events (for example, **Christmas will come after two weekends**).

Can tell ways objects are same and different.

Completes interlocking puzzle of 10 or more pieces.

Self-Help Skills

Dresses self completely.

Ties own shoelaces.

Brushes teeth unassisted.

Crosses street safely.

Fixes bowl of cold cereal or sandwich independently.

Independently brushes or combs own hair.

Social Skills

Independently makes friends with other children

Consistently problem solves in difficult situations.

Plays competitive games.

Engages with other children in cooperative play involving group decisions, role assignments, fair play.

Praises, supports or assists another child.

Verbalized positive statements about his/her uniqueness & abilities.

Independently completes all aspects of developmentally appropriate tasks.

Engages in independent work for 20 minutes.

States and routinely follows 5 classroom rules.

29

PART II

CHILD-CENTERED TEACHING

FAMILY PARTICIPATION

III.   FAMILY PARTICIPATION

Philosophy

Young children are dependent on their families for

- Their physical well-being, including food, shelter, clothing, and health care

- Their emotional well-being, including love, encouragement, and consistent and gentle reminders of what is right and wrong

- Their developmental well-being, including communication, opportunities to crawl, walk, run, climb, play, and new experiences to share

It is important that professionals acknowledge the primary role of family as first teacher. By the time preschool starts, families have taught children a vast array of things, ranging from how to drink from a cup or throw a ball to the pleasure of listening to stories. Preschool builds on this primary relationship between child and family by providing opportunities for families to participate in all aspects of the program.

The Step by Step Program is founded on the belief that family involvement is essential to reinforce and expand the classroom learning and to build on the interests and learning that occur at home. This reciprocity between learning environments — home and school — reflects the respect and sharing that the program promotes. One of the strongest arguments for parent involvement in early childhood programs was articulated by psychologist Urie Bronfenbrenner (1975), who asserted that ". . . programs that place major emphasis on involving the parent *directly* in activities fostering the child's development are likely to have constructive impact at any age, but the earlier such activities are begun, and the longer they are continued, the greater the benefit to the child" (p. 465).

The influence of the family on early childhood development cannot be overstated. Children are brought up in their families and are influenced by events that occur within them. Families are the ongoing caring, teaching, and decision-making people in the lives of their children. "Early childhood educators need to recognize, encourage, and enhance the primary attachment between parents and children" (Johnston, 1982, p. 51).

Families are diverse. They may be small, nuclear families or large, extended families. There may be many brothers and sisters or an only child. The child may be adopted or living with a relative. Acknowledging that children often have important relationships with adults other than their parents, such as aunts, uncles, grandparents, and close family friends, prompts the program to communicate with those who have an influence upon their lives. The Step by Step Program works with all adults who have close relationships with the children enrolled in the program.

Although families play a central role in the lives of their children, they depend on supports and resources from programs and the community. "Families are the critical element in the rearing of healthy, competent, and caring children. We suggest, however, that families — all families — cannot perform this function as well as they might unless they are supported by a caring and strong community, for it is community [support] that provides the informal and formal supplements to families own resources." (Hobbs et al, 1984, p. 46). For Step by Step Programs to promote growth and change, they must be aware of the priorities, interests, and concerns of the children they serve, their families, and their communities.

The Benefits of Family Participation

Involvement in preschool activities benefits the child, family, and program. The following describes how participation in an activity can provide emotional and physical benefits for everyone.

Emotional involvement allows us to feel

- Good about ourselves
- Productive
- Energetic
- Renewed and ready to face life again
- Happy and playful
- Like we have contributed to something or someone
- Like we belong to a group

Physical involvement allows us to

- Develop new skills
- Forget our worries
- Have fun and laugh
- Relax
- Get to know another person
- Manage stress

Attitudes

Both teachers and family members have had experiences during their own school years that will influence the way they react to families' presence and active involvement in the program. In many cultures, the role of family and that of school have been kept separate. Parents leave their children at the school door and have little knowledge of what occurs inside those doors. Teachers are accustomed to assuming responsibility for children during school hours and do not expect to interact with families. For cultures where this is typical practice, the concept of active family participation may be totally unfamiliar. Neither teachers nor family members know how to share information, plan jointly, or work together in the classroom. They feel uncomfortable with these new role requirements. It may be difficult, in these circumstances, to demonstrate the value of family involvement to teachers and families.

Even in programs where there is some experience with family participation, teachers may feel threatened by having parents in their classroom. They may feel that they have to be "perfect" and may worry about making a mistake or having a bad day. Parents may have had a negative experience with teachers during their own schooling and feel uncomfortable in the classroom. They may not easily express their concerns or questions. Others, by contrast, may have been in very supportive situations and feel at ease helping with preschool activities.

Mutual Responsibility

Teachers and parents share the responsibility of working together to develop a collaborative relationship. Communication, respect, accepting differences, and the best interests of the child form the basis for a good relationship. It is not always sufficient to change staff and family attitudes — often professionals and parents must also develop new skills and practices in order to establish quality interactions.

Opportunities for Collaboration

Family members are provided with many different ways and opportunities to be involved in the program. Visits to the home (planned at times convenient to the family) provide an opportunity for teachers to get to know the children and families in their own environment. Families are encouraged to visit the classroom at any time. They are invited to share a special interest or skill with the children, such as woodworking or stitchery. They are asked to comment on the student notebooks that are sent home by the teachers. When families notify teachers about special events in their lives, such as birthdays, new jobs, visiting relatives, or trips, it helps teachers understand any changes in children's behaviors and provides opportunities for discussion among the children.

The frequency and variety of opportunities for family members and teachers to work together, to communicate, and to share depends on family preferences. For instance, working parents may have limited time to participate in the preschool program. Creative ways to facilitate communication will be suggested, such as a quarterly Saturday breakfasts for families at school. In addition, the teacher may send home weekly notes telling parents about some favorite activities. In one family, a grandfather may care for the children while their parents work. He finds delight in participating in a weekly cooking activity in the classroom. This allows the child to have a family member share in his world; at the same time, the grandfather is able to provide insight and information to the rest of the family and to learn about the child's school activities.

Communication

Communicating with families is a critical part of the teaching team's responsibilities. All families are concerned about their children and want them to be successful and happy learners. Preschool may be the child's first experience away from his or her family, and family members will want to know about the child's progress. The teaching team will want to discuss the child's home and school activities, strengths, weaknesses, and areas of concern.

Developing open and trusting communication takes time. Some parents may have had negative experiences during their own schooling and may feel intimidated by teachers. Others may have been taught that teachers "know what's best" and hesitate to question them. Teachers may also have had negative experiences; perhaps parents may have told them how to teach. These attitudes or feelings can get in the way of good communication. It is important for the teaching team to talk with families from the very beginning of the program and explain what information they want from the families. Good listening skills are vital. Asking open-ended questions such as, "What does Ivan like to do at home?" or, "What does Eva tell you about what we do in school?" offers the family members opportunities to tell you about their children. Teachers should always use clear language that is understandable to the family and offer opportunities for them to ask questions.

Guidelines for Communication with Families

- Allow time, create opportunities, and encourage families to express their ideas, joys, goals, and concerns.

- Offer places to speak privately and always regard the information as confidential.

- Families share very personal information with teachers and it is important that the information be kept confidential. Step by Step Programs should have a policy on confidentiality and all staff and families must adhere to it.

In the preschool years, it is important that families and the school communicate freely about children and their experiences. School and home are linked closely, and the better the communication between the two places, the more support children can receive to make their early learning experiences positive. When teachers consider communication essential for children's success, it becomes part of the everyday activities.

Expectations

Many preschool programs have discovered that there can be differences in the expectations or goals of the school and teaching team and those of the family. It is important to discuss the program philosophy with families during enrollment and to continue the communication throughout the year. Differing views or expectations can cause misunderstanding or gaps in communication. It is also important to ask families what their expectations are for the child and what they want the child to gain from preschool. Have parents share what "success" means to them. Clarifying these issues early in the school year assists in later communication.

Strategies for Communicating with Families

This section presents examples of formal and informal communication strategies. A variety of communication strategies will best meet the needs of diverse families.

Informal Communication Strategies

Drop-Off and Pick-Up Times

Busy schedules often leave families with little extra time. Taking advantage of natural, informal occasions to talk with the family can help build the communication between the home and school.

For example, many teachers report that they talk with families in the morning when the children are dropped off and in the afternoon when the children are picked up. This is a good time to report on the day's activities, tell families about successes, and remind families of meetings or events. This informal time allows families to talk with other parents, ask the staff questions, request a meeting, play with their children or read to a group of children. It is not a good time to discuss concerns or problems, since the children are present. Set up a special meeting for that purpose.

To accommodate informal time with families, the classroom schedule must be flexible, building in relaxed beginning and ending activities. To ensure that families don't just leave the children at the door, the policy must clearly state that families must bring children inside and help them get organized for the day.

The first and last half hour of the day should be free time, during which children and their families can play and work together in the classroom. This time should be written into the daily schedule and become a regular part of the school day. Invite families into the classroom and offer coffee or snacks. Be sure that one member of the teaching staff is available to talk. Make sure all family members are greeted and offered an opportunity to share and receive information about the program and their child. As families become more comfortable in the program, you can encourage them to stay and help, to work in the Family Room, to bring in snacks, and to fix toys or do other things that need to be done.

Notes and Notebooks

Sending a short, informal note home with a child facilitates communication. The notes should tell of a specific accomplishment, new skill, or behavior. They might also thank families for something they did for the program. Families can be encouraged to send notes back to the teaching team. Such an exchange is particularly effective if the teachers are working on a specific goal with the child and the family is reinforcing it at home.

For ongoing communication, notebooks that circulate between the school and home are effective. This is an especially good idea if family members have limited time or do not have phones. These can be simple loose-leaf notebooks decorated by the child and carried back and forth by the child or family member. For a child with specific needs or problems, notebooks ensure continuous communication and can alert both the teaching staff or family members to successes or changes in status. This technique is most successful if used at least once a week, and works best for families who are comfortable putting their thoughts and ideas in writing. Other systems may work better for those families who are not comfortable with this technique.

Bulletin Boards

Bulletin boards are another way to communicate informally with families. Information on bulletin boards can be directed specifically to parents and can include notices of meetings, flyers on child development, nutrition, or other relevant issues. Bulletin boards can also show families what activities are going on at school. Boards display children's art, stories about field trips or photographs of children's family members. The schedule for the day, sign-up sheets, and instructions for volunteers can also be posted. Information on the bulletin boards may repeat or reinforce information mentioned in other forms of communication like newsletters or notes sent home.

It is important to make the bulletin boards bright and cheerful and to change them frequently. If they are filled with old information or look sloppy, families will not look at them. Changing the bulletin boards can be a revolving job assignment for the teaching staff. It is easier and more fun to create bulletin boards with another person. Be creative: let the bulletin board communicate the atmosphere and activities of the classroom.

Ask families to contribute to the bulletin boards. For example, if a father is a good artist, ask him to come to the classroom and draw or paint with the children, then post the group artwork on the bulletin board.

Tips for Using Bulletin Boards

√   Place information at adults' eye level.

√   Change at least some of the information on the board regularly.

√   Remember that everyone likes to see pictures and names of themselves and their children.

√   Display children's work.

√   Keep information brief.

√   Ask families to contribute to the bulletin board.

√   Post personal messages that acknowledge family accomplishments, such as a "thank you" sign to a parent who has helped on a project.

√   Assign two people to create bulletin boards. It's easier and more fun.

Newsletters

Newsletters or news sheets are another good way to communicate with families. A biweekly or monthly newsletter helps assure that all the families in the program receive consistent information. The intent and topics of the newsletters may vary. Some programs prefer a general format and use the newsletter to describe the events and activities that are happening in school and suggest ways to reinforce those activities at home. Others use a theme approach and discuss only activities and ideas that pertain to that theme. Some newsletters have different sections that feature current events, things to remember, and an article on child development.

Items to include in a newsletter:

- Announcements of a meeting, event, or community trip

- Requests for materials or help with a project

- Community information

- Discussion about the current focus of the classroom

- Suggestions for at-home activities

- Thank you notes to volunteers or requests for volunteers

Newsletters should be short and easy to read. It is more effective to send out brief newsletters regularly than long ones infrequently. Newsletter writers should include names of children in the program and family members as often as appropriate, making sure everyone is mentioned over time.

Formal Communication Strategies

There are times when formal, scheduled communication with families is desired. Formal methods of communication, which include parent-teacher conferences and written reports, are covered in Chapter V, *Observing, Recording and Reporting On Children's Development*.

Home Visits

Visiting children and their families at home is a practice common to many preschool programs. Home visits are typically made twice during the year, usually at the beginning and end of the year. The chief purpose of the visits is to get acquainted with the children and their families. Visits are a good way to establish communication and meet family members.

Sometimes both the teachers and families feel intimidated by the suggestion of a home visit. If the home visit is approached as a visit to an acquaintance's home and the manners and behavior associated with visiting someone in their home are observed, it will go smoothly. The children are usually so excited to have their teacher in their home that time should allow for a visit to the child's room and introduction to pets or toys. You may want to bring a new toy for the child to play with while you talk with the family.

Always schedule the visit at a convenient time for the family. If possible, try to schedule it when the father is home. Describe the purpose of the visit and how long it will last. Families may worry that a visit means bad news; be clear that the purpose is to get better acquainted and learn more about the child and family. Bringing a child's art or math work from school provides an opportunity for you to discuss the curriculum with family members.

At the beginning of the visit, review the purpose for the visit. Always start by discussing positives, even if the purpose of the visit may be to discuss concerns. If there is specific information for the family, write it down so they can review it after the visit. Don't do all the talking; always leave time for families to talk about the children and their ideas, concerns, and interests. Do not talk about the child in front of the child unless it is honest praise or other positive feedback.

Home visits can be rewarding for both the teaching team and families. The teacher can learn more about the family's culture, style of interaction, and special skills or talents. The family gets the personal attention of the teacher and sees how the teacher and child interact. The family can discuss any concerns, misunderstandings, or specific goals that they have for their child. The teacher can talk about the child's progress. If both the family and the teacher are clear about the purpose and intent of the visit, home visits can establish and continue to maintain good communication, which will enhance the child's and family's experience in the program.

Families in the Classroom

Making families feel welcome in the classroom requires more than a written notice or a one-time invitation. During the first home visit with the child and family, emphasize that the program's success is based on collaboration between the teaching team and families. Help family members understand that their participation is very much wanted through asking them to complete a written needs assessment (an example is located at the end of this chapter) and an explanation of the many opportunities for families to participate in the program. Ask about the family members' interests and skills and suggest ways that they can participate in the program.

Creating an atmosphere of trust requires mutual respect, which occurs over time. There are many benefits to family participation in an early childhood program.

Benefits for Families

Family members who visit the classroom, participate in and lead activities, will

- Develop a personal sense of ownership for the program

- Learn to view their child in relationship to others

- Understand more about child development

- Grow to know and respect the teaching team

- Learn activities that are fun to do at home

- Meet their children's friends

- Develop long-lasting friendships with other parents

- Be able to reinforce learning at home

Benefits for the Teaching Team

With the parents in the classroom, teachers will

- Spend more time with individual children or have the opportunity to work in smaller groups

- Learn how parents motivate their children

- See how family members help their children solve problems

- Learn more about diverse cultural practices

- Learn about special skills and hobbies that family members share with children, such as cooking or playing musical instruments

As teachers encourage family members to ask questions or express their concerns, a climate of joint planning and problem solving develops. Parents and teachers better understand a child's behaviors. The children realize that the presence of more adults can help individualize activities and enrich the classroom. Ongoing contact and communication form the basis for a collaborative relationship that helps overcome barriers and builds bridges between home and school.

Welcoming Families to the Classroom

The Step by Step Program recognizes families as experts about their children and as active participants in their child's learning. Making families feel welcome starts with their first encounter with the teaching team. All communications must convey this attitude. Respect and open communication regarding the program policies, procedures, goals, and activities help to make everyone feel part of the program.

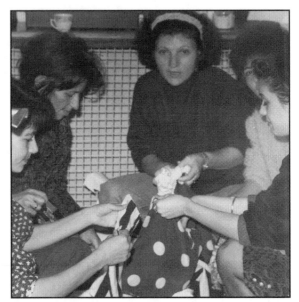

Families sometimes feel intimidated in the classroom or think that it is the teacher's "domain." They may feel reluctant for several reasons:

- They are not sure the teaching team really wants their help.

- They are afraid they may make a mistake.

- They do not know what to do and don't want to cause confusion.

- They don't feel they have anything to offer.

- The rules of the classroom are unclear.

It is the responsibility of the staff to encourage families to come to the classroom. At the beginning of the school year and regularly thereafter, it is important to explain that families are welcome to join the classroom activities any time they would like. Many programs have sign-up sheets on bulletin boards so families can sign up to participate for a certain time that fits their schedule.

There is no set amount of time that families need to sign up for. If a parent can come to help out during lunch or on the way to work, that's fine. Others may want to help a few hours each week. Some may come every day. Any amount of involvement is acceptable.

Introduction to the Classroom

Many programs hold the first family meeting in the classroom. The families go through the entire day's schedule as if they were children. They work with materials and play games, create an art activity, play outside, listen to music, and have a snack. It is a shortened version of the day, but the families experience what it is like for their children to be part of the program. Each activity center is clearly marked with a short explanation of what children learn in this area for families to read. (See *Explanation of a Preschool Dramatic Play Center* on page 49 for a sample description.)

This initial exploration helps families become comfortable with the classroom setting and the learning that occurs in different areas. This first meeting also allows teachers to explain different ways parents can assist in the classroom.

It is also very important for families to know the rules and specific procedures of the program. The teaching team can give a written copy of classroom rules to families at the beginning of the year and also post them on the bulletin board. Information can include techniques for discipline, clean up, and toileting.

Instructions for Activities

Hundreds of activities go on daily in a preschool classroom. Families who work with the children are not expected to know exactly what to do. Emphasize that when they help in the classroom, they can always interrupt you if they are uncomfortable or do not know how to handle a situation. If families are coming in on a certain day and time, give them directions about what will be helpful that day. A note with the person's name and instructions can be posted on a bulletin board. (See *Note for a Participating Family Member* on page 51.) The specificity of the instructions will depend on the comfort and skill of the family member coming to the classroom and the activity they will help with.

It is a good idea to display general information on ongoing activities in specific areas at all times. For example, the following explanation posted in the manipulative/table toy activity center would be helpful to parents.

Hello!

Thank you for helping us with the puzzles. Puzzles help us to learn spatial relationships, increase our problem-solving abilities, and work the small muscles in our fingers. Some of our puzzles have only a few pieces, and some have several. If we ask you for help, don't put the piece in for us. Just give a clue like "Turn the piece around" or "You may want to try and put the piece here."

Sometimes we pick puzzles that are too hard for us, and we do need extra help. If we are completely frustrated, help us put some in and then let us finish it, or suggest that we pick a puzzle with fewer pieces. At clean-up time, help us put all the pieces in the box and put the puzzles back in the rack. When you work with us, ask us about the colors, shapes, names of things in the puzzle.

Thank you. We like having you here.

Explanation of a Preschool Dramatic Play Center

Hello to Our Families –

Welcome to the Dramatic Play Center. This center is lots of fun and we have a good time here.

In this activity center we practice how to be big people and try new roles for ourselves. We practice cooking, cleaning, and wearing different clothes. We also learn how to get along with each other and practice our speech and language. We make friends and learn how to keep them. Sometimes the teachers add new materials to this area and we learn about bandaging the baby, combing hair, or being a farmer or postal clerk.

We learn about life here, and we often imitate you here, because you are our role models. When you see us "dressing up" at home, you will know that we are practicing our new skills.

Have fun here! We look forward to your visit and hope we can have "tea" together. Be sure and clean up. We must, too!

Love from the children.

(Adapted from "Motivating Parents" Workshop Handouts developed by Barbara Wolfe)

General guidelines for working in the classroom include information on storing materials, rules for handling disciplinary problems, a copy of the daily schedule, and information on how to interact with children in the different activity centers. Written information, like that on the sample *General Information for Families in the Classroom,* will help families feel more confident and encourage them to return to the classroom.

Some families will not be able to come to the classroom or are not interested in helping in that way. Remember, there are many other ways of participating in the program. Families contribute when they donate materials, attend meetings, help to build equipment or clean up the outdoor area, or bring in a book for the children to read. If people are uncomfortable coming alone, arrange for them to work with a parent who feels more comfortable or has more experience. Linking families with other families is a valuable way to introduce new parents to the program.

For those children whose families cannot participate in the classroom but are involved in other aspects of the program, it is important to let the children know this. You don't want any children to feel left out.

Showing Appreciation

Everyone likes to feel appreciated, and the families who come to help in the program are no different. They are using their valuable time to contribute to the program and deserve thanks and recognition. Always thank family members for coming and ask if they have any questions. Also ask if there is anything that would make their experience better the next time they come. (See *Showing Appreciation to Family Members* on page 53 for examples.)

Note for a Participating Family Member

Good Morning Mrs. _____,

When the children arrive, greet the children by name and talk to them about their morning. Help them take off their coats and put them away. Don't do it for them, but help them as they need it.

Today, we are working on identifying colors. Please take these children one at a time (give list of names) and work with them on matching colors using the lotto game. Show the child a color and ask him or her to find another one that looks like it. Praise them for the colors they can match. If they cannot match the color after a few attempts, show them which ones match and then ask them to try again.

Please help us set the table for snack by giving the snack helper the bowls and glasses to put on the table. Sit with the children at snack and talk to them. Ask them questions about what they did today.

Thanks for helping us today. We appreciate it.

(Adapted from "Motivating Parents" Workshop Handouts developed by Barbara Wolfe.)

General Information for Families in the Classroom

√ Participate in group activities. Sit with the children.

√ Encourage children to take off their coats, scarves, hats, mittens, or boots without help. Assist them only if needed.

√ Do not interpret children's art work, block building or wood work by giving it a title. Ask children what they call it. Have them explain it to you.

√ Ask the teaching team questions at appropriate times.

√ Wear comfortable clothes so you can sit on the floor or go outside with the children.

√ Do not discuss the individual children with other adults, their parents, or other family members. If you have comments, concerns, or questions, ask the teaching team or director.

√ Tell your ideas and suggestions to the staff so they can use them in the classroom.

√ If you have a special skill or talent, let the teaching team know.

√ Learn the discipline policy before you start working in the classroom. Ask the staff to explain what you should do if children get into fights with one another or have behavior problems.

√ Do not discuss children's behavior in front of them.

√ Give children enough time to do things for themselves before you offer to help or solve a problem.

Showing Appreciation to Family Members

√ Thank family members individually for helping.

√ Address them by name and remember to mention their child's name.

√ Plan meaningful activities for the families to do. Show them what you expect them to do and ask if they have any questions. Also ask them what they would like to do. Give them choices.

√ Be prepared to invest time training parents in the classroom. Show helpers around, explain things, introduce them to the staff, and indicate where they will work.

√ Arrange for a place for helpers to sit and relax and store their personal belongings.

√ Supply enough food so the helpers can eat with the children.

√ Designate a bulletin board for helpers.

√ Have teaching staff available to answer family members' questions and give them directions when they arrive.

√ Create a section in the newsletter that highlights family members' activities.

√ Have a section in the newsletter that recognizes and thanks families who have come to the center or contributed to the program.

√ Award plaques or certificates of recognition.

√ Hold celebrations or parties to honor everyone who made the program successful.

Be supportive of parents' efforts. Thank them and thank them again. Encourage them to come with a friend. Encourage them to bring their spouses. Include activities that fathers may feel more comfortable with, like building outdoor equipment or playing in the block area. Invite them directly. Grandparents may also be willing to help. Ask them what they would like to do or what talents they have.

Getting Men Involved

Every effort should be made to include and welcome the men who are in the children's lives. From the beginning of the program, schedule home visits, parent meetings, conferences, and other activities at times when fathers can participate. Include the men in all discussions. Ask them questions about the child. Address notes and invitations to both fathers and mothers. If reports need to be signed, ask for both signatures. This tells the father "You are important to us."

There are many ways to involve the men who are significant in the children's lives. The following strategies are especially useful:

- Plan special events oriented towards men. Invite children and their father or other important men, to an event or activity just for them.

- Ask the men how they would like to contribute to the program.

- Encourage two fathers to come together to meetings or the classroom so they can support each other.

- Plan "men-only" social events where fathers can exchange ideas and talk about their children.

- Offer parenting classes just for men, preferably led by a man. Emphasize activities men can enjoy with their children. These types of classes often form support groups and are very beneficial.

- Sponsor family nights and events that encourage both parents to participate.

- Designate a morning when fathers and other men are invited to the classroom before they go to work. Encourage men who are delivering their children to stay for a while. This can become a special time for both the children and the men.

- Sponsor family evenings, weekend events, and "share" suppers that encourage participation of both fathers and mothers as well as other family members.

Family Meetings and Gatherings

Family meetings and gatherings are an important part of the Step by Step Program. Some preschool programs have a parent meeting once a month. The families, teachers and administrators decide the topics and the types of meetings to be held. There are several types of family meetings including instructional, advisory, informal, and support.

An **instructional meeting** is an informative workshop. An outside speaker usually is invited to the meeting to discuss a certain topic with the families.

Adult learners need to be part of the decision-making process and participate in the workshops. Staff should use an interest survey or hold discussions with families to identify topics of interest to them. Certain topics, such as child growth and development, may be presented more formally. Others are participatory and give families a chance to practice new skills such as communication techniques.

A formal **family advisory committee meeting** is also recommended. The purpose of this committee, convened by the proper administrator and held quarterly, is to solicit information and ideas from families. Families are encouraged to share their ideas for program improvement or fund-raising strategies. Topics commonly addressed include encouraging family participation, parent-teacher conferences, community involvement, and social events. An advisory committee empowers parents to be active participants in all important  aspects of the program — from planning to implementation. Parents learn skills such as planning and facilitating meetings, running for and holding office, fund raising, working on committees, and strategic planning. Teachers and administrators must be responsive to the recommendations of the board or have sound reason for suggestions that are not taken. The program administrator works closely with the officers of the advisory committee, and they solve problems and generate new initiatives as a team.

Informal meetings are times when families gather to have fun, share experiences, talk with other families, and feel part of the program. Families plan these events with the staff. These gatherings may take the form of morning coffees, informal chats in the Family Room, field trips, picnics, family dinners, holiday parties, and game nights.

Support groups usually form out of a common need for several families to discuss an issue. In the course of an instructional meeting, several parents may find they want to discuss a particular issue or get more information. Families with a specific interest or need can get together and offer each other suggestions, resources, and support. These groups may be for fathers, mothers, single parents, new parents, or parents of children who have a disability.

Informal support groups that meet in the Family Room and discuss their issues. Staff should support these efforts as much as possible by providing coffee, chairs, and space.

Family Room

A space dedicated to families says, "Welcome, we want you here." Whether this is shared space or a room unto itself, an attractive area for families opens many options for family involvement. The room should have a rug and a sofa or comfortable chairs. If possible, simple snack food should be available as well as coffee or tea. Children's drawings and other art projects should adorn the walls. A box filled with toys provides entertainment for younger brothers and sisters. If this room is used for group events such as parent meetings, extra folding chairs should be available.

If the room also serves as an office for staff, it may be necessary to schedule times during the day when the room is closed. However, it is important that the Family Room be available for parents at regular times each day — at a minimum for two hours in the morning and an hour or two every afternoon. Other times might be more flexible, depending on the needs of the staff and the schedules of the families. Update the room schedule weekly and make it available to all families.

Lending Library

Books and toys should be available for parents to borrow for use at home. The toys can be kept in the Family Room. Use a sign-up sheet or cards to record who has borrowed a toy and when they should return it. A two or three week loan period generally works well. Families should be able to borrow toys as often as they wish.

Children's books provide a special time between parent and child, and reading at home promotes a love of literature that can last a lifetime. A similar sign-out process can be developed for books. The Family Room also should have books on child development and parenting available for families to borrow or read in the room. If no such books are available, teachers should write simple information on child development for parents to read. Family members may choose to use a parent meeting to share information on child rearing, and some of their ideas can be written down for others to read.

Family members can organize and maintain lending libraries by arranging the toys and books, checking the sign-out sheets, and sending reminders to families who may have forgotten to return an item.

It is important for families to feel comfortable borrowing toys and books, so assure them that normal use can sometimes result in a toy breaking or a book tearing. It is clear that families need to care for materials, but it is understandable that accidents happen. Remove broken toys from use because they can be dangerous. Broken toys and torn books should be mended if possible. Parents are often very good at fixing things, and that may be one way they can contribute to the program.

Discover Family Interests

Involving families in a meaningful way takes time, planning, and knowledge about the interests and limits of the family members. One way to find out how the family may want to help is to develop a checklist or inventory of ways to participate. To encourage broad participation, this inventory can be presented and explained at one of the first parent meetings. (See *Family Interest Form* on the following page).

The purpose of the interest survey is to inform families about how they can use their individual interests, talents and time to contribute to the program. Each family's contribution is valuable; however, all families will not participate to the same extent.

Involving families in the program takes time and dedication on the part of the staff. However, the effort is worth it because families grow and learn together. By involving them in the program, you offer them the opportunity to learn more about how to support their child's growth and development.

Family Interest Form

Parent's name(s)_____

Child's name _____

Program level_____

Dear Mr. and Mrs. _____

We are delighted that your child will be enrolled in the Step By Step Program this year. We look forward to working with you. As you know, we encourage families to be involved in our program as much as possible. To give us an idea of ways you would like to help, please check off your areas of interest below. Thank you. We look forward to seeing you soon.

FAMILY INTEREST SURVEY

I am interested in

_____ Attending monthly parent meetings

_____ Working in the classroom If checked, are there any activities you would especially enjoy doing with the children? Reading____ Art____ Puzzles____ Music____   Other____

_____ Building or making materials Outdoor equipment____ Doll clothes____ Other____

_____ Helping with community trips

_____ Planning special events (birthdays, holidays)

_____ Working with the teaching team to develop ideas for the classroom

_____ Sending materials from home

_____ Attending events for parents

_____ Participating in a support group

Choosing Topics for Family Meetings

Many programs use a checklist to ask families what topics they want presented at the monthly meetings. Families check off the topics they are interested in and prioritize their interests; the topics that receive the most votes are then selected for parent meetings. Ideas for topics include the following:

- Child growth and development
- Managing difficult behavior
- Childhood nutrition
- Childhood diseases
- Learning through play
- Building self-esteem
- Developing language
- Physical development
- Toy selection
- An overview of the program
- Community resources

In developing an interest checklist, give specific information about the workshop contents. A specific description gives families an opportunity to decide if the topic interests them and helps ensure they will attend the session. For example:

Techniques for Managing Behaviors
This workshop will focus on techniques to use when your child says "no" to you or engages in unruly conduct, such as kicking or biting.

Childhood Nutrition
This workshop will look at the nutritional requirements of children ages three to five years and discuss foods that children of this age usually like.

As you develop or review the format for discovering families' interests, make sure that the activities meet the following criteria. If you answer "no" to any of the questions that follow, consider revising your survey format.

Determining Family Interests: Staff Review Sheet

Does the process –

√   Ask family members how they would like to be
involved? ___yes ___no

√   Allow parents to be interviewed rather than just
to fill out another form? ___yes ___no

√   Ask families to describe their talents and interests?   ___yes ___no

√   Continue to solicit input and remain flexible? ___yes ___no

√   Respect culture and customs? ___yes ___no

√   Include interesting activities? (Show families a
picture album of last year's activities or ask parents
who have participated in past years to talk about
their experiences.) ___yes ___no

√   Include families' ideas? (Ask family members from
previous classes to help design the process.) ___yes ___no

Discovering the needs and interests of families continues throughout the year as relationships grow stronger. These relationships enable staff to elicit additional information on parents' needs, interests, and talents and thus plan more relevant topics for meetings. It is up to the program staff to plan useful activities and to point out the ways that new skills can be transferred into other settings.

Planning Informal Events or Gatherings

Since parents are asked to give up their spare time to attend meetings and participate in the program, the needs-assessment process should include information about what they enjoy doing in their free time. Once this information is obtained, it can be incorporated into the program planning process.

Questions that elicit this information include the following:

- What do you do in your free time?

- How do you and your family have fun?

- What activities would you like to do that you never have time for?

- What activities would you like to do that you never have done before?

A checklist format also works for these questions. Using a format similar to the one that follows, ask the parents to check the activities they enjoy doing in their spare time.

What do you like to do in your spare time?

Spend time with my family	____ Spend time alone
Play cards	____ Read
Cook	____ Visit with friends
Walk in the park	____ Spend time outside
Other _____	

Which activities do you do most with your child?

Play games	____ Tell stories
Enjoy the outdoors	____ Take them to the park
Take them to church	____ Visit with relatives
Other _____	

Scheduling

Families lead busy lives, and to accommodate the most people, times for events must be flexible. Fathers may be available for evening, weekend, or late afternoon. If the meeting is held at a convenient time, is well organized, allows people to participate, has a social element, and is fun, families will attend.

Activities to Promote Family Participation

Outside Activities

Hiking – A hike in a nature area can be a wonderful learning experience.

Sing-alongs – Singing, traditional or cultural games, and story telling involve everyone.

Ice skating and roller skating – If no one is very good, it doesn't matter. You will laugh a lot.

Fishing – Both children and adults like to fish and getting wet is part of the fun.

Building or improving the playground – Everyone can help. This is a good way to involve fathers.

Gardening – The children will learn about how food grows, and parents will have fresh food.

Kite festival – Have children and parents make kites together. Invite other classes, too.

Clubs or Classes. Groups of various types provide parents with friendship and support systems.

Sewing, art, exercise classes – Ask a local person to lead a class for the family and staff.

Fix-it club – Families help each other repair cars, equipment, clothes, and so forth.

Secret pals – Assign each parent to another parent. During the year, the parents will do nice things for their assigned person (sending notes, making small gifts, etc.). At the end of the year, the secret pals are acknowledged.

Big Brother/Big Sister – Ask family members who were in the program last year to serve as a Big Brother or Big Sister to new parents. They can answer questions and encourage parents to attend meetings. Parents who have already participated in the program are the best promoters of Step by Step.

Food and Fun

Food festivals are an excellent way to acknowledge various cultures. Encourage families to bring prepared foods or ingredients to the center. Have a group of parents and children assist preparing the meal. Offer music and dancing. Have children contribute their art work or stories.

As an alternative, hold *"favorite food night."* Have parents talk to their children about their favorite food, prepare it together, and bring it to an event.

These are only a few ideas for involving families in pleasurable, active ways. With all the information gathered from the checklists and your informal discussions with the parents, you can design innovative activities. Start small, and expand your ideas with each success. Join the parents as they have fun and learn at the same time.

How to Hold a Successful Meeting

To promote comfort and a relaxed atmosphere, use different methods of introduction. For example, have participants introduce themselves by giving their middle name, their favorite food, or the last thing their child said to them before they left the house. Teaching team staff, family members, the site manager, and people from the community may lead the meetings or the workshops.

- Encourage active discussion. This can be done by asking open-ended questions or by dividing participants into pairs or small groups to make speaking less intimidating.

- Hold the meeting in a comfortable, friendly environment.

- Provide baby-sitting services.

- Place chairs in a circle so everyone feels included.

- Use visual aids, media, handouts, games, or activities to reinforce messages.

- If you are discussing child development, use audiotapes or photographs of the children in the program.

- Send personal invitations and follow up with a conversation.

- Always allow time for families to talk with one another.

- Pair an involved parent with one who is not involved. Perhaps they could meet or talk beforehand.

- Keep presentations short. Adults have short attention spans, particularly after a long day.

- Include playfulness in the presentations. Laughter is good for everyone!

If families are unable to attend the meeting, you can send a note home saying what was discussed and express your hope they will be able to come to the next meeting.

Evaluating Family Meetings

Since family meetings are such an important part of the program, evaluate them to see if they address families' needs and interests. A simple form like *The Family Meeting Evaluation Checklist* can be used for this purpose.

Family Meeting Evaluation Checklist

	Yes	No
Were families encouraged to share opinions and experiences?	—	—
Was everyone physically comfortable?	—	—
Were the topics relevant to families' interests?	—	—
Was some part of the meeting fun?	—	—
Did the presenter use more than one medium to present the information? (handouts, activities)	—	—
Would you have attended the meeting if it were not your job?	—	—
Were child care and transportation provided?	—	—
Were family members introduced to each other?	—	—

Confidentiality

Confidentiality can be defined as preserving information that was received in confidence from a family member and disclosing information only to professionals for the benefit of the family.

In the Step By Step Program, staff encourage an atmosphere of open discussion and provide opportunities for families to talk about issues that concern them. Parents may sometimes give the staff sensitive information regarding their children or a troubling family situation.

All efforts to build a supportive program can be undone if anyone discovers that confidential information has been divulged about children, parents, or staff. All those who are associated with the program, staff and parents alike, must be aware of the necessity to learn to treat both conversations and records in a confidential manner. Keep records in a locked file and create a check-out system for a few key staff who have permission to use the records. Check-out forms should include the child's name, the staff member's name, the date of check out, and the date of return.

The program staff has the responsibility to protect all private information that is shared, whether it is obtained orally or in writing. The written permission of the family is required before the program can disclose information to others. Families must know how and what information may be shared. They must also be aware that they have the right to review their personal/data file at any time.

Staff in-service training should review confidentiality procedures at least once a year. Staff should also be reminded regularly that information learned through conversations and parent groups should not be repeated. Information written by staff must be factual, objective, and useful. Hearsay and rumors are usually not objective or useful. Reporting and recording only factual, objective information is the key for ensuring that staff will provide appropriate services to each family and child.

All programs should develop a written confidentiality policy. The policy should include the following:

- The process for releasing information to community agencies or individuals

- How the program will use confidential information

- Training and procedures for ensuring objective recording and reporting of information

- Parent's rights

- Procedures for getting staff the information they need

- Disciplinary action that will be taken for violations

- Procedures for staff and parent training

The confidentiality policy should state that staff members must not discuss families or children in the program with anyone outside the agency, including their own families and friends. The policy should also state that all staff will not convey confidential information to visitors or family members who are working in the classroom. This includes information from conversations, parent meetings, or discussions with families. If others request information regarding the address of the family or any other personal information, the family must consent to any information released.

(Information in this section was adapted from: Mental Health in Head Start: It's Everybody's Business, The Head Start Social Services Training Guide and ACF Region VII memo on Client Confidentiality for Head Start Programs.)

Suggested Guidelines for Maintaining Confidentiality

Families have the right to be assured that any personal information they reveal, whether orally or in writing, will be held in confidence by staff. The following principles should be kept in mind:

1. Parents should be the primary source of information about themselves, and information sought from them should be limited to that which is essential to serve them.

2. Parents and other volunteers are prohibited from reviewing records other than those of their own children.

3. Children's records and family records are open only to staff and special consultants on a "need to know" basis (only to the extent necessary to provide services).

4. Families are told about information that will be shared with other staff and the reasons why. (For example, a signed consent form that includes how information is shared and with whom could be helpful.) When in doubt about releasing information, obtain permission from a family member.

5. Do not release information to anyone outside the program without written consent from the family, except in reporting suspected child abuse and neglect.

6. Consult with other agencies and individuals only with the family's consent and within the limits of that consent.

7. On a yearly basis, with input from parents and staff, decide what information will be collected, how it will be shared, and with whom.

8. Include information on how forms will be used and how information will be released as a part of the agency's plan or policy for confidentiality.

9. Record only that information and maintain only those records that are essential to provide service and determine the use of records by agency function and with the consent of the family.

(Source: Head Start, *Social Services Training Guide*)

Suggested Opportunities for Family Participation

Home Visits
Early fall - September and October
Spring - April and May

Reports
December - in writing, using checklist with comments
May - in writing to send on to the next teacher

Regularly Scheduled Conferences
November - with all families
March - with all families

Written Communication
Communication notebooks - sent home weekly
Newsletters
Monthly calendars
Special notes - as warranted
Samples of children's work - frequently

Visits in the Classroom
Morning and afternoon visiting times - always available
Special occasions - birthdays, holidays
Working with children - planned in advance to help with an
    activity (cooking, reading, woodworking)
Spending time with a child

Parent Meetings
Explaining the Step by Step Program and curriculum -
    September
Child development meetings - to discuss areas of development
    and parenting concerns (as often as interest and time allow)
Special speakers and topics - to discuss appropriate issues
    (nutrition, health and safety, or music)

BUILDING COMMUNITY

IV. BUILDING COMMUNITY

Today's five-year-olds will be twenty-one-year-old adults in the early 21st century. Their world will be very different than the one we live in. Societies are changing. Communities are being redefined. How can parents and educators best prepare young children to be successful members of tomorrow's communities? What social skills will they need? The Brazilian activist Paulo Freire asserts that educators must be guided by "dreams and utopias." He declares, "I can't respect the teacher who doesn't dream of a certain kind of society that he would like to live in."

We have the opportunity to create the kind of community in which we can share dreams of success for all children. Building communities that will equip young children with the social skills they will need is a basic goal of the Step by Step Preschool Program.

In *Teaching Children to Care,* Ruth Charney has written, "In today's world, it is particularly urgent that we extend beyond the domain of self and the lessons of self-control. We need to find connections to others, and to feel ourselves members of many groups — intimate groups, community groups, and a world group. We need to teach children to give care as well as to receive care." (1992, p. 32).

Charney writes that teachers build community by expecting children to

- *Know names*   Children learn and use each other's names and get to know the interests and feelings of others.

- *Take turns*   Children learn how to take turns. As they get older, turn taking occurs often without arguing or quitting the activity.

- *Share*   Children learn to share attention, private time with the teacher, space at the sandbox, snacks, and crayons.

- *Make room in the circle*   Children learn to make room for latecomers to the circle and to sit with children who are not their best friends.

- *Join activities* — Children learn how to join small groups in a constructive manner.

- *Invite others to join* — Children learn how to extend invitations that will bring others into their activities.

- *Be friendly* — Children learn how to greet and express interest in others.

- *Cooperate* — Children cooperate on projects, solve problems together, and play games as a team or in a group.

- *Solve conflicts* — Children learn that by talking about problems and sharing feelings and points of view, conflicts can be resolved.

Setting the Tone

The teaching team sets up the room, selects materials, plans the daily schedule, and most important, truly sets the tone for everything that happens in that classroom. Attitudes of respect, sincerity, humor and fun contribute greatly to this tone, as Murphy and Leeper observe in the following passage:

The single most important influence on a child in a classroom, naturally, is the teacher. The entire program revolves around her. Adult helpers enrich and bolster the teacher's relationship with the children. . . . A skillful, understanding teacher, whose primary goal is caring for children, can provide a challenging program, even when the physical setting is not ideal. . . . A good teacher in a well-planned setting combines the basic elements for successful child care (Murphy and Leeper, 1974).

Ways to Show Respect for Children in the Classroom

√   Always use the child's name.

√   Speak to the child individually as often as possible.

√   Get down to the children's level when talking to them by kneeling or sitting on a low chair.

√   Listen to what children say to you and respond to what they say.

√   If you tell children that you will do something for them later, be sure to do it.

√   Express honest appreciation for a child's work.

√   Give children the opportunity to share their work and interests with the others.

√   Use children's ideas and suggestions and acknowledge their contribution.

There must be respect for one another in the classroom — among the teaching team and the children. Respect is an essential component of a healthy classroom community. Teachers model the kind of understanding, respect, and care that is expected of children. The quality of respect that the children experience is a key factor in the development of their own self respect. Self-respect provides a solid basis for satisfying relationships with the other children.

When the teaching team shows respect to every child, children learn how to accept all children — the child who is a slow runner, the child who is an excellent painter, and even the child with different or difficult behavior. When children see and feel that each of them is accepted and respected, they become comfortable and feel free to develop their own interests and styles.

The teaching team needs to recognize that like adults, children are sensitive to, and aware of, the sincerity shown them. Praise for a child's work must be individualized and honest; interactions should be natural and not forced.

Children enjoy and respond to age-appropriate humor and fun. Adults do not have to fear that they will lose control of classroom order if they laugh and joke with children. On the contrary, laughing together can enhance the warmth and friendship between teacher and child and encourage cooperation within the classroom.

Teaching about Diversity

Many of today's preschoolers will be working with people from around the world. Many of these people will be from different cultures and speak different languages. An ability to work smoothly and respectfully with others will be critical for success in the years ahead. Few children will be untouched by the potential problems that will occur if they are not at ease with diversity and not able to cooperate and collaborate with people who are "different".

Young children are gaining information about their ever-widening world and forming opinions about what they experience. They try to learn the significance of differences. Children look to adults in their lives, such as parents and teachers, for cues. The Step by Step Program believes that diversity is to be celebrated and appreciated, rather than avoided. It is the duty of parents and teachers to help children understand how hurtful prejudice and bias are. Issues of fairness, so important to young children, can be used as a springboard for helping children appreciate why it is unfair to categorize playmates and neighbors.

Adjusting to life in a multicultural society takes time and experience. The Step by Step Program helps children grow in their willingness to appreciate differences through positive real-world experiences. Issues of differences are infused throughout the curriculum. Time spent addressing these issues can significantly enhance the self image of children and support families as well. Teachers have reported that their classes have become more productive and less disruptive when issues of diversity are addressed.

The teacher can help children expand their thinking about similarities and differences by incorporating these guidelines into daily teaching strategies:

- *Pay close attention to children while they are talking.*

- *Set a calm, relaxed atmosphere so children have enough uninterrupted time in the conversation to form and express their ideas.*

- *Affirm the thinking with comments like: "I believe you."*

- *Clarify the thinking by repeating the idea back to the child using some other key words and phrases.*

- *Offer supportive, thought-provoking comments such as: "Gee, that's an interesting idea," "What makes you think that?" "Does anybody else have an idea?" "Once somebody told me..." "What do you think of that idea?"*

- *Avoid evaluating children's ideas by saying "good idea" or "good solution," because it gives children the impression that there is one right answer and that you are looking for the child to find the one right answer.*

Roots and Wings, Redleaf Press, New York, p. 119-120

The Step by Step Program encourages teachers to respond to discriminatory behavior in the following ways:

- Do not ignore it.
- Explain what was observed and engage participants in discussion.
- Do not fear conflict.
- Become aware of your own attitudes.
- Be understanding.
- Recognize your own frustration.
- Model expected behavior.
- Be ready to intervene.
- Be nonjudgmental.
- Distinguish between categorical and stereotypical thinking.

Adapted from Roots and Wing, Redleaf Press, New York

The learning environment and curriculum should reflect the language, culture, and customs of the children and families in the program. *Promoting Cultural Diversity and Cultural Competency,,* the self-assessment checklist found at end of this chapter, can be extremely helpful as you plan a culturally appropriate format.

Teaching Responsibility

Children are often far more competent at caring for their belongings, cleaning up after themselves, and working independently than adults expect. Good early childhood programs provide real-life opportunities for children to make decisions, take responsibility, and do as much as they can for themselves. As children overcome challenges, they develop mastery and self-confidence.

Teachers should not do for children what they can do for themselves. Feeding, toileting, and dressing are among the important self-help skills mastered by toddlers and preschool-aged children. When adults feed preschool children, clean up for them, dress them, and in other ways infantilize them, they give the clear message that the children are not capable. Instead, teachers should communicate to children that they are able to do many things on their own. Children feel pride and accomplishment when they can put on their coats by themselves or wash off the tables after snacks.

Teachers learn to distinguish between assistance and intervention: helping a child who is unable to complete a physically or developmentally difficult task, but not intervening when the child is trying hard to complete the task alone. Sometimes teachers intervene because it is faster, easier, or too painful to watch the child struggle, but the child who is unable to perform an entire task can at least carry out part of it. If, for example, a child is unable to cut his meat without help, the teacher might encourage him to use the knife to cut his potatoes, bread and carrots on his plate.

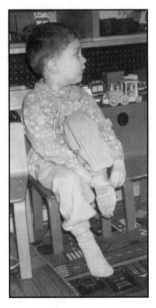

Responsible children grow up to be responsible citizens. Through practice, children learn to understand their impact on material objects and other people. The preschool environment provides children with many opportunities to practice this important life skill. Shelves that are labeled help children learn to put away their materials after each use. Making a job chart with rotating jobs such as waiter (snack helper, lunch table setter), janitor (floor sweeper), zoo keeper (pet feeder), botanist (plant waterer), teacher (attendance taker), musician (selector of songs), and librarian (book chooser) allows children to participate in the daily maintenance of the classroom.

When children help formulate class rules and then abide by those rules, they function as part of a democratic community. When teachers insist that children work out a solution to a disagreement, they learn to accept the consequences of their actions. In child-centered classrooms, children are viewed as competent and responsible. They are encouraged to do real work and participate in the decisions that govern this work. Teachers take pleasure in creating opportunities for children to become partners in the learning process.

Classrooms that function as communities are dynamic; they convey a sense of excitement and energy. As children are involved in their important work and play, they reflect their teacher's confidence in them. They feel competent, responsible, and are empowered to do their best.

Decision Making

Making decisions is fundamental to the child-centered classroom. Choosing activities, materials, foods and clothes helps children practice the decision-making process in safe, structured ways. They learn to take responsibility for their choices and understand the consequences of their actions. The child must ask herself, "If I play with the blocks now, I may miss the cooking activity. Which is more important to me?"

When the teacher asks the children to vote on the name of the class's new rabbit, they learn that they have the power to make something happen as a group. They also learn that the group democratic process may not always support their individual choices.

Making choices requires practice. The preschool schedule allows many opportunities for children to make choices: where to sit in the circle, which activity center to work in, who to play with, whether to throw the large or small ball, or what to make with clay. Effective choice making should not be confused with intelligence; rather, it is a skill that is learned through experience and practice.

Children in classrooms where choice is built into the learning environment will weigh the costs and benefits of their choices and make appropriate decisions for themselves. As children practice making choices, they become better at making decisions in an increasingly complex world.

Classroom Rules

The Need for Limits

In our own homes, each of us has rules, routines, and rituals. The way we do things makes us comfortable; it seems like the right way to do things. We think of our way as the "right" way. Children get accustomed to the way things are done at home, and it becomes the natural way for them.

Children in a preschool program are confronted with a set of rules and expectations that are necessary for group living and may differ greatly from those at home. The nature and extent of classroom rules also vary, depending on the teacher, the curriculum, the physical arrangement of the classroom, and the children in it. Most children are quite willing to accept the expectations of the preschool. They are more comfortable when they know what they may do or may not do and what they can expect of others.

Children vary in the degree to which they conform to a routine and accept some of the expected ways of behaving. One of the best ways to maximize conformity to classroom routines is to involve children in developing rules, changing rules, and making new rules when necessary.

A major objective in working with young children is to teach them self-control. Teachers can assist children to learn self-control by explaining the consequences of undesirable behaviors and helping children recognize and find solutions for problematic behaviors. Involving children in solving a problem can have long-term benefits that are superior to traditional reward-or-punishment techniques. Rules and expectations for classroom behaviors help children develop self-control.

The teaching team will find these general guidelines helpful when establishing rules:

- Teachers must be clear in their own minds about what is and is not permissible within the classroom setting.

- The teaching team must be consistent about what is acceptable behavior.

- The teaching team should develop rules with the children.

- Over time, children should come to understand that the rules serve all the class members.

Importance of Consistency

An adult who combines affection with fair and steady rules is modeling consistent behavior. Children feel secure when the adult is consistent. Clarity eliminates many potential problems. If children know that when they return to the classroom from the playground, they must put their jackets in their cubbies and then go to the reading area and select a book, they will have a routine they can follow each day and in which they can be successful. On the other hand, if children do not know what is expected of them when they return to the classroom, chaos may result: children may run around wildly and create a disruptive situation.

Consistency about what is acceptable within the classroom setting creates an environment that guides children in how to behave. It creates a climate that, both directly and subtly, establishes clear expectations for behavior.

- Apply rules to all children. For example, one rule may be "No hitting." You could express the rule as: "Treat others gently. You may not hit another child; I will not let anyone hit you."

- Always explain the reason for a rule to a child. For example, if one child is hitting another, first stop the hitting and then explain the reason for not hitting and the effect of hitting.

- State rules positively. Say, "Please walk in our classroom," instead of "Don't run."

Some rules or limits vary from teacher to teacher and group to group. For example:

- Individual tolerance for noise varies, as do the acoustical qualities of classrooms. Therefore, rules about using "talking" voices inside the building and allowing "shouting" voices outside might be determined according to the situation.

- The need for a rule curtailing running might depend on the space in the room, the number and nature of the children, and the opportunities for outside play.

Involving Children in Developing Rules

When a situation causes disruption or distress to children, it is appropriate to set limits and to involve children in developing the rules. For example:

Evan and Mikol are building in the block center. They are showing the teacher their grocery store building when Marianna runs through the area and knocks it down. This is not the first time such a situation has occurred. What do you do?

Sit down with the three children. Ask them:

- What was the problem?
- What caused the difficulty?
- What can they do so this doesn't happen again?

Once the children have identified running as the cause of the problem, they are ready to identify the solution. The teacher may need to guide the children to recognize that running should not be allowed in the block center. Once they reach this point, the teacher needs to ask how to share this decision with other children in the class. The children may decide to make a sign (or ask the teacher to make one) that says, "Slow down" or, "Come in only if you are walking."

Since the problem had concerned other children at other times, the teacher may want to identify this rule for all the children. When making the rule, the class should focus on the problem, not on the child who caused the problem.

Re-evaluating Classroom Rules

If children are not following the rules, the teaching team needs to consider the following questions:

- Are the expectations clear to the children?

- Are the activities too hard?

- Are the children expected to sit too long? To stand in line too long?

- Do the children have enough time to move around?

- Are the adults demonstrating and doing projects while the children merely watch?

- Are there specific reasons why an individual child is misbehaving? (For example: fatigue, physical problems, home problems, personal adjustment problems?)

When families and children are helped to understand rules, they are also assisted in the transition process from home to school. When children participate in creating rules, they acquire problem-solving skills and develop self-control. Families can practice this process of making family rules or guidelines at home.

PROMOTING CULTURAL DIVERSITY
AND CULTURAL COMPETENCY

Self-Assessment Checklist
for Personnel Providing Services and Supports
in Early Childhood Settings

DIRECTIONS: Please select A, B, or C for each item listed below.

> A = Things I do frequently
> B = Things I do occasionally
> C = Things I do rarely or never

PHYSICAL ENVIRONMENT, MATERIALS AND RESOURCES

_____ 1. I display pictures, posters and other materials that reflect the cultures and ethnic backgrounds of children and families in my classroom or program.

_____ 2. I select props for the dramatic play area that are culturally diverse (e.g., dolls, clothing, cooking utensils, household articles, furniture).

_____ 3. I ensure that the literacy area has picture and story books that reflect the different cultures of children and families in my classroom or program.

_____ 4. I ensure that table-top toys and other play accessories that depict people are representative of the various cultural and ethnic groups within my country or society.

_____ 5. I read a variety of books that expose children in my classroom or program to various life experiences of cultures and ethnic groups other than their own.

_____ 6. When such books are not available, I provide opportunities for children and their families to create their own books and include them among the classroom resources and materials.

_____ 7. I encourage and provide opportunities for children and their families to share experiences through storytelling, puppets, marionettes, or other props.

_____ 8. I plan trips and community outings to places where children and their families can learn about their own cultural or ethnic history as well as the history of others.

_____ 9. I select videos, films or other media resources that are culturally diverse to share with children and families in my classroom or program.

_____ 10. I play a variety of music and introduce musical instruments from many cultures.

_____ 11. I insure that classroom meals include foods that are unique to the cultural and ethnic backgrounds of children in my classroom or program.

_____ 12. I provide opportunities for children to cook or sample a variety of foods from culturally diverse groups.

_____ 13. If my classroom or program consists entirely of children and families from the same cultural or ethnic group, I feel it is important to plan an environment and implement activities that reflect the cultural diversity within my country or society.

_____ 14. I recognize and ensure that curricula I use include traditional holidays celebrated by my country/society as well as those that are celebrated by the culturally diverse children and families in my classroom or program.

COMMUNICATION STYLES

_____ 15. For children who speak another language, I attempt to learn and use key words in their language so that I am better able to communicate with them.

_____ 16. I use visual aids, gestures, and physical prompts in my interactions with children who are not proficient in the dominant language of my country or society.

_____ 17. When interacting with parents who are not proficient in the language of the dominant culture in my country or society I keep in mind that:

    *   limitations in language proficiency is in no way a reflection of their level of intellectual functioning.

    *   their limited ability to speak the language of the dominant culture has no bearing on their ability to communicate effectively in their own language of origin.

    *   they may or may not be literate in their language of origin or the language of the dominant culture.

_____ 18. When possible, I ensure that all notices and communiqués to parents are written in their language of origin.

_____ 19. I understand that it may be necessary to use alternatives to written communications for some families, as word of mouth may be a customary or preferred method of exchanging.

_____ 20. I use bilingual volunteers or staff to serve as interpreters for meetings, conferences, or other events for parents who would require this level of assistance.

_____ 21. I avoid correcting the language expressions of children who speak a non-standard dialect.

_____ 22. I accept and recognize the differences between language used at school and at home.

_____ 23. I encourage and invite parents to volunteer and assist in classroom or program activities regardless of their ability to speak the language of the dominant culture.

VALUES AND ATTITUDES

_____ 24. I avoid imposing values which may conflict or be inconsistent with those of cultures or ethnic groups other than my own.

_____ 25. I discourage children from using racial and ethnic slurs by helping them understand that certain words can hurt others.

_____ 26. I screen books, movies, and other media resources for negative cultural, ethnic, or racial stereotypes before sharing them with children in my classroom or program and their parents.

_____ 27. I provide activities to help children learn about and accept the differences and similarities in all people as an ongoing component of program curricula.

_____ 28. I intervene in an appropriate manner when I observe other staff engaging in behaviors which show cultural insensitivity.

_____ 29. I recognize and accept that individuals from culturally diverse backgrounds may desire varying degrees of acculturation into the dominant culture.

_____ 30. I accept and respect that male-female roles in families may vary significantly among different cultures (e.g., who makes major decisions for the family, play and social interactions expected of male and female children).

_____ 31. Even though my professional or moral viewpoint may differ, I accept the family/parents as the ultimate decision-makers for services and supports for their children.

_____ 32. I recognize that the meaning or value of education may vary greatly among cultures.

_____ 33. I accept that religion and other beliefs may influence how families respond to illnesses, disabilities, and death.

_____ 34. I understand that traditional approaches to disciplining children are influenced by culture.

_____ 35. I accept and respect that customs and beliefs about food, its value, preparation, and use are different from culture to culture.

_____ 36. I advocate for the review of my program's mission statement, goals, policies, and procedures to ensure that they incorporate principles and practices that promote cultural diversity and cultural competence.

How to use this checklist

This checklist is intended to heighten the sensitivity of personnel to the importance of cultural diversity and cultural competence in early intervention and early childhood settings. It provides concrete examples of the kinds of practices which foster such an environment. There is no answer key with correct responses. However, if you frequently responded "C", you may not be engaging in practices that promote a culturally diverse and culturally competent learning environment for children and families in your program.

Developed by Tawara D. Taylor, Early Childhood Special Educator, Georgetown University Child Development Center, University Affiliated Program, Washington, D.C. (June, 1989, revised 1993.) Adapted for CRI, February, 1995.

OBSERVING, RECORDING, AND REPORTING ON CHILDREN'S DEVELOPMENT

V. OBSERVING, RECORDING, AND REPORTING CHILDREN'S DEVELOPMENT

Observing and Recording

How do teachers know if the materials in the activity centers are of interest to children? How do they know if the activities are meeting the needs of children? How can teachers share information with parents in a way that accurately describes how their children are spending their time? How do teachers document a concern that they have about a child's behavior? How do teachers individualize an activity?

These are some of the questions that teachers should ask themselves as they plan activities, adapt the environment, and interact with children.

One method that teachers have found useful is to observe children in their natural environments — home, classroom, and outdoors — and to record their observations. In this way, they have concrete information that they can share with parents and other members of the teaching team.

Observation is the process of watching a child at work or play without interfering in the activity.

Recording is the process of documenting the observed activity or behavior. Although many teachers do this naturally, a systematic approach helps assure that children are observed participating in many different activities over time.

Teachers' observations must be sensitive and detailed. Young children are often unable to express in words what they express in action. A child might express frustration by throwing the paper on the floor when he cannot cut with scissors. A big smile might be the only indication we have that a child has climbed to the top of the slide for the first time. As Cohen and Stern observe,

> *"Children communicate with us through their eyes, the quality of their voices, their body postures, their gestures, their mannerisms, their smiles, their jumping up and down, their listlessness. They show us, by the way they do things, as well as by what they do, what is going on inside them. When we come to see children's behavior through the eyes of its meaning to them, from the inside out, we shall be well on our way to understanding them. Recording their ways of communicating helps us to see them as they are."* (Cohen and Stern, 1974, p. 5).

91

By recording their observations, teachers document children's work and the quality of that work or interaction. This information enables them to better evaluate and set goals for that child. Over time, observations of the child can reveal patterns of behavior, learning preferences, mastery of skills, and developmental progress.

Observation Guidelines

To function as an observer, the teacher must set aside the time to observe and have the right tools to record her observations. No teacher can be a totally objective observer. Teachers should try, however, to describe accurately the behaviors they record, without subjective interpretation or labeling. Objective observations do not include what the teacher thinks or feels happened; rather, they describe what the child actually did or said.

Objective observations are factual statements: "Jo picked up the block and threw it at Samuel," or, "Marie spent her time outdoors sitting under the tree."

Subjective observations are labels, judgments, or information recorded out of context: "Jo is aggressive" or, "Marie is lazy." Labels do not convey information that helps in understanding a child's development.

An observation should also be detailed and descriptive. For instance, recording "Adam chose to build with blocks in the block area," gives information about the choice Adam made and the materials he worked with. It does not provide as much information as the following, more complete, anecdotal observation: "As soon as Adam came into the classroom, he announced to his friends, Mica and Sol, that he wanted to 'build the biggest house in the city.' He invited them to join him. Together they used all the blocks available and built a house with seven rooms. Adam asked me to make a sign for his house, which I wrote out and he copied onto yellow paper. The sign said, 'The Big House.' Adam stayed in the block center for fifty minutes."

This record documents what Adam chose to work on. It illustrates that he had thought about and planned what he wanted to build prior to coming to school. It also indicates that he included others, shared his ideas, and expanded his block play into the area of literacy. Finally, he sustained attention for a long, uninterrupted period of time.

It did not take the teacher long to observe Adam and describe his activity in detail. When she reviews his records for planning, she will be able to encourage and expand upon his interests. She will also have an anecdote to share with his family.

Other types of observations can range from short notes jotted on a piece of paper to checklists that pinpoint specific activities.

Informal Observation Techniques

Anecdotal Records These are brief accounts of specific incidents. They tell a picture in words. They should give factual information about what happened, when it happened, where it happened, the stimulus for the activity, the child's reactions, and how the action ended. They can quote what the child said and describe the quality of behavior. The previous description of Adam is an example of an anecdotal observation.

Narratives or Diary Records These are daily notes or impressions of group and individual activities that are recorded at the end of the day. They tend to be somewhat subjective and often capture a quick impression or mood. They are useful for tracing some of the successes and failures of the day's events. For example:

> *The group activity of hide-and-seek did not go well today. The children were restless and quickly lost interest. They much preferred our nature walk and are looking forward to watching the salamander eggs hatch.*

Michelle was especially interested in exploring the stream today, examining the water with the magnifying glass and guessing what the squirming creatures were. She was reluctant to return to class, and I had to ask her to come three times.

Daily Health Checks   Every morning as children enter the classroom the teacher should take note of their health status. Is the child's nose running or stuffed? Does the child seem flushed or feverish? Is there a rash? Any bruises or lacerations? Are eyes tearful or running? Is the child scratching her head? Is the child hearing well, or might his ears be filled with fluid?   Is the child limping? Does the child have diarrhea? If the child is unwell, the teacher should let the parents know immediately and keep the child quiet and away from other children if possible. In addition to these daily health checks, routine vision and hearing screenings should be performed by the health department. A record of all required immunizations should be on file.

Teacher Observation Checklists   An observation checklist identifies specific behaviors to be observed. A developmental checklist structures the process of systematically collecting information on a child's level of functioning in various areas. It typically lists skills that have been sequenced in the order that they are generally learned. The checklist may assess domains such as fine and gross motor, expressive and receptive language, intellectual, social-emotional, and self-help skills. These checklists provide information about what a child can and cannot do in each developmental area. Teachers can use this information to help set goals for a child and plan activities that help the child progress. An example of a developmental checklist, *Observation Checklist for Teachers*, is at the end of this chapter.

Other checklists provide teachers with a record of what learning centers the children choose, or which materials they use most often. They are helpful in assuring, for example, that children who spend most of their free time in the art area are encouraged to explore other activity centers. The teacher can help the child make this transition by setting up a favorite art activity in another part of the room, such as painting clouds and the sky for a castle that will be built with blocks and small boxes.

Frequency Counts and Time Samples   These techniques help a teacher keep track of the number of times a behavior occurs. A tally is kept for a specified time ("Sue hit another child five times during outdoor play today,") or the length of time a behavior lasted ("Thomas cried for eight minutes when he was asked to wash up for lunch.") These records can be used to help a child reduce or diminish a negative behavior. For example, if the teacher discovers that Thomas cries whenever there are transitions from one activity to the next, she may be able to help him by alerting and preparing him before the transition occurs. This method is effective only if the behavior is overt and frequent.

Portfolios or Work Samples   These are collections of work that a child does over time. They can include drawings, dictated stories, attempts at writing words and numbers, and language samples, which are transcriptions of the exact words a child uses to express a thought or idea. In addition, a series of photographs can provide a visual picture of the child at work. Tape recordings of a child's conversation can also be included. These are highly individualized collections.

Children enjoy reviewing their work with teachers and reminiscing about when they did it and what it means to them. They may also be interested in selecting work to put in their portfolios themselves. Family members are often surprised to see the diversity of their child's work when teachers share the portfolios at conferences. Children should always be aware that teachers will share their portfolios with their parents.

Interviews and Conversations   Children are happy to discuss their thoughts, ideas, and work with adults if they trust that the adult is truly interested and respectful. When a teacher takes time to listen to a child describe an art project or talk about a favorite cousin, it makes the child feel valued and helps the teacher better understand that child. Open-ended questions, such as "Why are clouds in the sky?" or "How does an airplane fly?" provide insight into the level of the child's understanding about the world. Teachers can probe further by asking for more information or by offering another question, such as, "How are birds and airplanes alike?"

Do not contradict children. Accept all answers. The purpose of this kind of inquiry is to learn more about a child's thinking process.

Literacy interviews for five- and six-year-olds often give insight into their understanding of reading, writing, and speaking, as well as their readiness for more complex literacy experiences. A child who answers the question "How do you know how to read words?" with "Words are really lots of letters that each have a sound, and you move your tongue and lips in funny ways to make the sounds," may be ready for rhymes and books with a strong use of phonics. A child who responds "Words are like pictures that grown-ups know," shows that she thinks reading is an external process. She is not ready for more formal approaches toward literacy. That child should listen to stories, play with letters and numbers in a more concrete way, and see her words on paper.

These are methods of observing children and recording the observations. Teachers also need to decide when, where, and what they will observe. All children in the classroom should be observed in different areas of the room and outdoors, at different times of the day throughout the year.

Recording Techniques and Tools

Teachers use a number of techniques to record and organize their observations. One technique is to keep a pad of paper and pencil in a pocket at all times to catch a phrase or describe the key events in an interaction. Another is to keep scrap paper and pencils around the room to record information. At the end of the day, these short notes are transcribed in greater detail into a notebook or file. Some teachers spend time at the end of the day listing specific observations and general impressions into a diary. Other teachers create an individual file card for each student. By rotating the cards daily, the teacher can be sure to take notes on all the children. Checklists can be put on the walls around the classroom to keep track of the choices children make during the day. If a teacher wants to observe gross motor development, she can set up an obstacle course outside and use a developmental checklist to record the skills of all the children as they play on the balance beam, climb stairs, or bend and crawl under a board. Photographs and tape recorders provide long-lasting records of children. Gathering, recording, and organizing the observations of children leads to purposeful planning and individualizing of the curriculum.

What To Observe

Dimensions of the Individual

Accommodating the individual aspects of each learner is a cornerstone of effective teaching. It is important to respond to the individuality of each child and not judge or evaluate it. Understanding of the individual child requires that the teacher consider the following dimensions:

Family Culture and Diversity

The most salient characteristic of each family is its culture. Culture determines much about what individuals think and value and how they behave. Children are socialized in ways that are consistent with the culture of the family.

Home visits are essential, because they give teachers some insight into family and culture. Teachers should ask parents to discuss any important cultural considerations that can be accommodated in the classroom, such as dietary preferences (pork may be prohibited), religious practices (Hanukkah can be celebrated along with Christmas), language (the child may speak a different language at home), and time (some cultures view time as flexible). Teachers will also have a chance to observe how the family interacts with the children.

Some families prefer that children be "seen and not heard," while others include children in every aspect of activity and conversation. Some cultures considered it disrespectful for children to look adults directly in the eye. The insights gained through home visits will help teachers understand many of the behaviors that children exhibit at school and view them as culturally appropriate for an individual child.

Age

Obviously, three-year-olds act and think differently than four- or five-year-olds. Familiarity with the stages of child development is paramount for teachers. For example, most five year old children can concentrate longer, communicate more effectively, engage in more interactive play, and understand abstract concepts better than most three- and four-year-olds. Age is an important factor when determining what activities to provide, how to provide them, and for how long. (See *Developmental Guidelines* in Chapter II).

Developmental Level

Within any group of three year old children, there is great variance in ability and functioning. Some will function like two-year-olds and some like four-year-olds; most will be somewhere in between. To further complicate matters, the development of children is often uneven: a child may be advanced in language and communication, but delayed in motor abilities. There is a variance of at least two years in the developmental level within most classrooms of children of the same chronological age. If there are particularly gifted or developmentally delayed children in the class, the variance will be even greater. It is, therefore, not enough to consider chronological age alone; to individualize each learning strategy, the teacher must also consider the child's development level.

Personality and Temperament

There are many characteristics of personality and temperament and for each characteristic there is a continuum along which each child can be placed. These continuums include the following extremes:

- Serious/Lighthearted
- Energetic/Calm
- Extroverted/Introverted
- Curious/Indifferent

- Easygoing/Intense
- Fastidious/Messy
- Risk-taker/Cautious
- Trusting/Skeptical

Teachers need to be aware that their own personalities and temperaments may clash or mesh with those of individual children. By understanding these differences and accepting them, teachers can improve the quality of life of children.

To learn well some children need to talk and interact with others, while other children learn best when they work quietly on their own. By weighing such factors the teacher makes sure that each child is choosing appropriately and not, for example, isolating herself because she fears being rejected by others or lacks the skills to interact effectively. This may be difficult to determine, because children who cannot do something often simply refuse to do it.

Gender

Gender difference is so obvious that it is often overlooked when teachers consider the dimensions of the individual. Teachers often witness gender-based behavior, such as boys engaging in loud, physical, rough-and-tumble play and girls preferring language-based, social, and organized play. It is natural to allow children to select playmates and activities, even if these decisions are gender-based. It is equally important to encourage all children to expand their competencies.

Learning Style

Children learn at different rates. Learning rate is not necessarily an indication of intelligence, for some slow learners understand concepts more thoroughly than quick learners. Some children are highly dependent on others to learn well, while other children learn better on their own. Often a child has a primary sensory learning modality. This means that he may rely mostly on his visual sense to obtain information and to interpret the world. Another child may do the same with her keen auditory, tactile, or feeling sense. Like personality and temperament, learning style characteristics exist on a continuum. These characteristics are particularly noticeable when a child is at the extremes of the continuum. When this is the case, teaching strategies must be adjusted accordingly.

Interests

Most children have at least one particular interest. Some are fascinated by trucks and machines, others by dinosaurs, a certain sport, or a particular activity in kindergarten. Using these interests, the teacher can incorporate activities from all areas of the curriculum. Sometimes children express and pursue their interests only at home, so it is necessary to ask parents about them.

Strengths and Needs

All children have strengths (what they do particularly well) and needs (what they require help with to do better). Sometimes strengths and needs are inextricably linked. Good teachers build on abilities and interests, which are often the same, to help children overcome their weaknesses.

For instance, Judith is an excellent artist who chooses to spend much of her time in the art area. She shows little interest or skill in mathematics. Her teacher helps Judith practice math concepts through art. She asks Judith how many colors of paint she wants to use at the easel, then has her mix the paints using a recipe of one half cup of powdered paint to one cup of water. Another day, she asks Judith to prepare balls of play dough for the children sitting at the art table. Judith counts the children and divides the play dough into five equal portions. Judith feels comfortable practicing math using materials that interest her.

Self-Concept

Indicators of self-concept include how children perceive themselves, how realistically they know their own strengths and needs, and how they judge their own ability to undertake a particular task. All children come into the class with differing self-concepts. Some view themselves as incapable, others as extremely capable, and most fall somewhere between the two. Overconfidence, or overestimating one's ability to accomplish a task is just as problematic as a lack of confidence. Teachers can help children develop a realistic sense of themselves and teach them to identify resources to solve problems (an important part of self-efficacy) if they are able to determine accurately that a particular task is too difficult for a child to do on his or her own. Increasing self-efficacy has a positive effect on self-concept.

Behaviors to Observe

The following list summarizes some of the classroom behaviors that teachers may want to focus on:

- How a child responds to routines.

- How a child manages transitions, quiet and active periods, group and individual work periods. Watch the children as they separate from their parents, during mealtimes, using the toilet, dressing, washing, and resting.

- How and what materials are used. Watch for the quality of use (Is the brush held securely?), the variety of materials (Does the child use all the art supplies or only the paints at the easel?), the imaginative use (Does the child invent new ways to use the small blocks or always stack them?), skill level (How many pieces are in the puzzles he puts together?), and concept understanding (How complex is the mathematical thinking that is demonstrated as the child uses attribute blocks?).

- How a child interacts with other children. Does the child play with many children or only the same two children? Does the child share toys? Does the child initiate play or wait to be invited? What kinds of activities does he enjoy with others?

- How a child interacts with teachers and other adults. Is the child able to ask for help? Does the child require a lot of attention or direction? Does the child ask for constant praise? Does the child enjoy talking with the teacher? Does the child spend time with adult visitors in the classroom?

- Where the child plays in the classroom. Watch how the child moves about the classroom. Does he spend time in all the activity centers? Which one does he prefer to work in? Does she move easily from center to center or does she require help?

- How a child uses language. Is the child easy to understand? Does she make her wishes known? What is the quality of his voice? Does she speak with both children and adults? How extensive is his vocabulary?

- How a child moves. Watch the child outside. Does he climb, run, skip, jump? How is his balance? Is she able to catch and throw? Is he sure or tentative in his movements? Does he enjoy soccer, kickball, dance, and movement activities?

- Mood and temperament. Is the child easygoing or tense? Does he cry frequently? Does he laugh and smile? Is she able to express his feelings verbally? Can he negotiate with children and adults? Is he easily frustrated?

- The roles the child takes within the group (for example, leader, follower, listener, talker).

Teachers' observations, assessment data, and information provided by family members can be used to understand and plan for each child.

Using Information Gathered Through Observation

Individual Adaptations

One of the major purposes of observing the child is to gather information that will enable the teacher to structure classroom experiences to better meet the child's needs. The following techniques may be used to adapt classroom activities to needs identified through observation:

Building on Interests For a child who is reluctant to take risks by expanding her repertoire of activities, the teacher can expand a familiar activity by integrating a new activity. For example:

> Tal loves building with blocks but is reluctant to draw or write. The teacher adds markers, paper, and tape to the block area and asks Tal to make a traffic sign or a "Do not Disturb" sign for his building.

> Eva talks so softly that it is difficult to hear her in a group. The teacher gives puppets to Eva and a friend and asks that the puppets yell out a refrain in a song.

Pairing and Grouping Children Piaget suggests that children learn best from each other. Pairing a child who does not grasp a concept with another child who has recently mastered it may facilitate understanding. For instance, a child who has not mastered one-to-one correspondence watches as his friend demonstrates and "teaches" him to play with dice and beads.

Modifying Activities Teachers can have children play with various combinations of the same materials, depending on their knowledge or skill level. For instance, when children play with puzzles, the teacher can make sure that there are puzzles with different numbers of pieces available. While children play a group game, the teacher can ask one child to perform a harder task such as hopping on one foot, while another child jumps in place. Everyone participates in different ways.

Targeting Specific Needs A teacher may provide opportunities for a child to practice mastering a specific skill or difficult task. If a teacher has observed that several children have difficulty using scissors, she may plan activities that use small muscles, such as fishing for objects with tongs or placing pegs in a board, then move to tearing paper and, finally, to using the scissors.

Seeking Outside Consultation or Arranging Referrals

Occasionally, a teacher may find a worrisome pattern of behavior that does not seem to improve, even after individual adaptations have been made. The teacher may sense that there is an underlying problem. It is important to document any concerns and remediations and share them with the family. Together, teacher and family may decide to get more information. A physician, psychologist, or other health professional may need to evaluate the child and make recommendations about special interventions and supports. These recommendations can be used to set specific goals and plan individual activities for the child.

Formal screening tools and developmental assessments can provide additional information. They should be reliable and valid. Teachers should be trained before using these methods of assessment to ensure proper administration and interpretation. Some diagnostic tests should be administered only by personnel trained in a discipline, such as a special educator, psychologist, speech and language pathologist, or occupational and physical therapist.

Children With Disabilities

Including children with disabilities in preschool classrooms conveys a powerful message to society — that we value every human being. All young children are more alike than different, and with support from teachers and parents, children with disabilities can thrive in a classroom that values each child's individuality and uniqueness. Typically developing children learn to reach out to their peers with special needs in friendship, play and work.

Staff who have not worked with children who have disabilities are often concerned about their ability to meet the child's special needs. They need information on the characteristics of common disabilities as well as an opportunity to express their worries. Often parents are excellent sources of information on their child's disability as well as specific techniques that can be used to meet their child's special needs. They can also identify their child's strengths and interests as well as needs.

With parental permission, specialists such as speech or physical therapists can observe a child with a disability in the classroom and make recommendations for adapting materials and activities for the child. Specialists can work individually with the child or include the child with a disability in a small group activity with other children in the classroom. Teachers can request help in developing individualized plans for the child with a disability.

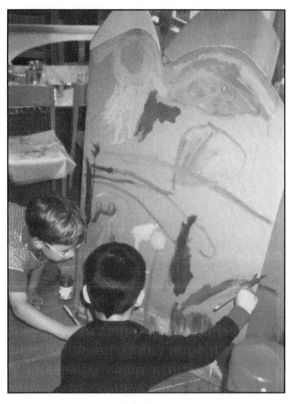

The following techniques, adaptions , and modifications will help teachers meet the varied needs of children with disabilities:

- **Physical Disabilities** The classroom may have to modified to accommodate a wheelchair. A ramp can replace stairs; an easel can be raised; a water table put on blocks; bolsters may help a child sit or lay in a comfortable position. Have fat crayons and pencils available; use tape to create a better grip on paint brushes; have puzzles with knobs on the pieces for easy removal; use adaptive utensils if available.

- **Language Delays** Model appropriate language using simple sentences. Use visual clues such as pictures or real materials to accompany language. Repeat information and directions, and have the child repeat new information. Make sure that the listener/teacher is accepting and nonjudgmental.

- **Hearing Impairments** If the child uses sign language, have someone come to the classroom to teach everyone simple signs. Check hearing aid batteries. Use visual clues such as pictures, photos, or real objects. Get the child's attention before telling a story or giving information. Demonstrate new activities and the use of materials.

- **Low Vision or Blindness** Use materials that appeal to many senses: for example, use sandpaper letters and numbers, or glue textured fabric onto puzzles. Make sure that the classroom is safe for the child's free mobility. Stay close or assign a peer to accompany the child in the classroom and outdoors. Use a bell to get the children's attention. Play music and sing songs. Help the child feel new materials and equipment.

- **Mental Retardation** Help the child feel successful by having appropriate materials and activities available. Learn how to break tasks down to their simplest parts. Give simple, clear directions and give feedback often. Help the child enter into play with other children.

- **Attentional Difficulties** Use short sentences and give clear directions. Keep group times short. Use visual clues. Have the child sit next to a teacher during group events. Have a quiet area of the room that the child can use for work that requires concentration or for a place to rest.

- **Emotional or Behavioral Disturbances** Help the child use words to express feelings and keep choices limited. Have a quiet place to which the child can retreat. Give positive feedback and set consistent rules and expectations. Use puppets, stuffed animals, and dolls to allow the child to express his thoughts and feelings. Help the other children set limits and feel safe without isolating the child. Allow withdrawn children to watch others before joining an activity and help them make a special friend.

Reporting Information to Families

Parent/Teacher Conferences

Much of the contact teachers have with families is informal. Informal contact is valuable and meets many needs of both families and staff. However, there are times when a formal conference is the preferred mode of communication. The purpose of such a conference is usually to allow teachers to discuss the child's progress and give the parents an opportunity to share their

observations, ideas, and concerns. Problems can be discussed and solutions generated by teachers and parents together. Individual goals can be set for children, and parents can provide information on strategies they use effectively at home. Conferences usually last from 30 to 45 minutes and are held between one and three times during the program year. The following guideline will help ensure successful parent/teacher conferences.

Guidelines for Successful Parent/Teacher Conferences

- Schedule conferences at a convenient time for the family. Evening or weekend conferences may be necessary for families unable to leave work during regular school hours. Tell the families the purpose of the conference. If you want them to bring any information, ask for it specifically and give an example.

- The Family Room or the classroom will offer families a comfortable and familiar place to meet. Have coffee or refreshments available. Ask another adult to care for the children. Start the conference with positive information about the child's progress and development.

- Give parents any written information or reports prior to the conference so they can read and review them before the meeting. Provide examples of the child's work to illustrate points that you will discuss. If portfolios are used, parents and teachers can discuss the child's development based on his work samples. Always give families opportunities to ask questions, express concerns, and share the successes or problems they see at home. The purpose of the conference is to share information both ways. Make the conference personal — ask families about activities the child likes to do at home, about a sick family member the child has mentioned, or a recent book the child liked.

- Behavior is the subject of many discussions between teaching staff and families, and it can be a cause of concern for both. Discuss the rules of behavior in the classroom and give examples of how appropriate behavior is reinforced and methods used if behavior is inappropriate. These conferences (along with meetings, newsletters, and workshops) can reinforce consistent management of behavior between the home and school.

- Respect the family's other obligations. If the conference is set for 30 minutes, respect the time limit. If all the concerns and information have not been covered, reschedule another conference for a mutually convenient time. Always end the conference on a positive note and give the family the opportunity to ask questions or provide ways to contact you if they have questions later.

Reports

Written reports are another formal method of sharing information with families. They provide a written record of the child's progress, overall development, preferences, and style of interaction. Reports should create a picture of the child during a typical day. Sample forms for two reporting methods are included at the end of the chapter: *Observation Checklist for Teachers* and *Sample Midyear Narrative Report*.

Write in positive language, stressing both strengths and needs. State concerns directly and objectively. Be careful not to be judgmental when writing reports or reporting behavior to families. Information should be observable and documented. Offer suggestions on ways to change behavior or to improve learning, and recommend any resources that may be helpful to the family. Be as specific as possible. Always sign the report and include a way for the reader to communicate with you.

If the report is to be sent to anyone other than the parent, such as the primary school or a psychologist or therapist, families should have ample time to review the report and request changes before it is distributed to others. Families should review, sign, and give permission for all reports that are being sent to other service providers or school personnel.

The information in written reports should never be a surprise to families. They should be familiar with any concerns from informal contacts, telephone calls, notes, visits, or conferences. The written information should be a review of the information that you and the family have already discussed.

Frequent communication between families and teachers promotes a successful experience for all — children, families, and teachers. Together, they can provide an experience that nurtures, challenges, and celebrates the successes of the children.

OBSERVATION CHECKLIST FOR TEACHERS

Name of Child _____

Date _____ Time _____

Name of Observer _____

Check those items that pertain to the child you are observing. Use NA for those activities and behaviors you do not observe an item. Note any concerns or qualitative information next to item.

Developmental Domains

Speech and Language Skills

Talks with children _____

Talks with adults _____

Is understood _____

Uses complete sentences _____

Talks during play _____

Uses language spontaneously _____

Initiates conversations _____

Expresses feelings in words _____

Perceptual Skills (visual and auditory)

Matches colors and shapes _____

Notices new materials or toys _____

Recognizes own written name _____

Identifies common sounds _____

Is tolerant of loud noises _____

Listens and understands directions _____

Listens to and comments on stories _____

Participates in music and movement _____

Large Motor Skills

Jumps with both feet over object _____

Balances on a board _____

Goes up and down steps easily _____

Throws a ball _____

Uses a dominant hand to throw consistently _____

Kicks a ball _____

Uses a dominant leg to kick consistently _____

Runs without falling _____

Rides wheeled equipment with ease _____

Uses the swing _____

Climbs up and goes down sliding board _____

Small Motor Skills

Buttons and unbuttons clothing _____

Zips and unzips clothing _____

Strings beads or other small objects _____

Completes puzzles _____

Stacks objects correctly _____

Traces around object _____

Cuts well with scissors _____

Draws simple shapes _____

Pounds nails into wood _____

Uses cooking utensils with little help _____

Cognitive Skills

Asks questions about materials _____

Counts accurately up to (insert number) _____

Recognizes some letters and numbers _____

Sorts by size, shape and color _____

Shows understanding of likes and differences _____

Makes believe in regard to dramatic play situations _____

Shows interest in books _____

Can recognize some words _____

Is able to read _____

Builds with blocks in long rows _____

Makes bridges with blocks _____

Makes enclosures with blocks _____

Routines of the Day

Chooses activity center without difficulty _____

Stays with activity until complete _____

Moves from one activity center to another with ease _____

Plays well with peers _____

Complies with classroom rules _____

Participates in large group activities _____

Manages bathroom routine without help _____

Eats most foods _____

Is eager to go outdoors _____

Is able to rest _____

Social and Emotional Skills

Gets along well with other children _____

Gets along well with adults _____

Is able to share _____

Is able to take turns _____

Can express anger in appropriate ways _____

Has one or more special friends _____

Helps in clean up _____

Joins group games _____

Works in small group with one or two children _____

Is able to give first and last name _____

Looks at person when speaking or being spoken to _____

Is respectful of and careful with materials _____

Separates from parent without tears _____

Smiles and seems happy much of the time _____

Rarely disrupts others' activities _____

Seems pleased with own accomplishments _____

Is not afraid to try new experiences _____

Is not unduly afraid of animals or insects _____

Child's Health

Is rarely absent _____

Is seldom ill _____

Has good endurance _____

Looks generally healthy _____

Seems to have few or no allergies _____

Rarely complains about feeling ill _____

Child's Favorite Activities:

Child's Favorite Books and Stories:

Other Comments:

SAMPLE MIDYEAR NARRATIVE REPORT

NAME: Anna

TEACHERS: Kris and Roxane

DATE: January 1997

Having Anna in our class this year has been a pleasure. Anna has been healthy so far this year, and has only missed school once when she had an ear infection. Anna is a hearty eater and tries new foods eagerly at breakfast, snack time, and lunch. Her favorite new food is yogurt with fruit, and she looks forward to having it as a snack. Anna is able to take her coat and hat off herself, and she can button her coat. She is trying to zipper, but still needs help with her boots. Anna is able to use the toilet without help and usually remembers to wash her hands.

As the year has progressed, Anna has been able to separate from her grandmother more easily. She now gives "Nanna" a hug goodbye and comes into the room on her own. She typically enters the classroom with enthusiasm, saying "hello" to her teachers and any children nearby. Anna eats breakfast immediately and then moves easily into one of the activity centers. She enjoys playing with other children and shares toys and materials without difficulty. She is able to initiate play as well as join in the play of others. Anna displays confidence in herself as she proudly displays her drawings and other art work to her classmates.

Anna moves from one activity center to another with ease, usually without teacher assistance. Anna's favorite activity centers are literacy, sand and water, art, and manipulatives. Anna has been building interesting and diverse structures with all the bristle blocks in the manipulative area: last week she used all the blocks to build a house for the toy animals to sleep in. Her small-muscle skills are very well-developed, as shown by her ability to cut with scissors and paste small pieces of wood together. She can spend up to one-half hour making a collage, working with clay or drawing pictures for the many books she makes.

Anna has started showing interest in letters and words and often asks us to write a story under a picture she has drawn. As you have seen, Anna has started trying to write her name. It is age-appropriate for her to reverse the direction of her letters, and she is able to hold her pencil with certainty.

While she is working at the manipulative center, Anna has worked with other children sorting colored blocks and matching shapes. She enjoys setting the table for lunch and is able to count up to seven objects, such as cups, napkins and silverware. These are all important logical mathematical concepts.

During large group activities, Anna often chooses to leave after five or ten minutes to work by herself at the literacy or art centers which, as you know, is an option for the children. During the time spent with the group, Anna is attentive and participates. She especially enjoys listening to books being read and music. Her favorite story is "Run Away Bunny" which she asks to read over and over to her and her friends.

Anna eagerly awaits outdoor time and is one of the first children to put on her coat and hat. Favorite activities outside include sliding down the sliding board and playing in the yellow house with several girls. They often pretend they are puppies or kittens that live in the woods. She has recently started playing kickball with other children and is not concerned about missing the ball much of the time. In observing Anna using an obstacle course, we noted that her balance is age-appropriate, as are her climbing and jumping skills. She runs with enthusiasm and is just beginning to use the tricycle.

Anna often talks about the places she visits with her family over the weekend. She was especially eager to tell her classmates about visiting her new baby cousin, Emile. This started a long discussion about babies and prompted many of the children to make a baby book with photos of themselves as babies. We have enjoyed having Anna's grandmother cook with the children. Anna is able to share her grandmother's attention with others and seems to like to join in the cooking activities.

Anna's contributions to the group have been many and we look forward to the rest of the year.

STUDENT PROGRESS REPORT

PRE-KINDERGARTEN

NAME _____ YEAR _____

TEACHERS : _____

DATE: _____

SECTION I:

In our reports to parents, it is our intention to share with you how much we see your individual child approaching and using the general program as it is offered to all the children. Therefore, we will begin the report with the following list of materials and activities which have been available to the children.

We have circled areas in which your child has chosen to work and have put a star (*) next to areas of particular interest to your child.

INDOOR SPACE:

Large hollow blocks

Small unit blocks

  xploration table (sand, water, seeds)

Books, storytelling, rhyming

Music (singing, movement)

Records

Puzzles

Films

Playdough

Chalkboard

Dramatic play

Small manipulative materials (Lego, pegboards, pattern blocks)

Easel painting

Cutting

Taping

Drawing (crayons. chalk and pencils)

Gluing

Snack

SPECIAL PROJECTS:

Bookmaking

Cooking and baking

Woodworking

OUTSIDE SPACE:

Sand

Swings

Tire swing

Turning bars

Seesaw

Snow play

Climbers

Sawhorses and planks

Playhouses

Wagons

Balls

SPECIAL SUBJECTS:

Music

Library

P.E.

N/PRE K-2

NAME _____   **YEAR** _____

SECTION II: DEVELOPMENT OF A KNOWLEDGE OF THE PHYSICAL WORLD, LITERACY AND LOGICAL MATHEMATICAL REASONING

All learning is integrated. For example when working with blocks, one child may be most interested in aesthetic patterns and images, while another might respond to mathematical relationships. As your child has worked in the areas and with some of the materials listed in Section I of this report, he/she is developing a knowledge or understanding of the physical world. This leads to and can include logical and mathematical reasoning. It also often incorporates and extends literacy development.

As _____ works with materials, we have observed that _____

WINTER			SPRING			
I	S	U	I	S	U	KEY: I = Infrequently S = Sometimes U = Usually
						explores and experiments with the physical properties (texture, etc.) of materials.
						observes others working with materials.
						plans what he/she will do as the work progresses.
						observes and responds to "what happens" (feedback from objects).
						discovers his/her own ways to organize materials.
						stays with a piece of work to its "natural" conclusion.
						observes changes in his/her environment.
						demonstrates mastery in work with materials.

COMMENTS:

NAME _____ **YEAR** _____

SECTION III: SOCIAL EMOTIONAL DEVELOPMENT

Each child comes to school with his/her own sense of self. This knowledge has developed primarily through a process of interaction with family and close friends (plus any former school experiences). In this section of our report we will share with you our observations of how your child has continued in this process of social emotional development within the school environment. Relationships with peers and adults as well as autonomy are aspects of this growth.

In working with _____ we have observed that _____

WINTER			SPRING			
B	S	U	B	S	U	KEY: B = is beginning to be S = sometimes is U = usually is
						comfortable with adults.
						able to use adult support.
						able to cooperate with adults.
						able to participate successfully in teacher directed group activities.
						comfortable with peers, one to one.
						comfortable with peers in small groups.
						comfortable with peers in larger groups.
						able to participate in child initiated group activities.
						able to select own task.
						able to care for self and belongings.
						able to express feelings verbally.
						able to observe others working.
						able to follow the ideas or examples of others.
						able to work alone.
						confident about his/her work.
						able to control impulses.
						able to take turns.
						able to settle disagreements with peers.

COMMENTS:

117

NAME _____   YEAR _____

In the area of Mathematics _____

WINTER			SPRING			KEY: I = Infrequently S = Sometimes U = Usually
I	S	U	I	S	U	
						explores comparisons and equivalents (larger, smaller, same, different, etc.).
						orders and seriates materials.
						becomes involved in sorting, classifying and estimating.
						notices and experiments with patterns.
						counts items.
						understands and uses one–to–one correspondence.
						associates number names with collections of items.

In the area of Language and Literacy _____

WINTER			SPRING			KEY: I = Infrequently S = Sometimes U = Usually
I	S	U	I	S	U	
						listens to what others have to say.
						understands information received aurally.
						responds appropriately to oral information.
						shows an interest in developing new vocabulary.
						expresses ideas verbally.
						speaks in sentences.
						shows an interest in books.
						shows an understanding of material read to him/her.
						dictates signs or stories.
						perceives writing as recorded speech.
						shows an interest in letters and words.
						experiments with making letters.
						recognizes familiar words and names.
						prints own name.
						recognizes upper case letters.
						recognizes rhymes.

COMMENTS:

N/PRE K-5

NAME _____ YEAR _____

SECTION IV: DEVELOPMENT OF A KNOWLEDGE OF THE SOCIALLY TRANSMITTED INFORMATION

Some knowledge is transmitted from person to person or generation to generation. The whole area of cultural and societal traditions can only be learned from other people (unlike mathematical knowledge.) Social Studies is a major curriculum area for this work in grades one to eight. However, each child acts upon this information in very individual ways. This personal process of working things through is consistent with the process we support and observe in all areas of learning.

In working with _____ we have observed that _____

WINTER			SPRING			
S	B	O	S	B	O	KEY: S = has not yet shown B = has begun to show O = often shows
						a sense of own family structure, home routines, own holidays, etc.
						a sense of other (than own) family patterns, routines, holidays, etc.
						a sense of the classroom schedule and routines.
						a sense of Green Acres (places and people) beyond his/her own classroom.
						a knowledge of the community beyond home and school.
						a knowledge of our culture's nursery rhymes, children's stories, TV shows, etc.
						an extensive vocabulary.
						a knowledge of language usuage.
						an ability to organize socially transmitted information in an individual way.

COMMENTS:

NAME _____   **YEAR** _____

SECTION V: PHYSICAL DEVELOPMENT

The child is gaining a knowledge of his/her physical self as he/she develops in this area. This is closely related to the child's development of a knowledge of the Physical World.

In noting a child's physical development, we observe the child involved in some of the following kinds of large and small muscle activities: walking, crawling, running, hopping, jumping, skipping, balancing, pumping, swinging, climbing, cutting, buttoning, zipping, fitting small items together, hammering, sewing, using pencils and crayons, pasting, taping, stapling, painting, dressing and undressing, pushing and pulling, lifting and carrying, pouring.

As _____ works with materials, moves around the classroom and uses our outside space and equipment, we have observed that _____

	WINTER			SPRING		
KEY: D = developing. A = age appropriate. O = outstanding.	D	A	O	D	A	O
speech is						
small motor control and coordination is						
large motor control and coordination is						
accurate judgement for moving body in space is						
ability to negotiate different physical environments is						
understanding spatial relationships is (under, over, in front of, behind)						
accurate perception of his/her own physical abilities is						
sense of his/her own endurance and physical needs is						
confidence in his/her physical abilities is						
willingness to risk new physical challenges is						

COMMENTS:

PLANNING THE INTEGRATED CURRICULUM

VI. PLANNING THE INTEGRATED CURRICULUM

Planning is an important part of creating and implementing the curriculum. Planning makes it possible for the teaching team to work together smoothly and unobtrusively. It helps eliminate confusion about roles and responsibilities. Teaching teams should schedule weekly planning meetings.

Curriculum content should come from at least three sources: from observations of individual children and the goals that a teacher has set for them; from the teacher's understanding of her particular class of children (their unique interests, strengths, needs, characteristics, concerns, and living circumstances); and from the teacher's general knowledge of children and their development. For example, she knows that three-year-olds usually need simpler, more concrete, and more sensory activities than six-year-olds.

Need for Long- and Short-Term Planning

Teachers should understand both long- and short-term planning. When doing **long-term planning**, the teaching team looks at the entire school year. They discuss what will happen when children first come to school, how they will be made to feel welcome, and how to involve the families. Discussions can also include ways to celebrate birthdays, holidays, special events, seasons, and the end of the year. Long-term planning does not encompass every classroom activity. However, it does give a general blueprint of the major events of the year. The teaching team should review the developmental milestones as a part of the planning process and then plan activities that lead children through these stages. Long-term planning facilitates any major changes to the environment, such as a new piece of outdoor equipment or staff expansion.

Short-term planning is done weekly. Teaching teams discuss the interests and problems of individual children. Through ongoing discussion, the team decides on projects to explore and changes they will make in the learning centers. They also decide who will be responsible for specific activities, gathering and preparing the materials that will be needed. They plan how best to use family members who are coming to work in the classroom, making sure that they are prepared and feel comfortable in their role. Team members agree on their own assignments during the day (one might stay with a small group participating in an activity, another might move around the room facilitating and observing), allowing for time with individual children as well as with groups of children. They plan balanced active and quiet times, structured and unstructured periods. They note and plan special events such as birthdays and holidays. They agree upon who will go to the library, call a parent, or obtain information about the flu that appears to be causing many absences. They plan activities that include family members and send a note advising a parent on the choice of a toy from the lending library. They discuss children's progress and set goals for individual children and for the group.

Importance of a Written Plan

Learning plans should be written. Teachers use different tools to help them plan. Some use calendars, listing major activities and responsibilities for the week or month. Others use matrices that list learning centers across the top and days of the week down the side, with activities and events noted in the boxes. Some teachers develop individual plans for children, identifying specific goals and activities to meet those goals. Other plans may be less elaborate, listing activities, materials, and teacher responsibilities for the week.

Written plans help provide structure to the program, by noting additional changes to the activity centers and keeping a record of activities. They provide useful information for visitors who will assist in the classroom. (See *Sample Daily Schedule for Three- and Four-Year-Olds* and *Sample Daily Schedule for Five- and Six-Year-Olds* at the end of the chapter.)

Another strategy used is a curriculum web. A curriculum web is a visual schema that depicts relationships between a theme and developmental domains or activity centers. Children's knowledge and ideas can be integrated into a curriculum web. (See *Friendship Web* and *Farm Web* at the end of the chapter.)

Planning the Daily Schedule

The daily schedule provides the structure for activities, work, and play. Schedules set forth routines that children get to know and feel comfortable with. Schedules should be created with the developmental needs of the children in mind so that three-year-olds receive more free play time, less teacher-directed activity time, and shorter group times than do five- and six-year-olds.

All schedules should be flexible enough to accommodate special events, like a community trip or a visiting parent who brings a new activity to share, as well as to reflect moods of the group or even the weather. If a beautiful day follows three rainy days, children should be able to spend more time outdoors, regardless of the original lesson plan. Flexible schedules allow for a flow of activity. They do not inhibit children [who are doing anything, not only busy playing] by forcing them to stop one activity to move to another.

Daily schedules reflect a balance of active and quiet times. They allow sufficient time for child-selected activities, for exploring a variety of materials throughout the classroom ,and for outdoor activity. The schedule builds in time for transitions between activities. It allows time for teachers to observe children, talk and work with them individually and in groups. Written schedules should be illustrated with pictures and posted.

This section provides a sample of how a program day might look. Program schedules vary with the age of the children and length of the day. (See *Sample Daily Schedule for Three- and Four-Year-Olds* and *Sample Daily Schedule for Five- and Six-Year-Olds* at the end of the chapter.)

Arrival and Breakfast

Before the children arrive, the teaching team should have prepared all the materials necessary for the morning work. A member of the teaching team should greet each child and family member and encourage them to settle in. Since the children may arrive at different times, the classroom should have quiet games, books, crayons, and paper available. Breakfast should be served to children when they are ready. Some children may need a short play time before they are calm enough to eat, while others may arrive ready for breakfast. After breakfast, children should put away their games, drawings, and books and come to the morning meeting.

Morning Meeting

This is the time for children to consider and plan what they want to accomplish that day. Teachers introduce special materials, discuss events of the day, and check the status of ongoing project work. For three-year-olds, the meeting is very brief. It may simply be a chance for each child to state where he or she wants to begin work, with prompts and reminders by the teacher. "Today, we have finger paints in the art area," "Remember, today we are going to visit the dairy," or, "Yesterday you built a sculpture out of cardboard. Are you ready to start painting it today?"

Four-, five- and six-year-olds can meet to review the daily schedule and discuss what they want to accomplish that day. Five- and six-year-olds may enjoy reviewing the posted daily schedule, the calendar or weather chart. The morning meeting provides an opportunity for children to share news or information about their home and community experiences, such as a visiting relative or an upcoming field trip. Some classrooms for five- and six-year-olds start the morning with a math challenge, a riddle or other "fun" activity.

Work Choices

During two periods of classroom activity, in the morning and afternoon, children work independently or in small groups. Teachers have planned and put special activities or materials in work areas. Children use the materials in the activity centers in many creative ways. They initiate their own play, or play an organized game such as lotto, cards or checkers.

Teachers circulate among the children, commenting on their work and asking questions. Older children can work on more teacher-directed literacy and math activities. This is also the time for children to work on ongoing projects or special activities, such as cooking or stitchery, facilitated by parents or other visitors. It is important for teachers to notice the choices children make, the quality of their work, whether they work alone or in groups, and how long they stay with an activity. Children's work should be fun and self-paced; the teacher's role is to provide challenging and creative learning opportunities.

Snack Time and Lunch

Some teachers like to have an informal snack available on a table so that children can eat whenever they choose. Other teachers prefer that all children have a snack together. Snacks should be simple and nutritious. Children can take turns preparing for snack and for cleaning up.

Lunch provides an opportunity to meet children's nutritional needs. It is also a social and cultural experience. Children sit at small tables, learning to help themselves, to taste new foods, and to take turns passing the food, as they engage in quiet conversation.

Children should have jobs in the classroom. Children's meal time jobs may include setting places (i.e., plates, bowls, eating utensils, napkins, cups, or glasses) for each person, carrying food to the tables, and clearing and washing the tables. Children learn many things when they help with meal time jobs. They practice their counting skills and one-to-one correspondence. If placemats with names are used, children practice name recognition. Teachers help set that tone, by sitting and eating with the children and engaging them in conversation. Meal time should be pleasant and relaxing for children. Also, remember that different children eat different amounts. Furthermore, some children eat very quickly, while others take their time. These differences should be allowed and encouraged. Children who finish first should clean up their places and be free to read a book or play quietly.

Tooth Brushing

Encouraging children to brush their teeth after meals promotes a very healthy habit. Each child should have his or her own child-size toothbrush. Each brush should be marked with the child's name so they cannot get mixed up. Brushes should be stored so they can air-dry and not touch other brushes. Ideally, each child should have his own brush, cup and tube of toothpaste. Each item should be labeled with the child's name. If individual toothpaste is not available, an adult should put the paste the each child's brush, making sure that the toothpaste tube does not touch any brush. This could spread germs. Tooth brushing needs adult supervision and should be done in small groups.

Explain and demonstrate the correct way to brush teeth to children during class. Make it interactive and fun. Have children practice and look at their teeth. Talk about their pretty smiles. Provide reinforcement and additional instructions to the children while they are brushing. All children will not brush perfectly. It is important, however, that they begin to learn the importance of taking care of their teeth.

Group Times

The teaching team may choose to have children meet as a whole group or to break into two groups for shared experiences. The length of time spent together depends on the age of the group. Three-year-olds usually become restless after ten minutes, while five- and six-year-olds can spend up to thirty minutes together. This is a time for social games, story reading, finger plays, singing, discussion of current events, review of work, group planning, and fun. Teachers should be prepared to change an activity or shorten the group time if children seem uninterested or restless. Teachers or volunteers should read aloud to children daily. Younger children may choose to leave group time early or choose to miss it entirely and continue working at an activity center.

Outdoor Times

All children need time outdoors. Equipment that encourages climbing, sliding, jumping, and dramatic play can be purchased or borrowed. Outdoor time, like indoor time, requires planning. A variety of equipment and materials should be available for children to use. Teachers can take some equipment, such as water tables, woodworking tables, and dramatic play materials, outside. Opportunities for nature study, construction, and physical science study using dams, bridges, ropes and pulleys, shadows and reflections, are perfect outdoor activities. Teachers should use this time to observe children's motor skills, group social skills, and understanding of rules.

Nap/Rest Time

Just as children's needs for food and use of the toilet are individual, so are their needs for sleeping. Some children need a long nap during the day, others need a short nap, and some need only to rest quietly. The schedule must accommodate these differences.

It is recommended that all children be required to have some quiet time. Children who are in an active classroom all day need to relax and rest, even if it is only for a short period. Children who want to rest or wake up sooner then others should be allowed to get up and look at books, draw or play with puzzles or other manipulative activities. Establish rules so children know where they can play if they do not need to sleep. Generally, younger children will require more rest than older children.

For those children who have trouble calming down, staff can play soothing music, read a story, rub the child's back, and ask families to bring a favorite toy from home.

Teachers often express the concern that if one child gets up to play, then the entire class will want to awaken. Allowing children choices and helping them learn when their bodies need rest is part of teaching personal responsibility. Some days children may get up and play because their friends are playing. On other days they will want to read quietly or choose to rest because they are tired.

Transitions

Transitions often pose problems for children and teachers. They are often rushed, tense times that occur as children move from one discrete set of activities to another. Transitions can be minimized by having a flexible schedule that allows children to work at their own pace. Although teachers have a daily schedule, they should allow ample time for children to complete their work before having to move on. Teachers can show respect for the work that children are doing by giving them options. The following list provides examples of how teachers can make transitions go more smoothly:

- Announce when a transition will occur. "When this record is over, it will be time to clean up for lunch," or, for older children, "We have ten more minutes before lunch," then, "We have five minutes . . ." and so on.

- Walk around the room and help children get ready for another activity. "I will help you put the clay back in the container."

- Give children enough time to finish what they are working on. Urge those who are already done to look at a book.

- Have a daily job chart that assigns children to help clean up areas of the room.

- Let children who are engrossed in an activity continue it by putting a "Do Not Disturb" sign on the game or materials so that children can return to them later.

Preparing Families for Preschool

The start of a program year is an exciting time for teachers, parents, and children. The teaching team must be prepared to take responsibility of caring for a new group of children and creating ideas on how to enhance the development of each individual child. They are establishing age-appropriate routines and rules for a smooth-running, happy classroom. They are also setting up a stimulating curriculum that includes individual, small-group and large-group activities.

Families are thinking about what it will be like to have their child in the care of other adults. They are adjusting their routines to meet the preschool schedule, getting to know other families, and trying to understanding the program and its requirements.

Good planning is needed to ensure that the transition from home to preschool goes well. Such planning should include the following considerations and stages.

Before School Starts

If possible, the adjustment from home to preschool should be gradual. The family and child need to get to know new people, places, and routines. The more familiar each of these aspects is to both parent and child, the more likely that the transition from home to preschool will be easy for each of them.

The teaching team can use several approaches to foster a natural transition from home to school:

- A visit to the classroom prior to the start of the program

- A prearranged visit to the home

- A prearranged small group play session

- A group meeting with the parents to discuss the new program year

Separation from Parents

Being separated from loved ones is a basic fear. It is very difficult for small children to leave their families to go to school. Many children have difficulties with separation. Children who have trouble separating from their parents need to be reassured and comforted. They need to know that their parents will return for them and that they will be cared for while they are away. Teachers and parents should work together to make the child feel secure and comfortable. Successful strategies include the following:

- Ask the parent to stay with the child for a short time each day as the child gets acquainted with the class and the children.

- Find out about toys and activities that the child is interested in and have them available when the child arrives.

- Provide extra attention and nurturing as the child adjusts to the environment.

- Provide time for the child to express feelings through drawing or talking with a trusted adult or "best friend."

- Encourage the child to bring a favorite toy or object from home to help with the transition.

Most important is to provide a secure and nurturing environment for all children.

Communication with Families

Communicating as often as possible with families is a critical part of the daily schedule. (This is discussed at length in Chapter III, *Family Participation*.) Schedule times to talk with families and to communicate with them through bulletin boards, notebooks, home visits and meetings.

Transition to the Next School

Going on to the next school is exciting. It can also cause concern for both children and families. Therefore, it is important that the teaching team to plan transition activities and discussions for the families and children.

Teachers and families can ease the transition by

- Visiting the next class and meeting the new teacher

- Setting up a corner of the room to "play school"

- Developing a report for the families to pass on to the next teacher (Do this only with the family's consent.)

- Meeting with the new teacher and the child's parents

- Inviting the new teacher to visit the preschool classroom

Planning Thematic Projects

Children learn and grow in an integrated manner. Each developmental domain grows in conjunction with all the others. When children pursue their interests, they learn facts and draw conclusions about newly acquired information. They may use mathematical reasoning, language skills, or trial and error to solve a problem. These learning skills are not separated into content areas but occur simultaneously. Learning is interconnected and integrated.

Recent research has shown that children are always learning new things because of the brain's "enormous capabilities to process concurrently vast amounts of information, sensory stimuli, emotions and awareness." (Fortson and Reiff, p.26). Brain development is dependent on environmental influences. A rich environment that provides various and complex  experiences is "conducive to mental agility. Throughout life, the brain's synaptic organization can be altered by the external environment." (Restak, R.M., 1984, p. 21.) Diverse, plentiful materials and activities that encourage creativity and optimize integrated learning. Teachers who help children make cognitive connections through projects and themes that affect them personally witness heightened motivation and learning. Reiff and Jackson point out that "excitement and involvement are created by bringing together content from a variety of sources, presenting the content through different types of experiences, and encouraging children to respond through different modes of expression" (p. 26).

The Step by Step classroom features activity centers that can be modified and changed to respond to individual children. The teaching team or the children themselves can initiate individual themes or projects. Projects should be based on a strong interest shown by a child or several children. If the children continue to display curiosity about a subject, a project based on that theme is conceptualized, developed, and expanded by the children and the teaching team.

Teachers can initiate projects or themes, but they are not effective unless the children find them compelling. That is, children will be motivated to pursue the topic if their questions are the basis for the exploration.

How to Develop a Thematic Project

Thematic topics can be developed from a variety of sources; however, a theme based on children's interests ensures motivation and successful learning. A teacher who listens to children and asks questions about the things they are interested in will find many ideas to develop for thematic studies. Is there a current event in school or the community that has captured the attention of the class? Has someone had a new baby brother or sister? Is the circus coming to town? If something exciting like the circus is actually happening, the children could decide to create a circus as a classroom project. The circus theme could be developed by the whole group for a month or more. The duration of the thematic project depends on the interest of the majority of the children as determined by the teacher. Themes and projects are most appropriate for children four years old and older.

One useful way of developing a thematic project is to use a model that asks three questions:

- What do we *know*?
- What do we *want to* know?
- What have we *learned*?

This technique is known as the KWL model.

"K" is for "Know"

First the teacher initiates a discussion session by asking children to share what they already know about a certain subject. If the topic under consideration is the circus, for example, the teacher asks, "What do you know about the circus?" or "Tell me something you know about the circus."

As the children respond, the teacher writes their responses on large chart paper for all to see. It is important to note each child's name next to his or her comment and include all the comments.

"W" is for "Want to Know"

The second question is "What would you like to know or what do you want to know about the circus?" Again, she lists the responses on the news print. Answers to the question will determine the content of the theme project. All questions are listed, regardless of how silly or illogical they may seem. Then the teacher asks, "How can we find the answers to our questions?"

Children may suggest the following ways to get information:

- Look at books
- Ask parents
- Ask an expert
- Try an experiment
- Visit or go to the place
- Recreate an object or event

The teacher then organizes the children's suggestions into a logical learning plan of activities:

- Reading a story about the circus

- Going to the library to get books about the circus for the classroom

- Inviting an expert with a related area of expertise, such as a mime, clown, or animal trainer, to come to the classroom and share their talents

- Creating a circus with children choosing to take roles of clowns, animals, jugglers, or gymnasts

"L" is for "Learned"

The third component of the KWL model poses the question "What have we learned?" It enables the teacher to assess children's learning. Teacher assessment of the project is crucial for active learning. The teacher's analysis of the different activities will help improve the quality of later projects. Useful questions include these: What parts of the project were successful? What should be changed next time? What new information did the children learn? What did not go well? Why?

Next, evaluate the project with the class as a whole. Ask the children to think about all the circus-related activities they have done. Refer to the list of questions developed at the beginning of the project that asked what the children wanted to learn about the circus. Review each question and have children take turns responding. Clarify, through discussion, any misconceptions or misinformation that might exist. Questions you might ask include these:

- Who learned something new?
- What did you learn that you didn't know before?
- Did you learn something about the circus that surprised you?
- What was your favorite part of the activity?
- What should we change the next time we do the project?

The process of creating the circus can be documented by making a class book. Each step of the project can be described by the children and noted through drawings and dictation. The children will enjoy reviewing the book, and will especially enjoy seeing their own circus drawings and paintings. The project book should also recognize the contributions made by the parents and other community members.

Based on the assessment, suggestions for improving and extending the activities will probably include the following:

- Ways to modify the activity to make it more successful
- Ideas for individualizing
- Ways to include children with special needs
- Related topics for exploration

Example of a Thematic Project

One ongoing project was built around several children's interest in whales. The teacher asked a group of children, including the three who had been discussing whales, to talk about them. She asked what the children knew and found out that one child knew that there were several different species of whales and named two: the blue whale and the nurse whale. Another child disagreed, saying that there was only one kind of whale. The teacher suggested that the children ask the rest of the class about whales, and this became a large-group discussion. At the end of the day, the children were told to ask their families about whales.

The next day, one child came to school with a book about whales and another said her mother studied whales at the university. The children eagerly listened to the whale book, pored over the pictures in the book, and dictated an invitation to the mother/scientist asking her to come to school and share information with the class.

Over the course of several weeks, children went to the library to get more books about whales, drew their own pictures of whales to go in a whale resource book, built aluminum foil whales for the water table, and listened to whale "songs" on the record player. They became interested in the conservation of whales and wrote letters to an environmental group expressing their concern over the killing of whales.

In a discussion about the size of whales, the teacher asked the children to estimate how much area a small whale might cover. The children measured their classroom with tape measures and found that a whale was even bigger than that. They then discussed using the park to build a whale out of blocks. After carting their blocks to the park in wagons, they found that there were not nearly enough to fill the whale space. With encouragement from the teacher, the children continued the project—measuring out the length of the whale by using balls of string.

This whale project captured the interest of all the children for part of the time and was sustained by the constant interest of three children for over a month. This illustrates the capacity that children have for deep exploration and learning. It called for problem solving, literacy and mathematical skills, and knowledge of the physical world. Children were able to work individually and in groups. The teacher became a learner along with the children. It involved parents and the community. Such projects expand and stretch the use of materials and often extend the learning environment beyond the classroom.

In summary, thematic projects are most successful if well planned by the teacher. The format described in the preceding section is suggested as a possible planning tool.

The *Thematic Project Planning Sheet* may be used to record the planning, implementation, and outcome of a thematic project. It permits documentation of projects in a professional way so that ideas can be shared with colleagues.

Thematic Project Planning Sheet

I.   Topic and origin of the topic:

II. Related activities to be developed and corresponding concepts to be explored:

II. Materials needed:

III.   Introduce the activity by asking:

What do you know about _____ ?
(elicit prior knowledge)

What do you want to know about _____ ?
(learning content)

How will we find out about _____ ?
(plan for learning)

IV.   Assessment: What have we learned? (Use the child's point of view
and the teacher's.)

VI.   Suggestions for improving and extending the project. Include:

- Ideas for individualizing
- Related topics for exploration
- Ways to modify the activities for improvement
- Things to eliminate or add

Factors to be Considered in Planning

Child Development

One source of ideas for planning activities and how to present them comes from the teachers' expertise about children. Some topics are important to a majority of children between three and seven years of age in most cultures. The list includes families, familiar animals, babies, water, cars and trucks, separation, fairness, favorite foods, music, friends, scary things, and shopping—in short, all that children experience directly in their daily lives. Almost any of these topics, if adjusted according to the age, ability level, culture, and character of the group, can be the basis of a successful and engaging preschool educational experience.

The teacher would present a theme on water very differently to a group of two and three year old children and a group of six and seven year old children. Most of the activities planned for the younger group would involve sensory experience and would be simple and concrete. The activities could include providing a variety of materials (funnels, tubes, sieves, cups) with which to play in water; freezing and unfreezing water (tasting ice); walking in the rain and splashing in puddles; drinking water; and water coloring. More complex and abstract activities would appeal to older children: looking at pond water under a microscope to identify one or two micro-organisms; determining the freezing and boiling temperatures of water; visiting different types of bodies of water (river, sea, lake, pond); demonstrating the processes of evaporation and condensation; and determining the path of water from its source to the tap.

Dimensions of the Group

The second factor that influences planning is the particular group of children. Each group of children is unique. They and the teacher form a little community that has its own culture. Curriculum ideas and their manner of presentation must respond to this group; what is engaging to one group of children is not engaging to another. One teacher developed a two week theme about spiders after noticing her children's intense interest in a spider found in the outdoor play area. Another teacher planned a theme about bears when her children became fascinated by a "bear" character in a book. Another teacher planned a theme about the birth of babies when she observed that three of the children's mothers were pregnant and a fourth had just given birth. Hospitalization became a theme in another class when two children were scheduled for surgery. Fishing became a theme for a group of children when the teacher observed the children's excited reactions to people fishing along a river during a walk. Fire fighting and fire safety became a theme after a neighborhood house burned down.

139

The activities conducted within these themes are adjusted to the skills, age, and interests of the children. To illustrate the bear theme, the teacher made a twenty-five piece puzzle of a bear cub and a mother for a group of children who love to do puzzles. For another group of children who liked art activities and bears, the teacher organized a group project constructing a life-sized bear from boxes and cartons. The construction of this bear — planning, organizing, building, painting, and fixing — lasted over two weeks.

The teacher can incorporate children's individual goals within the activities of the theme. For example, the children whose goal is to count to ten can count all the boxes available and then the specific number of boxes required to construct the bear.

Individualization of Learning

By observing children and talking with their families, teachers get to know each child's strengths, needs, and interests. Based on this knowledge, teachers can formulate learning **goals** for each child. For one child, the goals are to participate in a variety of activities in the classroom and to learn to negotiate taking turns with other children more easily. For another child, the goals are to count to ten and to contribute more to discussions at meal time and during small-group activities. Social, emotional, cognitive, language, health habits, and all other areas of development are considered when setting goals.

Strategies are specific methods for helping children achieve their goals. They are based on a child's interests, strengths, learning style, and personality. It is a good idea to develop several possible strategies for implementing each goal. Strategies for helping a child who is independent to count to ten might involve opportunities to count in solitary games, activities, and routines. The teacher might suggest that the child stack ten square blocks on the shelf when putting the blocks away. Strategies for helping a child who is more social count to ten might involve small-group activities, such as counting with the teacher or a capable peer, pairing the child with another to count out the plates for the lunch table, and interactive counting in a game with other children.

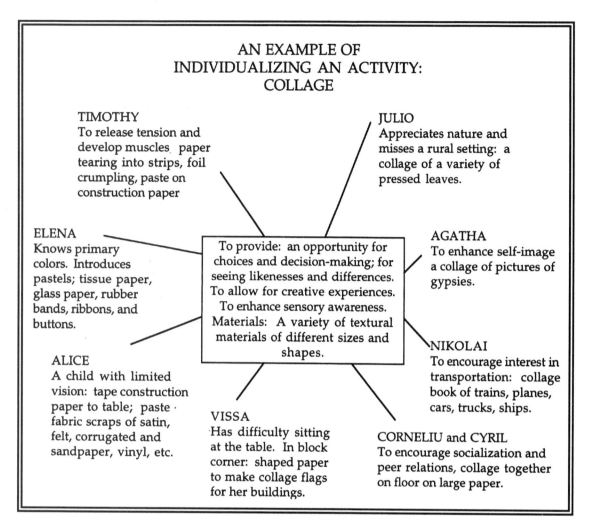

AN EXAMPLE OF
INDIVIDUALIZING AN ACTIVITY:
COLLAGE

TIMOTHY
To release tension and develop muscles. paper tearing into strips, foil crumpling, paste on construction paper

JULIO
Appreciates nature and misses a rural setting: a collage of a variety of pressed leaves.

ELENA
Knows primary colors. Introduces pastels; tissue paper, glass paper, rubber bands, ribbons, and buttons.

To provide: an opportunity for choices and decision-making; for seeing likenesses and differences. To allow for creative experiences. To enhance sensory awareness. Materials: A variety of textural materials of different sizes and shapes.

AGATHA
To enhance self-image a collage of pictures of gypsies.

ALICE
A child with limited vision: tape construction paper to table; paste · fabric scraps of satin, felt, corrugated and sandpaper, vinyl, etc.

NIKOLAI
To encourage interest in transportation: collage book of trains, planes, cars, trucks, ships.

VISSA
·Has difficulty sitting at the table. In block corner: shaped paper to make collage flags for her buildings.

CORNELIU and CYRIL
To encourage socialization and peer relations, collage together on floor on large paper.

Documenting and Tracking Individual Progress

The teacher's observations and records, as described in Chapter V, are valuable planning tools. It is useful to maintain this information in a file for each child. Observations should be ongoing, so that when a child's goal is met, a new one can be established. When preparing lesson plans, it is helpful to have a one or two page form that lists all the children in the class and a summary of the goals and strategies for each child. The lesson plan should include brief information about the ten children who will participate in an individualized activity: their names (or symbols or initials); how and when an activity will be presented to them (strategies). Lesson plans should describe the individualization that will occur. Many teachers are very creative and can conduct highly effective individualized activities spontaneously. In this case, the teacher should document the activity and its results on the planning forms and in the children's individual files. In reality, the forms serve both a planning and documentation purpose.

Sample Daily Schedule for Three- and Four-Year-Olds

7:00 - 10:00	Arrival, Breakfast, Morning Activity Time. Children arrive, are greeted by the teacher, and offered breakfast. As they finish, they can choose an activity center to begin their work.
10:00 - 10:15	Group Activity Time One large or two small groups meet with the teacher. Children who are busy at work may choose to continue working and not participate in the group activity.
10:15 - 10:30	Snack and Clean-Up Time
10:30 - 11:30	Outdoor Play
11:30 - 12:30	Wash up, set tables, and have lunch.
12:30 - 12:45	Group Story or Individual Book Time
12:45 - 2:15	Rest and Quiet Time
2:15 - 3:15	Afternoon Free Time. Children choose among activity centers.
3:15 - 3:30	Snack and Clean-Up Time
3:30 - 4:30	Outdoor Play
4:30 - 4:45	Group Activity Time. One large or two small groups meet with the teacher. Children who are busy may choose to continue working and not participate in the group activity.
4:45 - 5:30	Quiet Activities

Sample Daily Schedule for Five- and Six-Year-Olds

9:00 - 9:15	Morning Meeting. Choices for beginning activities. Teachers discuss special activities and materials for the day, and children choose where they want to work. Children share news and events.
9:15 - 10:30	Work Choices. Children work in the area they selected and move as they complete their work.
10:30 - 11:00	Clean-Up and Snack
11:00 - 12:00	Outdoor Choices
12:00 - 12:45	Wash up, set tables, and have lunch.
12:45 - 1:15	Group Story or Individual Reading Time
1:15 - 2:30	Rest and Quiet Time
2:30 - 3:10	Work Choices. Children continue to work at their selected activities.
3:10 - 3:30	Clean-Up and Snack
3:30 - 4:15	Outdoor Choices
4:15 - 4:45	Group Time. Children discuss activities of the day, play games, sing, or listen to stories.
4:45 - 5:30	Quiet Activities. Time with family members

Friendship Theme

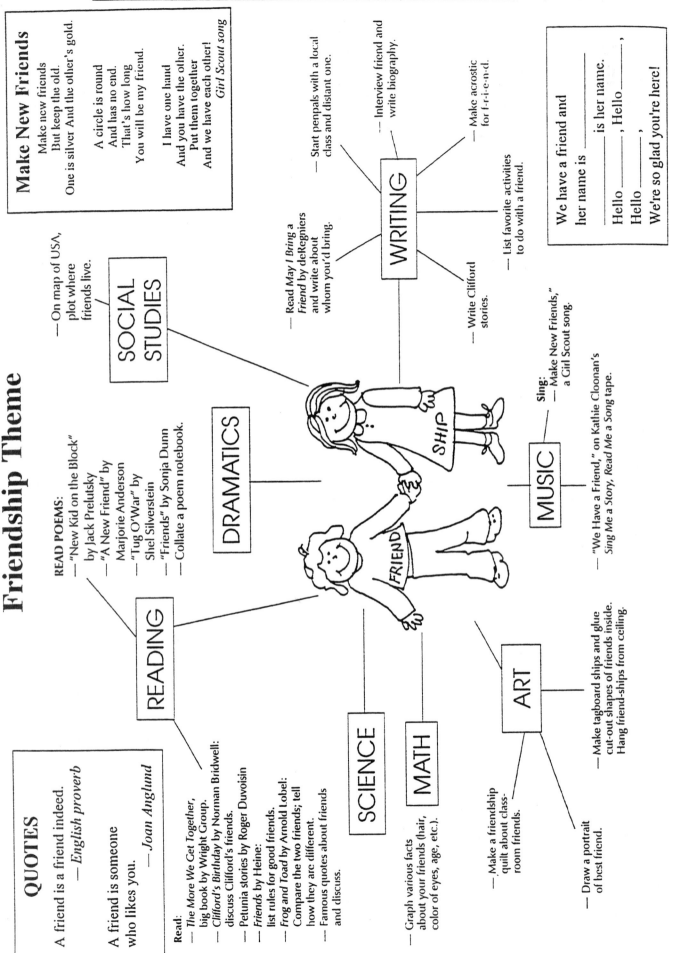

Make New Friends

Make new friends
But keep the old.
One is silver And the other's gold.

A circle is round
And has no end.
'That's how long
You will be my friend.

I have one hand
And you have the other.
Put them together
And we have each other!
Girl Scout song

QUOTES

A friend is a friend indeed.
— *English proverb*

A friend is someone
who likes you.
— *Joan Anglund*

READ POEMS:
— "New Kid on the Block"
  by Jack Prelutsky
— "A New Friend" by
  Marjorie Anderson
— "Tug O'War" by
  Shel Silverstein
— "Friends" by Sonja Dunn
— Collate a poem notebook.

Read:
— *The More We Get Together,*
  big book by Wright Group.
— *Clifford's Birthday* by Norman Bridwell:
  discuss Clifford's friends.
— Petunia stories by Roger Duvoisin
— *Friends* by Heine:
  list rules for good friends.
— *Frog and Toad* by Arnold Lobel:
  Compare the two friends; tell
  how they are different.
— Famous quotes about friends
  and discuss.

SOCIAL STUDIES
— On map of USA,
  plot where
  friends live.

READING

DRAMATICS

WRITING
— Interview friend and
  write biography.
— Make acrostic
  for f-r-i-e-n-d.
— List favorite activities
  to do with a friend.
— Start penpals with a local
  class and distant one.
— Read *May I Bring a
  Friend* by deRegniers
  and write about
  whom you'd bring.
— Write Clifford
  stories.

We have a friend and
her name is _____ is her name.
Hello _____, Hello _____,
Hello _____,
We're so glad you're here!

MUSIC
Sing:
— Make New Friends,"
  a Girl Scout song.
— "We Have a Friend," on Kathie Cloonan's
  Sing Me a Story, Read Me a Song tape.

SCIENCE
— Graph various facts
  about your friends (hair,
  color of eyes, age, etc.).

MATH

ART
— Make a friendship
  quilt about class-
  room friends.
— Make tagboard ships and glue
  cut-out shapes of friends inside.
  Hang friend-ships from ceiling.
— Draw a portrait
  of best friend.

Ann Lessard

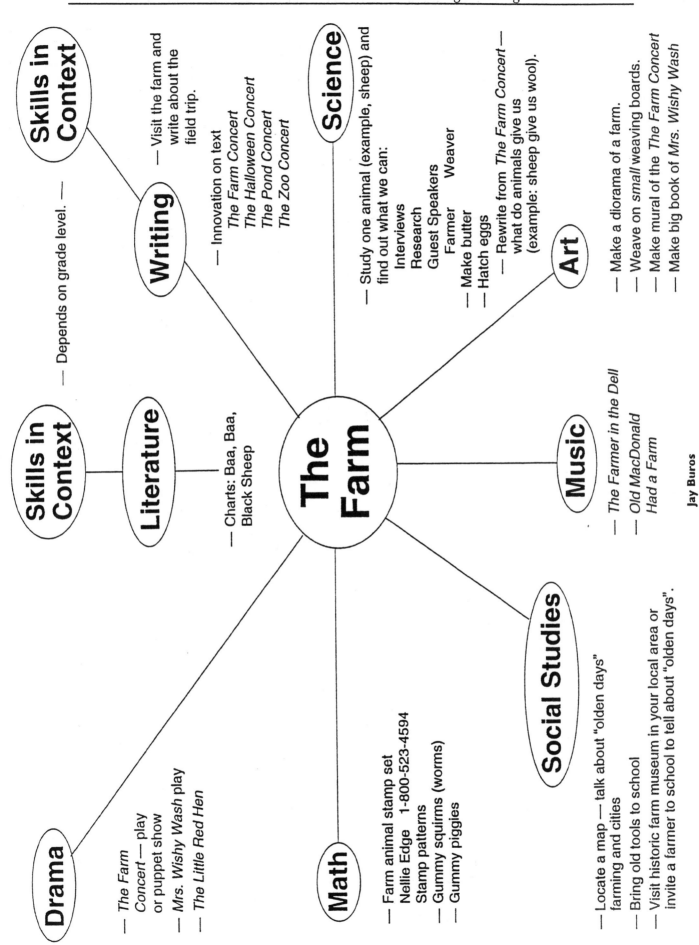

Skills in Context

Writing

— Depends on grade level. —

— Visit the farm and write about the field trip.

— Innovation on text
   The Farm Concert
   The Halloween Concert
   The Pond Concert
   The Zoo Concert

Science

— Study one animal (example, sheep) and find out what we can:
   Interviews
   Research
   Guest Speakers
   Farmer   Weaver
— Make butter
— Hatch eggs
— Rewrite from *The Farm Concert* — what do animals give us (example: sheep give us wool).

Skills in Context

Literature

— Charts: Baa, Baa, Black Sheep

Art

— Make a diorama of a farm.
— Weave on *small* weaving boards.
— Make mural of the *The Farm Concert*
— Make big book of *Mrs. Wishy Wash*

The Farm

Music

— *The Farmer in the Dell*
— *Old MacDonald Had a Farm*

Jay Buros

Drama

— *The Farm Concert* — play or puppet show
— *Mrs. Wishy Wash* play
— *The Little Red Hen*

Math

— Farm animal stamp set
   Nellie Edge   1-800-523-4594
   Stamp patterns
— Gummy squirms (worms)
— Gummy piggies

Social Studies

— Locate a map — talk about "olden days" farming and cities
— Bring old tools to school
— Visit historic farm museum in your local area or invite a farmer to school to tell about "olden days".

WEEKLY SCHEDULE

	MONDAY	TUESDAY	WEDNESDAY	THURSDAY	FRIDAY
Morning Meeting	Read book about the river. Discuss water/bridge.	Discuss field trip and ask children to take paper and crayons. Have clipboards to share.	Tell children to plan to write in their News Books today. What might they write?	Remind children about store. Give out play money.	
Art	Add new collage materials.	Only afternoon. Add new paint.	Sponge art.	Make sculptures for store.	Set up table for cooking activity.
Literacy	Have books on rivers and bridges.	Have books on rivers and bridges.	News Books. Miss P. will help.	Begin pricing for store.	Have blank books available (use colored paper) with markers.
Blocks	Add blue colored paper so children can make rivers.	Add blue colored paper so children can make rivers.	Teacher can settle in this area to help with bridge building.	Add boats and people.	
Family/Drama	Include doctor kit this week.			Put rocker/boat in area with sailor hats.	Put rocker/boat in area with sailor hats.
Sand/Water	Not open - will be outside today and Tuesday.	For afternoon only.	Put boats in water table.	Add cars, planks and boats.	Add cars, planks and boats.
Manipulative	Introduce new lotto game. Teacher will join the group.	In afternoon, play lotto again.	Remove stones from sorting tray.	Begin pricing new items for store.	Have buttons for sorting.
Outdoors	Take water table outside. For building bridges, use stones.	Water table outside in afternoon.	Free Play Nature Walk	Set up balance beam.	Balance beam.
Group Time	Music - Mrs. Z. will play guitar and teach songs.		Language experience story - visit to the bridge.	Have store time.	Read their language experience story. Play "Who is Hiding?"
Other Activities	Snack - make carrot sticks at square table in afternoon.	Visit to covered bridge.	Collect wood on nature walk.	Mary's birthday - cake at lunch.	Cooking - make fruit salad for afternoon snack.

SPECIAL THEMES - Water and Bridges

TO DO: Remember to send note home about trip to bridge. Invite parents to come.
      Ask Jo's aunt to help with News Book time on Wednesday.
      Send note to Mrs. Z - Thank her for guitar playing.
      Mary has a birthday on Thursday.

MONTHLY SCHEDULE

MONDAY	TUESDAY	WEDNESDAY	THURSDAY	FRIDAY
Art - Leaf collage. Story or news books. Mrs. Z. helps. Trip to library. Introduce card game.	Mix paints. Make snack mash potatoes. Soap and sponge to water table. Read new books.	Make play dough. Cars and trucks to blocks. Nature walk - collect leaves. Evening Meeting: Children and Play.	Art - Leaf rubbing. Science - float and sink toys in water table. Put leaves and acorns in sorting tray.	Bake bread. Mr. Y. helps. Science - float and sink toys in water table. Make leaf chart for wall.
Art - Make finger puppets. Story or news books. Mrs. Z. helps. Add leather scraps to woodwork.	Art - make finger puppets. Add magnets to table toys. Put puppets in family center.	Lara's Birthday. Have cake. Make cards and decorations. Build puppet stage out of box - children paint.	Art - Paper for puppets on sticks. Make play dough. Puppet Show.	Discuss trip - where does food come from. Trip to market. Mr. Y. and Miss A.L. help. Write language story.
Set up family area as market for the week. Story or news books. Mrs. W.P. helps. Read book on food.	Make play money for store. Have paint for floor painting mural.	Make clay "food" for market. Add scale to weigh food.	Make vegetable soup for lunch. Mrs. B. helps. Pick lettuce from garden for soup.	Use scale in table toys to weigh different materials.
		Balance Beam outside all week -- Observe children's balance.		
Story or news books. Mr. Y helps. Add cotton to art center.	Collect rocks to weigh and paint. Pull carrots and wash for snack. Introduce new board game.	Music with Sara - she will bring violin. Put musical instruments in family corner.	Read book on music. Put leaves, sticks and acorns in sand table.	Uno's birthday. Make cards and decorate. Cook applesauce. Add markets and make books.
		Large and Small Balls outside -- Observe catch and throw.		

147

PART III

CHILD-CENTERED LEARNING

DESIGNING THE LEARNING ENVIRONMENT

VII. DESIGNING THE LEARNING ENVIRONMENT

The physical environment includes all the space and surroundings of the preschool. The floors, walls, shape and size of the classroom, outdoor play area, furniture, materials, equipment, and toys all affect the preschool experience. Classrooms that are aesthetically inviting and comfortable help children and teachers feel good. Neutral colors with bright highlights, and warm and natural lighting create a happy atmosphere. The arrangement of furniture provides information on the use of the space and affects traffic patterns, safety, noise levels and teacher observation. The design of the indoor and outdoor space should be purposeful and carefully planned. A well-designed environment promotes complex play, independence, socialization, and problem solving. Children feel excited and compelled to initiate learning, explore materials, and discover new information. (See classroom diagrams at the end of this chapter.)

The classroom belongs to the children and the environment should reflect their interests and culture. Their art work is displayed attractively around the room. Their science experiments are labeled and clearly visible for everyone to watch. Block creations are allowed to remain in place overnight so construction can continue the next day. Artifacts, books, and food reflect the unique cultures of the children. Themes and projects transform the room into a garden, shop, or space station.

Respect for materials balances with children's curiosity to see how things work. Children are encouraged to care for materials and toys as well as help maintain the order of the room by putting things back in their proper places. Shelves and bins that are clearly labeled make this task easier.

Classroom materials and equipment are organized into areas that encourage children's play and work. These areas are called activity centers. Each classroom includes the following:

- Art
- Blocks
- Cooking
- Dramatic Play
- Literacy

- Mathematics/Manipulatives
- Music
- Outdoors
- Sand and Water
- Science

Activity centers contain a variety of materials that children use creatively. Materials are carefully selected by teachers to encourage exploration and displayed attractively on shelves for easy use. Children are encouraged to work independently with materials.

Many authors and theorists support the idea that play is children's work. For young children, learning is play and play is learning; the two should not be separated. Encouraging children to play promotes the natural development of skills and competencies. The Step by Step Program uses play as the basis of education by placing appropriate, compelling material in each activity center and providing planning and support from the teaching team. Children also learn from each other: activity centers and working in small groups provide them with opportunities for natural interactions. This gives them the opportunity to solve problems, make decisions, practice expressing themselves, learn about differences, become more independent, and learn from their peers.

As teachers plan and create activity centers, they should think about the kind of space required. For example, the block area must be large enough for several children to work together or alone and to safely build their sprawling creations. It is a good idea to have a carpet or other floor covering in this area because it reduces noise and is more comfortable to sit on. The dramatic play activity center is often placed next to the block center. Both are noisy, active areas. Children often combine block play with dramatic props such as dolls for block houses, stuffed animals for stables, and fire hats for a fire engine built out of hollow blocks. If possible the science center should be designed around a sunny window on which plants and small seedlings can grow. The literacy area should be smaller and more intimate, with carpeting, pillows, soft chairs, and a table for writing and drawing. The location of a sink in the classroom may affect the placement of the art activity center because it is helpful for children to have easy access to water for clean-up. The sand and water table is also placed close to the sink for easy filling and emptying of containers. Activity centers are divided by shelves, peg board, foam board cut to size and other pieces of furniture. This separation provides definition to the area, limits the number of children in each center, and promotes safe traffic patterns. Each child also needs a cubby or drawer that is marked with his or her name and photograph to keep their personal belongings.

Each center should have a variety of materials so that several children can use them at the same time. In the art area, for example, one child might be working with play dough, another making a collage, another painting at the easel, and two children sharing crayons to draw a mural together.

Activity centers become laboratories for child-initiated learning through play and interaction with materials. Children are allowed to choose materials and to play with them as they like. In this way, Legos become a house for one child, while another uses them to count, and yet another uses them to sort by color.

Children move freely from one activity center to another. Time spent in any one center varies from child to child. When children are actively engaged in play, creatively using materials, they will move less frequently and spend longer periods of time at their work.

The teaching team changes the centers by removing materials that have become very familiar and introducing new ones. They can individualize the centers by building on children's interests. The dramatic play area, for example, can become a spaceship for a child who wants to learn about astronauts when teachers add aluminum foil, space helmets, and a cardboard instrument panel. A child who is interested in snakes will be pleased to find reptile books in the library area. A child who likes to build bridges will be happily surprised to find that boats and cars have been added to the block center.

Classrooms are dynamic. Teachers should evaluate how effective the room arrangement is and feel free to change it during the school year. *The Classroom Environment Checklist* is a useful evaluation tool.

THE CLASSROOM ENVIRONMENT CHECKLIST

_____ Is space divided into defined activity centers — outdoors, art, dramatic play, literacy, mathematics/manipulatives, blocks, sand and water play, music and science?

_____ Are materials that encourage math and science exploration included throughout the classroom?

_____ Are materials grouped logically and located in appropriate areas of the room?

_____ Are activity centers clearly delineated? (Shelves, floor covering, storage containers, easels, tables, and lofts can all be used to divide space.)

_____ Are materials and activity centers labeled?

_____ Are the furniture and equipment positioned to promote safety and allow children to move around the classroom? (There should be no clear pathways across the room which encourage running.)

_____ Do areas in the classroom allow for individual play and small and large group activities?

_____ Are quiet and noisy areas separated so children are not disturbed? (The volume of noise influences the desire to move, anxiety level, creativity.)

_____ Are soft areas such as pillows, a covered foam mattress, and bean bag chair, available for reading, resting, listening to music?

_____ Are hard surfaces such as linoleum or wood flooring used in the art and sand and water play areas?

_____ Are there enough tables and chairs for the children to sit comfortably to eat breakfast and lunch? (Tables should be in a separate eating area.)

_____ Is the classroom set up so the teachers can see the activity centers and the children playing?

_____ Do the children have access to outside play areas?

_____ Are materials and children's work displayed at children's eye level?

_____ Do children have places to keep their personal things?

Classroom Safety

The children's emotional and physical safety are primary responsibilities of the teacher. An outdoor safety checklist is available in Chapter XV, *The Outdoors*. Emotional safety is discussed in Chapter IV, *Building Community*. Indoor safety requires careful planning, record keeping and maintenance of equipment. The following checklist will help to keep children safe and healthy.

SAFETY CHECKLIST

_____ Does the classroom have smoke detectors and a fire extinguisher?

_____ Are cleaning materials, medications, and other hazardous materials out of the reach of children?

_____ Are the telephone numbers of the nearest hospital, poison center, ambulance, and fire department posted by the telephone?

_____ Are all exposed electrical outlets covered? Are electrical cords and appliances in good repair?

_____ Are poisonous plants identified and out of the reach of children?

_____ Is there a first aid kit in the classroom?

_____ Is a staff member trained in cardiopulmonary resuscitation and first aid procedures?

_____ Are furniture and toys free of splinters and sharp edges?

_____ Do children and staff know what to do in case of fire?

_____ Is there a health form for each child listing allergies, doctors' names and numbers, parents' and other responsible adults' name and daytime phone numbers?

The following chapters (VIII - XVIII) describe each activity center and include information on the developmental goals of each center, materials and equipment, roles of the teaching team, and suggested ideas for activities and projects. Each teacher will individualize the curriculum, adding activities and ideas for materials that make it alive and appropriate for the children and families enrolled.

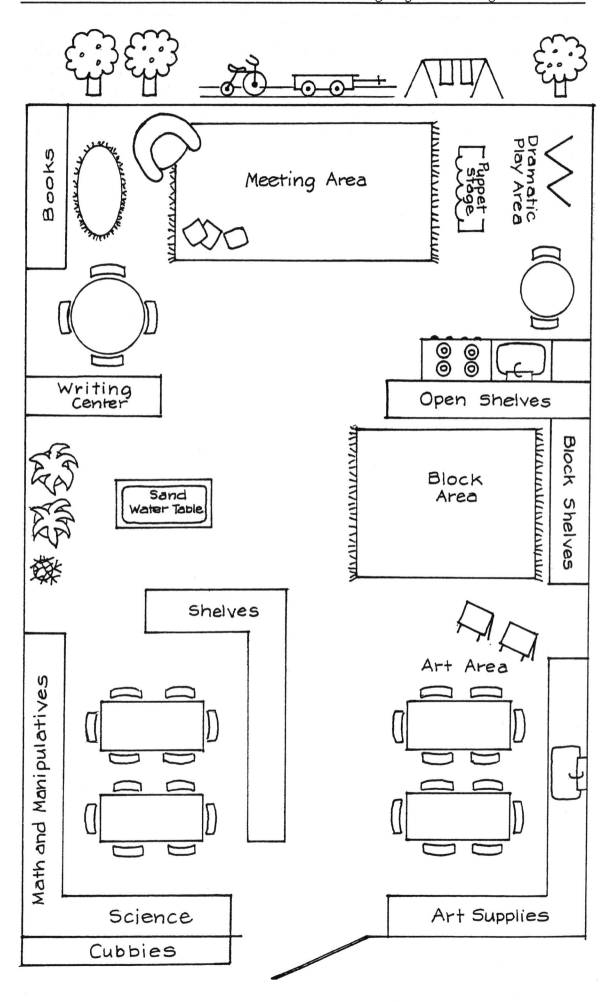

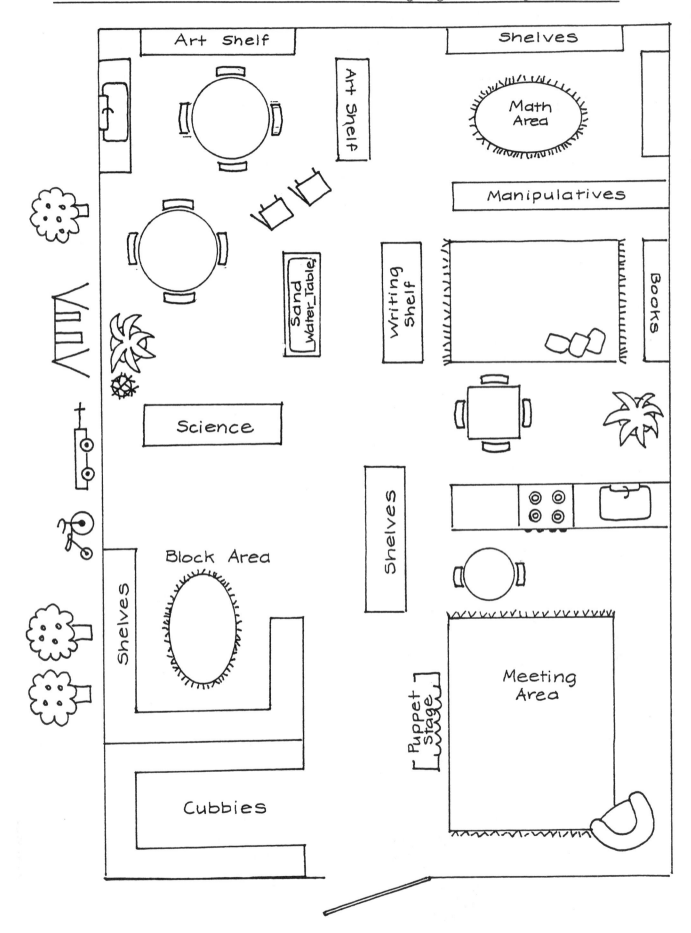

ART

VIII. ART

Children at Play: The Art Activity Center

The art activity center brings joy, excitement, and satisfaction to young children. Its major purpose is to nurture children's creativity, curiosity, imagination, and initiative.

If children are given time, opportunity, and freedom to experiment with creative materials, to make discoveries, and to test ideas, they develop a foundation for both academic and adult achievement.

E. Paul Torrance, author of *Developing Creative Thinking Through School Experiences,* defined creativity as:

> *"The process of forming ideas or hypotheses, testing them, and communicating the results. Implied in this definition is the creation of something new, something which has never existed. . . . [This process] involves adventurous thinking, getting away from the main track, and breaking out of the mold. It represents a successful step into the unknown. Creative ideas ultimately become evident in such things as scientific theories, inventions, improved products, novels, poems, designs, paintings, and the like."*

Children become intensely involved in the art activity center. They explore different media. They paint with brushes and with their fingers. They use clay, crayons, markers, yarn, sticks, brushes, collage materials, paper of all colors, weights and sizes, chalk, paste, scissors, and a host of other materials. An important point to remember is that the exploration process itself is the most vital activity.

A high-quality art education program provides creative experiences through a variety of materials. Children create both two-dimensional (painting and drawing) and three-dimensional (construction and weaving) products. The program also allows children opportunities to look at art and talk about art. These activities give them a chance to discuss what they like, what is pleasing to them, and how art makes them feel. They acquire information on culture, and history, and become aware of the community around them.

Children become excited about what they are doing, even though their final product may not be recognizable to an adult. Sensitive teachers respect each child's feelings and accept her efforts. They also keep in mind that children of the same age may be at different developmental levels.

In the early stages of painting or drawing, a child's muscular activity leads to scribbles (ages two to three years old). This first stage is a sensory kinesthetic experience and a very important developmental stage. Between the ages of two and four years, the child begins to draw distinctive shapes such as circles, squares, and triangles. One day, the child may accidentally make a circular shape with two little circles and will joyfully exclaim, "I made a face." This usually happens between the age of four and five. Practicing over and over again, the child begins to develop motor control. Later, depending on the range of experience, she begins to create intentional forms and may imaginatively tell stories about these forms. By the age of five, many children are drawing pictures that include people and can tell stories about their pictures. It is important for the teacher to keep a file or portfolio of children's drawings so that progress can be documented and discussed with families. It is important for parents to know about the stages of art development so they can encourage and praise their child's efforts.

The preschool teaching team should serve as facilitators who encourage children's originality. Teachers sometimes unwittingly limit children's creativity by presenting them with patterns and models. Trying to imitate adult models can cause frustration, since young children's eye-hand coordination and hand dexterity are not fully developed.

Developmental Characteristics

The following pages present characteristics of children's art from a developmental perspective.

The Three-Year-Old

- Children at this age begin to associate lines and shapes with tangible objects.

- There is a transition from "marking" to drawing.

- Art work is determined by factual and kinesthetic activity more than vision.

- Compositions reflect motor activity and a part-by-part thought process without regard for adult notions of visual or logical coherence.

- Size relationships are largely determined by the scale of the children's motor activity and nature of the medium. They may exaggerate size relationships in order to show parts of the work that are of special importance to them.

- Color choices are governed by personal preference and children's access to new or easily reached colors as well as by their expressive intent or perceptions.

The Four-Year-Old

- Children become consciously aware that lines and shapes can stand for people, animals and objects.

- They begin to verbalize a narrative account of their work. They should be encouraged to do so . This reinforces their awareness that visual forms are related to life experience.

- Four year olds begin to formulate ideas for expression before they begin working. This does not happen immediately but becomes part of their learning style in a gradual way. They are conscious of the need to discover visual means to communicate what they have in mind. This effort begins more noticeably by the age of five. The "early expressive" stage of development has really begun.

- Their eye development is still not complete and children at this age still tend to be far-sighted. Detailed work at a close range is often difficult and produces eye fatigue.

- They are more aware of size and color relationships. They are usually happy if placement of an image is judged appropriate by them .

- They are also now aware of doing art in group settings. Basic skills in listening, sharing materials, getting along within a group and assuming responsibility for materials (gathering and putting them away) are beginning to be understood now.

The Five-Year-Old

- Children at this age enjoy discovering that different art mediums allow them to create images and objects Their interest span continues to grow and they will now work for extended periods of time on one project.

- Their painted and drawn images are more involved Narratives about their work are more involved and longer. Growing competencies allow them to feel in control and confident.

- Three-dimensional work reflects growing skills in using and joining parts together. This skill is closely related to physical strength and motor control.

- Children approaching the age of five (or six) show a preference for using the right or left hand.

- Their color choices are now are apparent and deliberate. They want to please adults and want to use the "right" colors. (The sky is blue, the grass is green, and so on.)

- Children at this age become interested in repeating images from earlier work. They may be trying to master a skill and will practice it over and over again. They will move on to new images as they grow tired of repeating themselves and see another image they want to master.

- They also enjoy learning words or vocabulary that help them to express their visual ideas more precisely: for example, scissors, glue, paint, brushes; twist, rub, and roll.

Impact on Developmental Areas

The art activity center plays a significant role in a comprehensive curriculum. It contributes to all areas of development: emotional, physical, social, intellectual, and creative.

Emotional Development

The art activity center fosters emotional development by

- Offering opportunities to communicate without words

- Providing an outlet for the expression of feelings

- Permitting the release of emotional pressures

- Giving a sense of power

- Providing self-gratification in the creation of an individual piece of work

Physical Development

The art activity center promotes physical development by

- Developing small-motor control

- Developing a sense of touch

- Enhancing visual discrimination

- Encouraging body movement

- Giving experience in eye-hand coordination

Social Development

The art activity center enhances social development by

- Encouraging children to make decisions and solve problems

- Fostering independence

- Affording opportunities to work with others and take turns

- Learning to assume responsibility for the care of materials

- Encouraging respect for each other's ideas

Intellectual Development

The art activity center strengthens intellectual development by

- Increasing vocabulary

- Helping to learn about cause and effect — how and why things happen

- Learning about line, color, shape, and texture

- Helping children recognize their own names. (Teachers put names and dates on work or children begin to write their own names on their work)

- Increasing the attention span

- Learning to arrange, sequence, and plan

Creative Development

- Encouraging divergent thinking through open-ended solutions

- Building an appreciation of cultural and artistic heritage

Setting Up the Art Activity Center

Crayons, washable markers, scissors (right- and left-handed), collage materials, paste, glue, and paper

(construction, newspaper, used paper, and magazines) should be on an open shelf so that children can reach everything by themselves. Recyclable materials like wire, tape, staples and string should also be available for making three-dimensional constructions. These materials should be available at all times.

Children should have opportunities to paint every day. Set up the easel with large sheets of newsprint (24" x 36") and water-based paints (red, blue, and yellow) in small paint containers. Use small amounts of paint so there won't be much to spill and so that brush handles don't get sticky. Refill the containers promptly.

Have a long-handled brush available for each color. Younger children or children who have little experience with an easel will need short-handled brushes, which are easier to manipulate. A combination of brushes will give the children a choice and a variety.

Hang paint smocks or old shirts close to the easels. Children should wear them as they paint so that they do not stain their clothes. They may need gentle reminders to wear the smocks.

Moist clay should also be available in the art center. Cover it with a wet cloth and keep in a large can or crock. Keep clay boards and clay hammers on shelves.

The Teaching Team's Role

Opportunities for painting should be available daily, and paint should be introduced in the first week of school. Some teachers use all three primary colors at once; others prefer to put them out one by one. One color can be put out first, another can be added a day or two later, and a third can be introduced thereafter. The children can then use these basic colors to mix the secondary colors. Eventually, they can learn how to create pastel colors by adding white.

During the year, changing the shape of the newsprint can motivate children at the easel to try new approaches. (For example, you might cut the sheets to make large circles.)

Children should not be limited as to the number of paintings they do unless other children are waiting a turn. If the number of easels is limited and children often have to wait, they can try table painting. Painting on the floor is another option. Protect the floor with newspapers.

To vary the experience, you might also let the children paint with

- Smaller brushes
- Old toothbrushes
- Squirt bottles
- Cotton-tip swabs
- Cut-up sponges or vegetables
- Spools or cardboard rollers

Many teachers encourage experimentation by setting up an art table with a special activity. This might include finger painting, soap painting, string painting, blot painting, wax-resist painting, or materials for making puppets or mobiles.

Stimulating Creative Activity

Almost anything motivates children to experiment and be creative. Some children are naturally very inventive while others feel less comfortable expressing themselves. The teacher provides many objects, ideas, and motivators to assist and expand children's interest in art.

The teacher can

- Bring art objects to class for the children to see and discuss
- Display copies of famous art works around the room
- Discuss art in children's books
- Collect natural objects to discuss and use in art projects
- Have children draw and paint to music
- Provide sensory experiences of tasting, smelling, hearing, feeling, moving and encourage children to express these sensations through an artistic medium

Take the children on field trips to museums to look at art and learn about art history. Ask a local artist to come to the classroom and work with the children Both activities will be interesting and fun. Integrating art into all activity areas and reinforcing children's creativity, innovation, and natural affinity for making things magical allow children the freedom to explore and feel confident about themselves as artists.

Positive, practical suggestions for adults involved in art activities with young children cover "what to do" as well as "what not to do." This is partly because children will ask adults to do their work ("Make me a dinosaur"). It is tempting for adults to acquiesce, not only because it is hard to resist children's repeated requests but also because the materials themselves may tempt adults. Many adults have not had opportunities to be creative, and they may want to get involved. Someone once said that the teacher sets the stage, but is not the performer. Doing for the child may make her fearful of trying.

"Do's" and "Don'ts" for Encouraging Children's Interest in Art

DO	DON'T
Provide enough space for each child to work comfortably without interfering with others.	Do not model or show children exactly how to make something, such as how to make different kinds of lines with a brush or how to blend colors with crayons.
Provide choices of color, a variety of options, and a generous amount of materials so that several children can work side by side.	Do not tell children what to make. Give ideas, offer suggestions, and bring in models and many varieties of materials for them to explore.
Sit near a child who needs encouragement. Show enthusiasm and interest.	Do not emphasize the final product. Emphasize and reinforce the process.
Respond to all children as they work and evidence appreciation of their efforts. A smile, a pat, a comment on color, line, or a combination of textures can go a long way. Comments such as "You've really worked hard," are helpful, if they are sincere.	Do not tell children, "You have enough." They may never have had enough of anything.

DO

Comment judiciously and honestly on children's work. Remember that your body language may not be correspond to your words. If you don't think it's beautiful, don't say so.

Allow children time and freedom to experiment. Children need "to mess" as they explore. Process is primary.

Help children put on their smocks for easel painting. Encourage children to use the easel by having it available every day.

Put names and dates on all children's work. If children spontaneously tell you about their painting or drawing, put this information down, too.

Encourage painting to music for children whose body movements are tight. Painting with fingers, hands, toes, and feet is fun, too!

Realize that "wrong" proportions may represent children's feelings or an experience. They may also be due to the child's developmental stage.

Understand that children's feelings toward art are different from adults. Appreciate their work on its own merits, not by adult standards.

DON'T

Do not ask what the child is making. They may not have anything in mind. If they do and you can't recognize it, you are telling them that they are failures. Be careful about saying "It's beautiful." They may have been painting a scary monster! If you want to encourage discussion, ask *how* a child did something.

Do not hurry children.

Do not compare children's work. Competition interferes with the development of positive peer relationships.

Do not hang only the "best" examples of children's art.

Do not feel you have to comment on every piece of a child's work.

Do not allow tools or materials to be misused.

Do not expect that children will be able to clean up at first without adult help.

Do not omit the child's name or put it on the back of the picture. Print it on the front.

DO

Hang some of each child's work on the walls at children's eye level, as well as on bulletin boards, for parents to see.

While it may not be feasible to display every child's work every day, make sure nobody is neglected. Help children respect one another's work.

Allow children to take their work home. Early in the year, preferably at the Orientation Session, describe the stages of children's art work to parents.

Encourage care in the use of materials. Model correct use.

Encourage children to help in the clean-up, but work alongside them.

Activities and Projects

Finger Painting

Finger painting takes space, so it is best to do it with a small group at a time. Put children's names and date on the dull side of wet-glazed paper before putting water on the paper. Press out the wrinkles before a child begins. Children should wear smocks.

Tell children that in finger painting, they can use their fingers, hands, and fists. No brushes! This activity allows children to mess in a socially acceptable way. You may need to set limits. Because the activity is so enjoyable, children will accept these limits.

Finger painting can also be done without paper on a plastic-topped table. You can make a print of what is on the table by pressing easel paper over the design and pressing down. This makes it easier to clean the table when children are done.

Although finger paint is available commercially, it can also be made in the classroom using any of these three recipes:

Cornstarch Finger Paint

=   Use one part cornstarch to three parts water.

=   Mix cornstarch with cold water until it is smooth.

=   Cook until it is clear and has the thickness of pudding.

=   Add vegetable coloring while the mixture is still warm.

Small groups of children can help measure and mix. They can also help with the cooking, under close and careful adult supervision.

Laundry Starch Finger Paint

=   3 parts laundry starch

=   3 parts cups of soap flakes

=   8 parts boiling water

=   1 part talcum powder

=   Poster paint or food coloring

Mix starch with enough water to make a smooth paste. Add boiling water slowly, mixing constantly. Cook over low heat until glossy. Stir in soap flakes while still warm. Add powder and paint when cool. If liquid nontoxic starch is available, mix it with either liquid tempera paint or powdered paint.

Soap Flakes Finger Paint

Whip soap flakes to the consistency of cake batter. Add a small amount of washable paint for color. If some children seem reluctant to put their fingers in the soap flakes, involve them in the whipping process and let them paint with brushes on plastic table tops with the mixture.

Other children can use the mixture to finger paint on the table. When the tabletop has been "painted," it can be cleaned with sponges.

Sponge Printing

Cut several sponges into different shapes. Dilute tempera paint with water and put it into shallow bowls. Have children dip the sponges into the paint and make prints on paper. Some children will rub the sponges over the paper instead of printing. In time, they will grasp the idea of printing.

Found-Art Printing

Collect large buttons, cardboard rollers, plastic forks, bottle caps and other objects. Place paint in shallow plastic dishes or in a cupcake baking tin.

Have children choose an object and cover it with paint. Each results in different patterns. Teachers can start by showing the activity as the children watch. Students quickly catch on and make their own designs.

Blot Painting

Children drop paint (it is easiest to do this from a plastic bottle with a narrow tip) on one side of folded paper. They then fold the paper together and press or rub the two sides against each other. As they open the paper and see the design that has emerged, they talk about what they see. This activity is useful for language development as well as for expressing fears.

Depending on the age of the children, teachers may have to fold in half the paper on which the children will work. If you do this, let the children watch. Soon they will pick up the idea and do it on their own.

String Printing

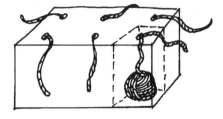

Children dip string in paint and pull it through a piece of folded paper. Repeated pulls make interesting designs. Smocks should be worn.

Wax-Resist Painting

The children crayon heavily on paper. They might even use candles as crayons. Then, using paint that has been thinned with water, they cover the whole picture. The wax resists the paint, and the drawing shows through. The children often call this "magic." The teaching staff should refer to it as a science experiment.

Play Dough

Play dough is available commercially. It can also be homemade. Children enjoy helping to make play dough.

Play Dough Recipe

= 4 parts flour

= 2 parts salt

= 1 to 2 parts water

Mix flour and salt. Add water and stir well. (Adding 1 tablespoon of salad oil makes a smooth mix.) Add tempera paint or food coloring to color.

Play dough does not harden. Keep in a closed container.

To provide variety, start with uncolored play dough. The second time, add one color. Thereafter, you can keep changing the color.

Puppets

Puppets are an integral part of several activity centers. Purchased puppets may be used for dramatic play in the manipulative center, the block center, the family corner, the literacy center, or the music center. In the art center, children can create their own puppets; this adds the dimension of imagination and creativity to their value.

Puppets can be made in many ways. Begin with simple ones and allow children to repeat making these before moving on to more complex ones. Puppet making should take place with small groups or with individual children. Don't press for realism. Let the children's imagination take hold.

At first, short impromptu performances are best for either small groups or for the total group. Plan group performances around familiar stories or books. Stages can be constructed with blocks. They can also be made out of large cartons: just remove the back section and cut an opening in the front.

Paper-Bag Puppets

Use small paper bags that fit easily (but not too loosely) over the child's hand. Show children how to put their hand inside the bag and, with their fingers, open and close the fold. This will help them to think about where the mouth should be.

Children can use collage materials and glue (buttons for eyes, cut-up straws or pipe cleaners for mouth, precut shapes for nose and cheeks) or tempera paint, crayons, or colored markers to make a face.

Another way to make paper-bag puppets is to have children fill paper bags with torn-up, crushed newspaper to form a ball shape. Staff will need to tie the shape with string. This becomes the head. The children can either paint or use collage materials to make their puppet. Puppets can be an animal, a make-believe creature, or a person.

Stick Puppets

Cut pictures of people, animals, cars, trucks, or machines out of magazines. Paste them to thin sheets of cardboard or heavyweight paper. Trim. Glue the stiffened shape to a tongue depressor or stick. As children mature and begin to paint representational figures, use their paintings instead of pictures from magazines. When using stick puppets, hold the stick below the stage and move it back and forth so that only the picture is visible.

Stick Masks

Stick masks are another version of stick puppets. Young children are sometimes fearful of over-the-head or eye-covering masks. Stick puppets can be used as a mask, providing a way for children to dramatize or role-play without fear.

Sock or Mitten Puppets

Materials needed include socks or mittens, buttons, yarn, trimming, glue, and felt pens. Staff should demonstrate the idea by putting the sock or mitten over the hand. Children may need help in cutting holes for fingers to protrude.

Stabiles

A stabile is best described as a standing mobile or a three-dimensional collage. Stabiles are easy to make.

Make a base from hardened clay, play dough, or Styrofoam. Used Styrofoam from packing cases can be cut into rectangles approximately 6 centimeters by 8 centimeters. (This has the added benefit of demonstrating to children the value of recycling.) Insert uprights into the base. These can be small branches, popsticks, wire, pipe cleaners, or dowels. Fasten collage-type materials to the uprights with hole punchers, paste, glue, wire, staples, or paper clips.

Mobiles

Mobiles are for older children, since they involve balancing. Use a clothes hanger or a large dowel for the crossbar. Children use string and paperclips to hang items. They must slide them to different spots for balance.

Weaving and Stitchery

Children can weave with strips of paper, yarn, natural materials, and other found objects. Once children learn the basics of weaving, they can create their own weavings.

Children can also do simple stitchery using big needles and yarn. Adults should show the children how to use needles safely and be present when children are using needles.

Art activities appeal to everyone. The more varied the materials, the better. The art activity area is a place where extra hands are always needed and parents are actively involved.

The art ear can always use new materials. Encourage parents and family members can contribute any of the following:

Boxes	Buttons
Cans	Fabric
Styrofoam	Newspapers
Magazines	Old shirts
Old paint brushes	(for smocks)
(for painting outside)	Sticks and twigs
Seeds	Yarn, string, ribbon
Wood scraps	

IX. BLOCKS

Children at Play: The Block Activity Center

In the block center, children play either alone or in groups using blocks of different sizes and shapes. Children are naturally drawn to this area of the classroom because it is active, creative, and fun. Teachers should encourage children to explore the blocks, build structures, and engage in dramatic play.

Blocks are critical to children's development in many areas, including language, social skills, science, mathematics, motor skills, and skills in social studies.

The block center allows children to construct buildings, learn about heights and weights, recognize shapes, cooperate, improve eye-hand coordination, and learn how to clean up and put things away.

As described below, children go through developmental stages with block building, as with other learning activities. The teacher's expectations will depend upon the age of the child. Young children carry and hold blocks. At the next stage of development, they line them up and stack them. The nature of blocks is such that children can create, develop, repeat, or change what they are doing in any way they wish. There is no right or wrong way to build with blocks. They use blocks to develop simple structures and, later, more complex ones.

Stages in Block Building

- **Carrying** Blocks are carried around, not used for construction. This is the activity of the very young child.

- **Rows** Children make horizontal rows across the floor or vertical stacks.

- **Bridging** Children connect two blocks with a space between by adding third block.

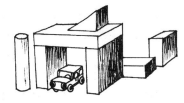

- **Enclosures** Children place blocks in such a way that they enclose a space. Bridging and enclosures are among the earliest "technical" building problems that children solve. These building skills develop shortly after a child begins to use blocks regularly.

- **Decorative Patterns** When children have acquired a more facile ability with blocks, decorative patterns appear in their block play. These patterns are usually very symmetrical. Buildings are generally not named at this point.

- **Naming for Play** Naming structures in relation to their function for dramatic play begins. Before this, children may have named their structures but now the names are related to the function of the building.

- **Naming and Use for Play** Children's buildings now symbolize actual structures. The structures may be reproductions of known buildings or creations of their own design. There is a strong impulse toward dramatic play around the block structures.

Impact on Developmental Areas

Language Development

Language can be expanded through playing with blocks. This can be done by building a structure, naming it, talking about what has been built, describing the sizes and shapes of the blocks, discussing and planning a block construction with another child, dictating a story about the construction, listening to books pertinent to activities with the blocks, and acquiring comparative vocabulary such as "same" and "different" and "long" and "short." Children label and make signs for their constructions in early attempts at functional writing.

Social Skills Development

Children develop social skills while playing with blocks. This happens when they use the blocks alongside another child, observe what another child has done and copy it, build with several other children, agree and disagree with another child, share the planning and building, use the structure together, let others use what has been built, and participate in dramatic play centered on the structure. They learn to respect the efforts of others. They develop a sense of competence as they reach their self-set goals. They feel a sense of satisfaction as they play together.

Development of Science and Math Skills

Blocks can be used to explore the following concepts:

- Size, shape, weight, height, volume, space, direction, patterns, mapping

- Observation, classifying, sequencing, predicting

- Different uses for the same object (for example, placing a block horizontally or vertically)

- Equilibrium, balance, and stability

- Measurement and counting

- Similarity and difference

- Equivalency (two unit blocks equal one double unit)

- Ordering on the basis of size or shape

- Problem solving

- Creative and imaginative thinking

- Stability, gravity, interaction of forces, properties of matter

- Trial and error

Motor Development

Playing with blocks develops small and large muscles. Children learn to control blocks of different sizes and weights, balance objects, and use their fine- and large-motor abilities. They also learn to work within a designated physical area. They develop eye-hand coordination and precision. Manual dexterity is refined as they grasp and lift and fit pieces. Visual perception is strengthened as they judge for delicate balance.

Development of Social Studies Skills

Children can learn about their environment by building a model of their community. Finding out more about the blocks themselves is a reasonable way to learn about wood, how blocks are made, and why standard measurements are important. The interdependence of people can be explored, as well as people and their work. Questions about how people have made their buildings over time can be explored.

Setting Up the Block Activity Center

Select an area away from highly active, busy areas of the classroom. Blocks should be in a protected place, where they will not be knocked down by children moving from one part of the room to another. The block center should not have to be used for other activities, so that block structures can remain standing from one part of the day to another, or from one day to the next.

Because much of the work is done on the floor, some sort of floor covering is desirable. A carpet reduces the noise in the area and provides a comfortable place for children to build.

Activities in the block center frequently involve dramatic play and may focus on acting out family/home situations. For this reason, and also because of the activity levels of each of these centers, it is suggested that the block center and the dramatic play center be placed next to, or close to, each other.

The number of blocks, the variety of shapes of blocks, and the amount of space needed for blocks will vary, depending on the age of children in the class. Large, hollow blocks, cylinders, long boards, half circles, triangles, and ramps are all used to build large structures. Cardboard blocks may also be available; they are lighter and easier for some children to use. Wooden blocks can be mixed with cardboard blocks for interesting effects.

Unit blocks are usually available in the classroom. They are small and can be used on the floor or on a table. They can also be used in conjunction with the large blocks. For example, a group of children may build a castle with the large blocks and create intricate decorations with the small blocks.

Blocks are displayed on open shelves at an appropriate height so that children can remove and replace them easily. Blocks of similar shapes and sizes should be grouped together. The blocks must be placed on the shelf so that the entire length of the block is visible; they are not to be placed with just the short end showing.

The block shelves should be marked so that children will know where to find and replace blocks. To do this, a sign exactly the size and shape of the block can be cut out and attached to the back of the shelf, or a picture of the size/shape block can be placed on the front edge of the shelf. The first method is preferable.

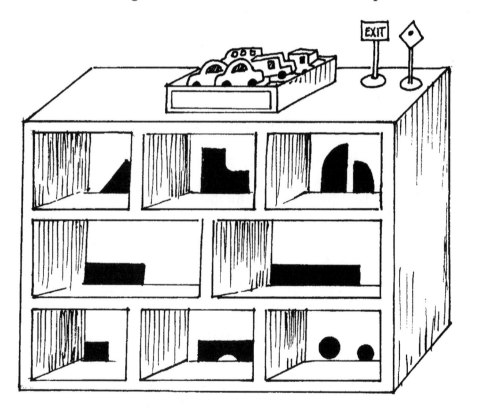

Containers with block accessories (for example, toy people, animals, small cars, planes, boats, pieces of fabric) should be placed on the shelf with the blocks. Many additional items should be available (for example, hats used by work people, tickets for the train conductor to give out, play money, pulleys and ropes) to complement block play. Large cars, trucks, planes, and boats also need a specific place in the block area.

As with all classroom equipment, blocks should be properly cared for. They may need to be washed with soap and water from time to time. Rough edges should be smoothed with sandpaper.

The Teaching Team's Role

The first responsibility of the teaching team is to set up the block center so that it is accessible and appealing to children. The amount and complexity of blocks and accompanying materials will depend on the ages of the children. Regardless of the children's age, however, not all materials should be displayed at the beginning of a program year. Materials should be added, put away, exchanged, and created as the children's interests emerge and change.

The teacher's role in supervising and assisting in the block center is to

- Observe the level of the children's involvement, the kind of structures they make, and whether they work alone or with other children

- Encourage all children to spend time in the block center (are the blocks are used by both boys and girls?)

- Comment constructively on children's work ("I see you have three blocks of the same shape," or, "You put your blocks on top of each other to make a tall building," or, "How did you get that bridge to stay up?")

- Ask questions that help children solve their own problems rather than supplying the answers

- Add materials as needed

- Find and read books that pertain to the subject of the children's building

- Plan field trips to supplement information on a particular building or topic and to follow up on children's suggestions

- Write signs for buildings

- Allow children to keep buildings up overnight when desired and possible

Learning about balance, height, and weight involves experimentation and trial and error. Structures fall down; that is part of block building and part of the learning process. Children learn from what they do: this is part of problem solving. Therefore, each situation needs to be handled individually. Rules should not limit the height of a building, but if a child or group of children repeatedly builds and knocks down structures in a way that is disruptive or dangerous to others, they must be redirected.

Another aspect of supervising the children's work in the block area is monitoring the number of children who can work there at one time. This depends on the size of the area, the particular children who are working there, and the kinds of structures they are making. There should not be a strict rule about the number of children working at one time; however, if it does become necessary to limit the number of children in the block center, this should be treated as a problem-solving situation and decided with the children.

When appropriate and possible, a block structure should remain standing over-night. This will not be necessary every day, only if a child or group of children has put a great deal of effort into the structure and is still elaborating upon it or using it for dramatic play. Moreover, always having to put away the blocks minimizes the value of children's work. Therefore, in those situations in which play and learning will be supported and encouraged, it is recommended that a structure be allowed to remain standing.

Clean-up can be an enjoyable learning experience, if you say

"Who is going to take the unit blocks?"

"Can you find all the squares?"

"Everybody take two blocks."

"Today let's take four blocks at a time."

"You can make a train with the blocks."

"Carry one big block and one small block."

Two children can be the "block store workers" who receive the blocks and put them on the shelves, while the other children are 'delivery people" who bring the blocks over to the shelves.

Activities and Projects

At times it may be appropriate for the teacher to initiate a project in the block center. For example, after a field trip to the local fish store, there may be several follow-up activities in the classroom such as writing a story about the trip, drawing pictures, cooking fish, and building a fish store. The teacher might enhance the building project by asking the children what other stores or buildings they saw on the trip.

Block play can involve other activity centers. A block house structure may need some furniture, which could be made at a workbench; house play may expand into the dramatic play center for dress-up clothes or it may use pots and pans from the cooking area.

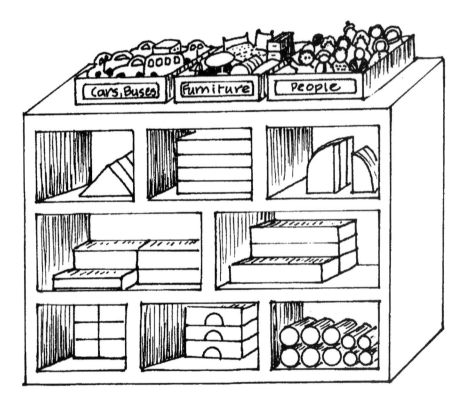

Materials created in the art activity center will also add to the play of the children in the block center. Children can make traffic signs, store signs, and other signs to identify their work. Using construction paper and sticks to make "stop" signs will help guide car and truck traffic in a block city, and children will learn about community helpers, rules, and the symbolic use of colors. If a building project centers on bridges and boats, children may decide to paint a river on paper and make that part of the project.

Children may also want to use art materials to draw pictures of their structures before they are taken down. They can make graphs of the sizes and shapes of buildings and individual blocks. They can use blocks to compare weights of different classroom objects.

Children also enjoy building a classroom obstacle course with the large blocks. This activity can take up a lot of space, so other activity areas may need to be moved. Balancing, climbing, crawling under tables, and walking on boards on the floor are all fun activities for the children.

COOKING

X. COOKING

Children at Play: Cooking and Learning About Food in the Classroom

Food is essential to our very being. We eat to nourish our bodies and sustain our energy. However, to most people, food is much more than sustenance. It carries memories or reminders of special moments and people. The smell of fresh bread conjures a picture of grandmother, in her apron, taking steaming loaves of bread from the oven, to be cut and spread with sweet butter and honey. A fragrant pork roast might remind us of holiday dinners with aunts, uncles, and cousins sitting around the dining table sharing family stories. Food carries cultural meaning, identity, and pride.

Through food experiences, children can learn about other people and other lands. Teachers can introduce a favorite regional food, such as dumplings, and let the children make it for lunch or snack. Using books and stories, the teacher can explain that dumplings are made by families all over the world, although they have different names, slightly different ingredients, and may look a little different. For example, in Italy they are called *ravioli*, in Israel *kreplach*, in China *won tons*, in India *samosas*. The children can make many different kinds of dumplings and discuss the countries they come from.

For families who struggle to find ample food for their children or who have lived through famine, food is precious. Parents may worry that their children are malnourished, and spend hours standing in line to buy whatever food is available. Children living in such circumstances may learn to never waste food, and eat everything that is offered to them.

When given the opportunity, all children enjoy helping with simple cooking chores. Even two- and three-year-olds can mash potatoes, spread jam on bread, or help knead dough, and feel a sense of accomplishment as they do real work.

Diverse experiences with a variety of nutritious foods help children establish lifelong eating habits. They learn that certain foods contribute to health and growth, while others may cause health problems. Children must be taught to make healthy food choices by learning about what the body needs.

Teachers can use beans, grains, vegetables, fruits, seeds and nuts to help children learn the fundamentals of food origins and preparation. It is exciting for children to sprout wheat seeds, plant and watch stalks of wheat grow, or feel the silky tassels of the wheat on the stalk. They can grind their own flour, make dough and take bread from the oven, enjoying the yeasty aroma and tasting the crunchy crust and soft center.

In the classroom, children can help make snacks, cook part of breakfast or lunch, or prepare a special food for a holiday celebration. Recipes that are appropriate for children range from simple ones, with only two or three ingredients, to more complex concoctions, with many ingredients that require greater skill. To promote maximum learning about food experiences, cooking and other activities related to foods can be integrated into other activity centers.

Cooking is an activity that promotes development and learning in all developmental domains.

Impact on Developmental Areas

Literacy

As children learn to decode recipes with words and pictures, they begin to scan from left to right and translate symbolic characters to concrete actions. They enjoy "reading" and some may enjoy copying the recipe in front of them. They practice sequencing as they proceed step by step through a cooking activity. Asking children to describe the cooking activity at a later time reinforces the sequence of the process and provides a rich language experience. They have the opportunity to build vocabulary, using words like sift, knead, and blend. As children perform the tasks, words like *squeeze* the lemon, *dissolve* the gelatin, and *melt* the butter become part of their vocabularies.

Mathematical Thinking

Children learn about quantities and measuring when they pour one cup of juice or two spoonfuls of sugar into a mixing bowl. They explore the meaning of numbers as they count three eggs, five spoonfuls of vanilla, and one–fourth cup of milk. Children grapple with the concept of fractions as they cut a cake into fifteen portions or fill a measuring cup half way with flour. They begin to develop a sense of time as they bake a cake for one hour or boil pudding for ten minutes.

Scientific Knowledge

Cooking is based on the sciences of chemistry and physics. As children observe yeast proofing and bread rising, they pose hypotheses about what is happening and why. They watch as heat thickens gravy or melts chocolate. Children learn to compare and contrast by tasting and describing foods like lemons and oranges, or eating carrots prepared in a variety of ways — raw, cooked, or baked in a cake. They learn about the origins of food as they plant seeds, water the seedlings and young plants, and finally cut lettuce for a salad. Children can discuss where eggs come from, thereby perceiving the relationship between chicken and egg as part of the life cycle.

Physical Development

Scooping, peeling, sifting, beating, and pouring build motor coordination and increase small-muscle control. As children pour salt into a measuring spoon, and then add it to a mixture, they must coordinate their eye and hand movements. Kneading bread and mixing batters requires strength in arms, shoulders, and backs.

Social Skills and Cultural Knowledge

Children learn to take turns as they pass a jar filled with cream around a circle and shake it until it turns to butter. They learn to share a finished product, making sure that everyone has a portion. They work together to create a snack. They realize that people are different as they discover that one child loves the taste and texture of coconut, while another finds it distasteful. Children learn about different foods that families eat and cultural differences in food choices.

Emotional Development

People often turn to food for comfort, and children may have foods that they prefer when they are sad or when they are celebrating a special occasion. Following a recipe and sharing the result with friends is very rewarding. A child's self–concept is enhanced by creating something real. On the other hand, it is disappointing to put a lot of time into baking bread that does not rise. In this case, children can profit from their mistakes by analyzing why a recipe did not work.

Concept Development

Colors are introduced as children make orange juice, red beet soup, or green salads. Shapes become meaningful when children roll dough into a cylinder, make triangular dumplings or cut carrots into circles. All senses — taste, smell, touch, and sight — are active as children participate in a cooking activity.

Setting Up for Cooking

Many centers do not have actual kitchens. Any classroom with electricity, however, can accommodate a temporary cooking area. If you are lucky enough to have access to a kitchen, an adult can supervise a small group of children in the kitchen. Also, children can prepare foods in the classroom, using the kitchen only for cooking. The refrigerator can be used to store foods and the sink used during clean-up. The goal is to create an atmosphere that encourages children to explore foods, and experience the pleasures and challenges of cooking.

When setting up a portable cooking area, keep it near a sink, if possible. The art area often has a table and a sink that can be used on a temporary basis. If the classroom does not have a sink, you can set up the cooking activity any place in the classroom that has an electric outlet nearby. In order to organize the equipment needed, it is a good idea to keep things together on a cart or stored in several boxes that are easily accessible. If a refrigerator is unavailable, an ice chest filled with ice can provide temporary cold storage.

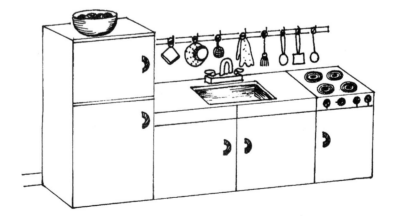

Basic Cooking Materials

Bread pans
Cake and cookie pans
Can opener
Cookie cutters
Cutting boards
Frying pan
Funnel
Graters
Juicers
Measuring cups
Measuring spoons
Mixing bowls
Mixing spoons
Potato masher
Rolling pin
Rotary beater

Sauce pans with lids (small and large)
Scales for weighing ingredients
Scissors
Sharp, small knives
Sieves and sifters
Smocks, old men's shirts or aprons
Soup ladle
Spatula
Timer
Vegetable peelers
Whisks
Wooden spoons

Electrical Equipment

- Oven (use a toaster oven if a stove is unavailable)
- Stove top (a hot plate can be used instead)
- Electric fry pan
- Blender

The cooking area should be separate from other activities, easy for an adult to supervise and safe for a small group to work in. The surface of the table should be easy for children to clean with sponges and soapy water. The floor should also be easy to clean or covered with newspapers. Expect spills and messes — they are part of the learning process.

Cooking activities should be part of the program's budget. The budget should include funds for utensils, storage containers, and food supplies. Families can be asked to provide special ingredients needed for a specific recipe. An outdoor compost pile (for fruit and vegetable waste) and small garden can complement the cooking area, and reinforce children's understanding of where our foods come from.

The Teaching Team's Role

The more opportunities children have to cook, the more confident they will be about their cooking skills. Children should be introduced to cooking techniques individually or in small groups of five or six. They should always be supervised by an adult.

Parents and other family members are valuable resources. They can help by supervising the children, planning the cooking activity itself, organizing the ingredients, sharing a special recipe, working in the garden, and contributing homemade foods. The teaching team should inform any adult helper of important cooking techniques and safety requirements. Cooking should be fun for children. Adult helpers should be aware that the process and experience of cooking are more important than the finished product. The activity's goal should be to promote the children's sense of competency, independence, and experimentation. The children should do the work, while the adult watches and guides!

Planning the Cooking Activity

Make sure you have all the ingredients and utensils available and well organized before the children start the activity.

Start with simple projects: peel and slice a banana, pop corn, spread honey on bread, take peas out of pods. Over time, the recipes can include more steps and become more complex. Describe the tasks that the children are doing so they begin to learn the vocabulary of cooking: "You are peeling the apple, rolling the dough, squeezing the lemons, cracking and whisking the eggs."

Be receptive to the children's ideas about what they would like to make. Try to accommodate their choices.

Build on the ideas that emerge during other classroom activities and that promote food experience ideas. For example, children who have read a story about apple trees may begin to talk about their favorite apple foods. The teacher can build on this interest by organizing a cooking session using apples :— apple pancakes, applesauce, apple pie, baked apples, or sliced apples in honey. Use foods for science and math activities as well. Be alert and take advantage of spontaneous opportunities!

Post the recipe where children can see it clearly. Use pictures and words to il-lustrate the utensils needed as well as the measurement of ingredients. Any one of several formats can be used to present the recipe sequentially and visually. The most appropriate format for the youngest children is to post each step of the recipe on a separate piece of paper or card and display them in proper sequence along the back of the cooking table. Other useful formats include a paper folded accordion-style, with each fold having a step of the recipe, or an easel or flannel board to hold large–sized paper with the recipe printed in magic marker. For the older or more experienced children, use a loose-leaf notebook with a separate page for each recipe. Keep the "cook book" handy so the children can look at it whenever they want. Older children may also want to draw and write or dictate their own recipes.

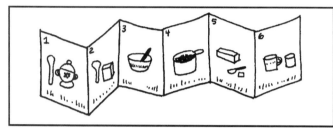 

Cooking Tips

- Remind the children to wash their hands and to put on a smock or shirt. Post a sign with hands being washed as a visual reminder.

- Make sure that the work surface is clean or have the children wash the surface before they begin.

- Review the recipe with the children, pointing out the names of the utensils and the ingredients that will be used.

- Demonstrate the proper use of utensils, and let everyone have a turn.

- Have as many children as possible in the small group participate in the activity at the same time. Some recipes allow for all children in the group to work at the same time (making cheese sandwiches for lunch), while others can accommodate only one or two children at a time (baking a cake).

- Keep a bowl of soapy water and a sponge nearby for quick clean–ups.

Safety Is Most Important

- Show children the safe way to handle and use sharp utensils. Let children use sharp utensils only while an adult is watching.

- Point out the hazards of cooking — the danger of burns from hot objects, the need to keep flammable materials away from heat, the importance of turning appliances off, and the need to turn all pot handles away from the front of the table or stove.

- Show children how to use appliances. The youngest children may need to watch the adult do the actual cooking, such as stirring a boiling soup or frying dough, while the older children may be able to do this themselves. Make sure you know a child's individual skills and abilities before you let him undertake a cooking task that might be dangerous.

- Teach children to use pot holders and how to place hot foods on a trivet or heat-proof surface.

- Find out if any children have food allergies, and make sure that all adult helpers know that these children must avoid certain foods. Have another food choice available for children with allergies.

- Make sure that children wash their hands with soap and water before handling food. Clean and disinfect your work surfaces.

- Have adequate adult supervision during the entire time children are cooking.

- Use electrical appliances with care. Make sure that children understand "hot" and that they are very careful around ovens, stoves, blenders, hot plates, electric pots and pans. Do not permit children to crowd around appliances that are being used.

- Plug appliances into outlets that are out of the way of traffic so children do not trip. Keep appliances unplugged when not in use.

- Make sure that cooking containers are unbreakable.

- Ask children to sit when using knives, peelers, graters, and other sharp utensils.

- Require teachers to be trained in first aid and able to respond appropriately to cuts, choking, and burns.

(Adapted from: "Setting Up for Cooking" October 1994.)

The Cooking Activity

Children should be able to see, feel, smell and, whenever appropriate, taste the separate ingredients before they begin to combine them.

Encourage children to observe and talk about the ingredients — their shape, texture, color, size, similarities, and differences. Ask children questions to stimulate discussion: "How does this taste, sweet or sour? Does the yogurt feel the same as or different from the jam? Which taste do you prefer, the strawberry or the rhubarb? Why?"

Talk with the children about the chemistry and physics of their cooking. What happens when ingredients are combined? For example, what happens when yeast is dissolved in sugar and water? What happens when the food is heated or chilled? As children are cooking, explain that water is a liquid, that when it boils it becomes a vapor called steam, and that when it is frozen it becomes a solid called ice. Make frozen ice pops and have the children guess what will happen if they are heated. Record their ideas and the results of the experiment. Have them reinforce their accomplishments by reviewing the cooking experience at the end of the day.

Use complete sentences to describe the process of cooking as you comment on a child's work. "You have added all of the liquid ingredients to the dry ingredients. What are you are going to do with the rolling pin? How has the texture of the potatoes changed now that you have added milk?" Accept the language that the children use to describe their observations.

Allow enough time to complete the cooking activity. All children who want to participate should have an opportunity to rotate in and out of the cooking area. Post a waiting list for children to sign their names if they want a turn; then children will not be waiting by the table for others to finish. Remember to call on the children who have signed up before letting others join. If there are not enough ingredients or time for all interested children to have a turn, repeat the same or a similar cooking activity the next day or soon thereafter.

Allow everyone an opportunity to taste what he has cooked. If possible, make enough for the whole class to enjoy.

Everyone who cooked should have a clean-up responsibility. Have basins of water and sponges available. Have a broom and mop nearby. Supervise the cleaning of utensils. Put aside the dangerous utensils or pots that need to be soaked; an adult can finish the job later. Remember that children may not clean as well as an adult can. Do not criticize their efforts; instead praise and encourage their help.

(Adapted from Goodwin and Pollen, 1974.)

Activities and Projects

Food Experiences That Do Not Require Cooking

- Using cooking tools (cups, bowls, beaters and whisks) with water

- Measuring and pouring dry ingredients (rice, flour, corn meal)

- Tasting and comparing fresh fruits and vegetables (green and red peppers)

- Tearing, breaking, and snapping (lettuce, beans, and peas)

- Pouring liquids (Mark the cup with a rubber band to show the child when to stop pouring.)

- Stirring and measuring (cocoa in milk, jam in yogurt)

- Spreading with knives (butter, honey, peanut butter)

- Rolling with both hands (cheese balls)

- Juicing with a manual juicer (lemons, oranges)

- Peeling with fingers (cooked eggs, banana, orange)

- Cutting with a knife (progressing from soft foods—a banana—to hard foods like an apple)

- Peeling with a scraper (potatoes, carrots)

- Grating with a hand grater (cheese, potatoes)

- Using the blender (fruit, milk and yogurt drinks)

(Adapted from *Cooking In the Head Start Classroom — An Everyday Affair.*)

Theme: Exploring Vegetables

If you ask children whether they like to eat seeds, roots, stems or leaves, they probably will say "No!" But ask if they like peanuts or potatoes or celery, or lettuce, and they will probably say "Yes!" They often are not aware of the many varieties and parts of vegetables. A theme-based project like growing a garden can be an excellent opportunity for children to learn about plants and to taste new foods.

Begin by reading stories about plants, discuss how they are grown, what they are composed of, and where roots, stems, leaves, flowers, fruits and seeds are located on different plants.

Have children cut out pictures of plants and draw their favorite plants.

Let the children plant some fast–growing seeds such as radishes and water them and watch them grow.

Guide the children as they investigate the different parts of plants: roots, stems, leaves, flowers, and fruits.

Roots

Bring in different root vegetables, such as beets, carrots, potatoes, or radishes. After they have cleaned and cut the vegetables, let the children taste them raw. (The teacher may need to cut these hard vegetables for young children.) Ask them to describe the differences in shape, color, and taste.

Demonstrate how to make potato prints by cutting a design in relief, dipping it in paint, and printing onto rolls of paper. After children have made their prints, show examples of woodcuts in art books and point out that they, too, are artists.

Cook the vegetables and ask the children how they have changed. Make boiled potatoes and baked sweet potatoes. How do they differ? Ask the children to describe the differences between raw carrots and carrots grated and baked into muffins.

Stems

Bring in celery, rhubarb, or asparagus. Show children the whole plant with the leaves, explaining that it is the stem that we eat. Rhubarb leaves are toxic, so be sure the children do not taste them. Help them observe how the stem connects the roots with the leaves.

Have children soak celery stalks in water colored with vegetable dye and observe how the water is carried up the stalk to the leaves.

Ask the children to guess how many "celery stalks tall" they are. Next, line up the stalks end to end on a piece of paper and ask the children to take turns measuring themselves. Make a graph showing how many celery stalks tall each child is.

Cook rhubarb with the children. Have them taste it before and after it is sweetened with sugar or honey. Ask them to describe the different flavors.

Let the children stuff celery stalks with soft cheese for a snack.

Ask them to watch what happens to the color of celery and asparagus as it steams in a little water in an electric frying pan.

Leaves

Take the children to a garden to pick a variety of fresh leaves, such as cabbage, lettuce, chard, spinach, kale, and parsley. If this is not possible, buy some leafy vegetables at the store, or take the children on a trip to the farmers' market or grocery store to purchase the produce.

Have the children identify how the leaves are different from and similar to one another. Record their ideas.

Have the children grate cabbage to make a slaw, stir-fry the spinach, and wrap lettuce leaves around a piece of meat to make a lettuce roll–up.

Flowers

Children are often surprised to discover that broccoli, cauliflower, and brussel sprouts are flowers. Let the children examine the vegetable under a magnifying glass to see how each floret is a bud waiting to bloom. If possible, show them a stalk of broccoli that has flowered into yellow blooms.

Have the children taste the raw vegetable and compare it with the cooked version. Let the children puree broccoli in a blender with a little milk and cheese for a completely different taste and texture.

Fruit

A tomato is actually a fruit, as are squash and pumpkins. Cut the stem and top off a pumpkin, so that the children can use spoons or their hands to scoop out the stringy insides. Wash the seeds, then salt and bake them in the oven. Some children like the messy texture of the pumpkin's insides, while others do not. Carve a face on the pumpkin and talk about the U.S. tradition of Halloween. (Food is often a wonderful way for children to learn about foreign customs and holidays.)

Let the children taste tomatoes raw, make tomato sauce to put on rice or pasta, or make tomato juice.

Celebrate the vegetable theme by reading a children's story about a garden or making soup. *Stone Soup* is a favorite folk tale. Have each child bring a vegetable from home. Invite the parents to come for a vegetable lunch. Serve vegetables in all forms: raw stems, roots, leaves, flowers, and fruits. Cut them into small pieces for salads or for eating with dips. Let the children make vegetable soup. Some of these foods can be prepared several days ahead and stored, covered, in the refrigerator. Ask the children to share their drawings, plants, and new knowledge about vegetables with their parents as they eat together.

(Adapted from Church, 1994.)

Breakfast for Fathers

It's often difficult for preschool programs to involve fathers in the classroom. To solve this dilemma, one program invited fathers or other important male relatives for breakfast the first Friday of each month. The children planned the menu, prepared the food, made decorations for the tables, and enjoyed sharing their culinary efforts with their fathers. It was a great success. This idea can be adapted for any family members.

Recipes

Most recipes can be adapted for use with children. Try to keep them simple. Remember that the children should do the cooking. The availability of foods may vary, depending upon the season. Try to be creative and use whatever is available. Recipes can be changed and ingredients can be substituted.

The following recipes can easily be prepared in the classroom.

Single Portion Recipes

These can be made by one child at a time or by a group of children working individually.

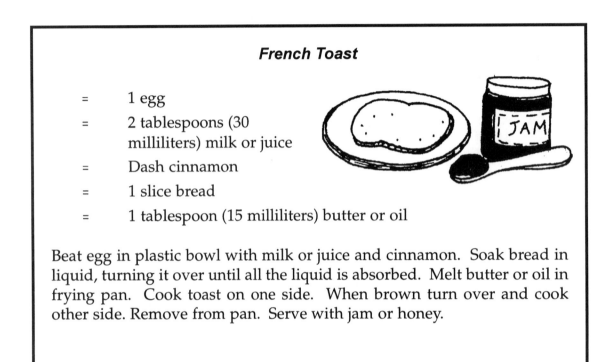

French Toast

= 1 egg
= 2 tablespoons (30 milliliters) milk or juice
= Dash cinnamon
= 1 slice bread
= 1 tablespoon (15 milliliters) butter or oil

Beat egg in plastic bowl with milk or juice and cinnamon. Soak bread in liquid, turning it over until all the liquid is absorbed. Melt butter or oil in frying pan. Cook toast on one side. When brown turn over and cook other side. Remove from pan. Serve with jam or honey.

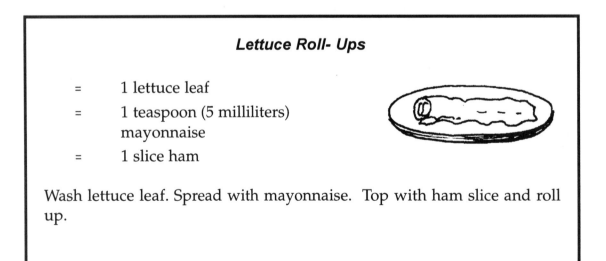

Lettuce Roll- Ups

= 1 lettuce leaf
= 1 teaspoon (5 milliliters) mayonnaise
= 1 slice ham

Wash lettuce leaf. Spread with mayonnaise. Top with ham slice and roll up.

Apple Salad

=   1 apple
=   1 slice celery
=   2 walnuts
=   10 raisins
=   1 tablespoon (15 milliliters) yogurt

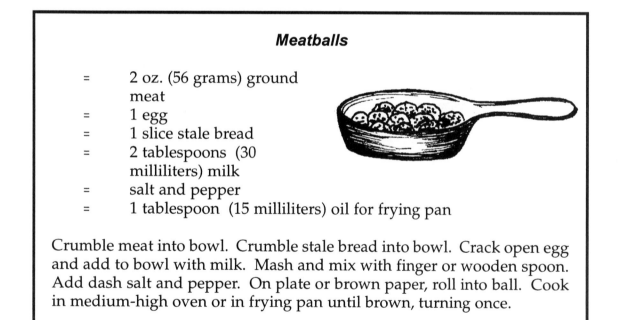

Wash apple and celery. Slice apple and remove core and seeds. Chop apple. Slice and chop celery. Chop nuts. Put chopped ingredients in bowl and add yogurt. Mix well.

Meatballs

=   2 oz. (56 grams) ground meat
=   1 egg
=   1 slice stale bread
=   2 tablespoons (30 milliliters) milk
=   salt and pepper
=   1 tablespoon (15 milliliters) oil for frying pan

Crumble meat into bowl. Crumble stale bread into bowl. Crack open egg and add to bowl with milk. Mash and mix with finger or wooden spoon. Add dash salt and pepper. On plate or brown paper, roll into ball. Cook in medium-high oven or in frying pan until brown, turning once.

Group Cooking Recipes

These can be prepared by children working in small groups.

Split Pea Soup

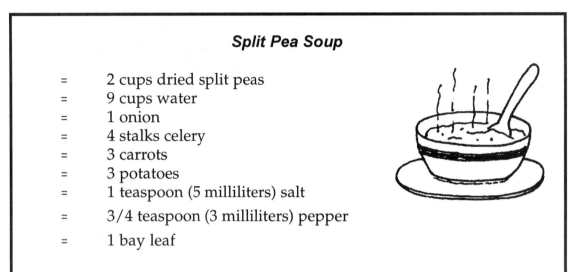

- = 2 cups dried split peas
- = 9 cups water
- = 1 onion
- = 4 stalks celery
- = 3 carrots
- = 3 potatoes
- = 1 teaspoon (5 milliliters) salt
- = 3/4 teaspoon (3 milliliters) pepper
- = 1 bay leaf

Have children cover the peas with water and soak them overnight. Drain peas. Wash and chop onion, celery, potatoes, and carrots. Add chopped vegetables, peas, and nine cups (2.14 liters) water to a large pot. Add salt, pepper, and bay leaf and simmer, partially covered for three hours. Add more water if soup is too thick.

Soft Pretzels

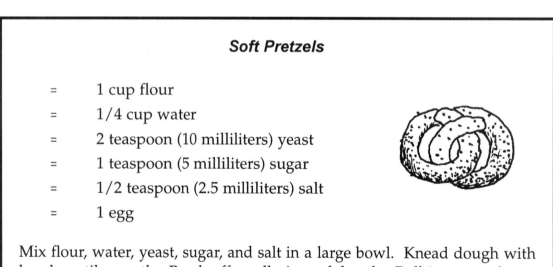

- = 1 cup flour
- = 1/4 cup water
- = 2 teaspoon (10 milliliters) yeast
- = 1 teaspoon (5 milliliters) sugar
- = 1/2 teaspoon (2.5 milliliters) salt
- = 1 egg

Mix flour, water, yeast, sugar, and salt in a large bowl. Knead dough with hands until smooth. Break off small piece of dough. Roll into any shape. Beat egg in bowl and brush pretzels with egg. Bake in hot oven twelve to fourteen minutes.

Apple Crisp

- =   6 apples
- =   1 lemon
- =   1 cup rolled oats
- =   1/4 cup flour
- =   1/4 cup sugar
- =   1 teaspoon (5 milliliters) cinnamon
- =   1/4 cup butter

Wash and slice apples. Put in buttered baking pan. Cut lemon in half and squeeze juice over apples. Melt butter, cool slightly. Combine flour, oats, cinnamon, and sugar in bowl. Add melted butter. Mix with fingers until crumbly. Sprinkle over top of apples. Bake in medium–hot oven for twenty to thirty minutes or until apples are tender.

Pasta Salad

- =   3 cups noodles or macaroni
- =   9 cups water
- =   2 cucumbers
- =   3 carrots
- =   4 stalks celery
- =   8 eggs
- =   1/2 cup yogurt
- =   1/2 cup mayonnaise
- =   1 lemon
- =   salt and pepper

Boil noodles in water until soft. Drain and chill. Cook the eggs until hard. Wash all vegetables. Chop celery and cucumbers. Grate carrots. Peel and slice eggs. Squeeze lemon. Combine in bowl with noodles. Add yogurt, mayonnaise and lemon juice. Season with salt and pepper.

DRAMATIC PLAY

XI DRAMATIC PLAY

Dramatic play is a spontaneous, self-directed activity through which children test, clarify, and increase their understanding of themselves and their world. Although the details of children's play vary in different parts of the world and in different cultures, the themes of their play are similar. In their play, children recreate places and scenes that are familiar to them, imitate the behaviors of family members, and appropriate the roles of various people in their communities. They reproduce the world as they understand it or as it confuses or frightens them.

From earliest childhood, children imitate the sounds they hear and activities they see. Delighting in make-believe, children respond to new situations through movement and sound. In short, they play. This play, when encouraged, develops into drama: an art form, a socializing activity, and a way of learning.

In *Understanding Children's Play* (1964), Ruth Hartley and co-authors define dramatic play in this way:

> *Dramatic play is the free play of very young children. It is one way for them to explore their universe, imitating the actions and character traits of those around them. It is their earliest expression in dramatic form, but must not be confused with drama or interpreted as performance. Dramatic play is fragmentary, existing only for the moment. It may last for a few minutes or go on for some time. It even may be played repeatedly if the child's interest is sufficiently strong; but when this occurs, the repetition is in no sense a rehearsal. It is, rather, the repetition of a creative experience for the pure joy of doing it. It has no beginning and no end and no development in the dramatic sense.*

Creative drama and play, especially in young children, cannot be isolated or confined to a definite time and place. Creative drama and play, whether in the classroom, at home, or in the community, helps children to assume responsibility, develop new interests, and, particularly in classroom situations, seek new information.

Drama is one of the most completely personal, individualistic, and intimate learning processes. Creative drama, however, is not formal drama. It does not consist of performers who memorize lines and use props and costumes to entertain an audience. In creative drama, children can spontaneously invent, enact, and interpret familiar situations and themes for themselves. For instance, preschool children most often enact situations based upon real or imaginary roles they have experienced, such as taking care of a baby, driving a car, or going to the zoo. In dramatic play, children create a world of their own from which to master reality. In this imaginative world, they try to solve real-life

215

problems. They repeat, reenact, and relive these experiences. Thus, dramatic play helps the child develop from a purely egocentric being into a person capable of interacting with others.

Impact on Developmental Areas

In dramatic play, children often spontaneously take on a role or behavior of someone else (pretending to put out a fire as a fire fighter), use an object to stand for something else (sitting on a block and driving a "truck" through the streets), and use make-believe to act out familiar events (going to the market to shop for food). For the preschool age child, this is the ideal arena for exciting and meaningful learning. All areas of a child's development are affected in dramatic play. If the teacher structures activities correctly, both mind and body are exposed to developmentally appropriate experiences.

In creative drama and play, the preschool child can experience activities that:

- Assist in the development of the five senses
- Foster expressive and receptive language
- Help them find patterns and understanding relationships
- Make connections
- Facilitate creative thought and problem solving
- Enhance self-esteem
- Develop the expression of emotions and feelings
- Develop fine and gross motor skills
- Celebrate the joy and freedom of childhood

Through dramatic play, children learn to concentrate, exercise imagination, try out new ideas, practice grown-up behaviors, and develop a sense of control over their world. Likewise, children gain a heightened awareness of the beauty, rhythm, and structure of their environment and their bodies while learning more about communicating their own thoughts, feelings, and emotions.

Social Development

Dramatic play almost always involves other children; consequently, it can make a significant contribution to a child's social development. Drama often includes joint planning and cooperation: "I'll be the mother and you be the baby, okay?" or, "Let's pretend we're going shopping. Bobby can be the father." It also provides practice in conflict resolution: "I want to wear the hat with the feathers. You can't have it!" Although children may argue and become upset with one another, such struggle leads to the development of techniques for dealing with others. Children will learn that working and playing with others is a rewarding and pleasurable experience.

Emotional Development

Children bring to play what they know about life: information and misinformation. They may bring hopes, fears, and, sometimes, painful memories. Young children who do not yet have much facility with language often use play as a way of processing the world around them.

Children's play reflects their understanding of societal roles and relationships. For instance, they know through their own experiences what goes on in a family: who prepares meals, who washes clothes, who goes to work, whether their parents talk or argue, and whether their family life together is enjoyable. Likewise, children share knowledge about a variety of occupations such as doctor, nurse, teacher, and storekeeper. Children act out these roles as they understand them.

Children may also dramatize events that they have experienced or heard about. They may act out frightening events as a means of coping, or they may recreate fond memories in order to experience the joy once again.

During make-believe play, children may dress up and be anyone they wish. The child can become the all-powerful parent or the intimidating doctor. The fearful child can be brave, or child who has a new baby sister at home can pretend to be a baby again. Children portray people and events not only as they are, or as they seem to be, but often also in ways that may express their wishes, frustrations, or fears. Play gives children the chance to express negative feelings that they may not be able to put into words.

In dramatic play, children replay life experiences, selecting and arranging roles and events for emotional safety. Through dramatic play, children develop a greater awareness of their personal strengths and weaknesses, their likes and dislikes, their abilities to lead or persuade, or their tendencies to follow. Such an awareness contributes to a child's sense of self.

Intellectual Development

Through dramatic play, children develop cognitive skills by learning to make connections, understand patterns, and organize information. They test ideas and learn through trial and error, formulate and execute plans, and develop ideas of past, present, and future. Children use memory to recreate people and events. They also use materials and toys in novel ways to suit their purposes. Thus, dramatic play encourages intellectual development not only by fostering creativity but also through the use of language skills critical to thinking and communicating.

Role of Dramatic Play in the Preschool Curriculum

Dramatic play relates not only to abstract concept formation but also to subject areas we recognize as part of the school curriculum, such as social studies, math, science, and reading.

Social Studies Concepts

Children develop understanding about people, their roles, and their behaviors. These, together with the development of interpersonal and social skills, are among the important contributions dramatic play can make to a child's living and learning.

Math Concepts

Dramatic play affords children the opportunity to explore introductory math concepts. In the dramatic play center, children are readily capable of categorizing materials and equipment. They might place dishes in one subcategory of kitchen items and pots and pans in another. Piaget termed this "classification," and it is crucial to an understanding of logic. Since it is impossible to add (or subtract) apples and chairs, the child must understand what constitutes a set or category.

Children practice the concept of one-to-one correspondence when setting a table for a make-believe meal. Making sure that there is one chair, one plate, and one fork, knife, and spoon for each person leads the child to an understanding of concepts like *enough*, *too few*, *more than*, and *the same as*. Children also use concepts like *bigger* and *smaller*, *wider* and *narrower*, *taller* and *shorter*, and *heavier* and *lighter* while engaging in dramatic play. Clapping, chanting and marching all provide opportunities for children to learn patterns that will assist them as they learn counting, sequence and repetition.

Science Concepts

Dramatic play also fosters concepts associated with science. Children may experiment in their play: "What would happen if...?" or verify: "Would the same thing happen if I did it again?" Children learn through observation (a necessary scientific technique), by comparing items or events on the basis of similarities and differences. They identify problems and generalize from specific situations. Such behaviors will benefit children in their later encounters with science.

Reading Readiness

Vocabulary and concept development are necessary for success in reading and comprehension. In dramatic play, children use language to communicate and exchange ideas, thereby increasing their fluency and vocabularies. Keeping materials and equipment in an orderly fashion, storing like objects together, and separating them according to similarities and differences help make children more sharply observant, and the recognition of similarities and differences is of utmost importance to recognizing letters and words in reading.

Children organize their ideas when they follow a theme in their play. This leads to greater reading comprehension where the understanding of plot and the logical order of events in a story are crucial.

Telephones in the dramatic play center show the letters of the alphabet. Empty food cans and containers, with either their original labels or teacher-made labels, help children make the connection between the written word and what the words represent.

Integrating Creative Drama and Play with Activity Centers

Dramatic play need not be limited to the Dramatic Play Area; it can be integrated into other activity centers.

The **Literacy Activity Center** provides many opportunities for creative drama and play. Books, pictures, songs, toy animals, and other items from this center can be incorporated into drama activities.

The **Music Activity Center** supports creative drama and play by providing songs, musical instruments, recordings, and percussion materials.

The **Block Activity Center** supplies building materials for many creative drama and play activities. A simple pile of blocks can become a fire engine, a tower, or a castle. Cardboard boxes and an old sheet can become a hide-out or fort.

Materials from this center should be taken freely to support creative drama; later, they can be returned to their proper places.

Teachers and children will look to the **Art Activity Center** to decorate, enhance, and embellish drama projects. This center will provide paint for a make-believe castle, paper to make role-play hats, cardboard to make mustaches, and string that will become a tightrope for circus performers.

Setting Up a Dramatic Play Activity Center

There are any number of ways to arrange classroom space to provide an intimate, semi-enclosed space that invites children to engage in make-believe play, is easily supervised from any part of the classroom, and is flexible enough to adjust to the needs and interests of the children and the changing themes of their play.

The Dramatic Play Center is usually set up in a corner, a location that affords a convenient way of setting the center apart from heavy traffic and shielding it from distraction by children who are not participating in the play. Block play also fosters dramatic play, and there is often positive interaction between the two areas. It is, therefore, helpful to situate the two areas close to each other.

The space for dramatic play should be clearly defined. Boundaries should discourage children who are not involved in the play from inadvertently running through and disrupting those who are. Boundaries should give children within the center a sense of privacy; at the same time, they should leave enough of an opening to permit children who might want to enter into the play the freedom to do so. Boundaries can be formed by the walls of the room or by furniture or shelves. The furniture or shelves should be low enough to permit adults to see over them at all times.

Teachers should also support the movement of pretended play from place to place. Dramatic play often begins in the house area with "dress-up" and moves to the sand table, which then becomes a beach. Once children begin to pretend, they often discover that they need additional locations; therefore, they might "go to school" in the book area and "go to the store" in the manipulative area.

Materials

Basic Materials

The major pieces of furniture in the Dramatic Play Center usually include a play stove, a sink, and a refrigerator or ice-box; a bureau, shelves, or a rack for dress up clothes and doll clothes; a doll bed that is large enough to hold a child; a cabinet or shelves to store dishes, pots and pans, cutlery, and make-believe groceries (empty cans and containers); a table and four chairs; and a full-length, unbreakable mirror.

A dramatic play center should have several dolls, including one that represents a child with a physical disability. It should have two telephones. There should be a clock (it does not have to work). An unbreakable hand mirror as well as a full length mirror is useful. A plastic basin for bathing dolls or washing clothes is also useful.

Dress-Up Clothes

Every dramatic play center must have dress-up clothes. These should include men's and women's hats, men's vests and ties, women's dresses and skirts (cut to a length that children will not trip over), beads, scarves, purses, men's and women's shoes, wallets, keys, a briefcase or a small suitcase, aprons, and whatever else might be appropriate for playing family roles. There should also be doll clothes for dressing and changing the "babies," and a mattress and blanket for the doll bed.

Materials for Food Preparation and Eating

Child-sized pots and pans are good for make-believe food preparation; plates and cups, spoons, forks, and knives are necessary for serving and eating. A plastic baby bottle is required for feeding the baby. A kettle and/or coffee pot, wooden spoons, a ladle, a sifter or a sieve, an egg beater, measuring cups and spoons, mixing bowls, and a rolling pin may be helpful. Empty food cans, carefully checked to make sure that edges are smooth, with either their original labels or teacher-made labels with food names and pictures (for example, peas, beans, peaches) should be available, as should empty boxes from rice, noodles, or other dry foods.

Cleaning Materials

A child-size broom, a dustpan and brush, and a mop and pail are useful items in this center. Empty bottles of laundry soap can be used. These, too, should have their original labels or be labeled by the teacher. They should be well rinsed.

Collecting Materials

One of the wonderful things about incorporating creative drama and play into the preschool classroom is that the needed materials can be introduced gradually. The class does not need a full

221

complement of materials to begin. Collecting appropriate materials for use in the creative drama centers is a continual process that should involve parents, the community, and local businesses.

The materials for many activities will already be in the classroom, and a quick "call for help" will easily supplement what is available. Use the classroom bulletin board, positioned where families can easily read it, to request what is needed.

The following is a partial list of useful materials for creative drama and play:

An old horn	Glue	Recordings of
An old steering	Hats	animal sounds
wheel	Kitchen utensils	Scarves
An old telephone	Large mirror	Shoe boxes
Bells	Large, hollow	Shoes
Blocks	blocks	Socks to make
Boots	Make up	puppets
Buttons	Masks	Sticks
Capes	Mats for tumbling	Storage boxes
Cardboard	Mirrors	Story books
Cardboard boxes	Musical	Straws
Colored paper	Instruments	String
Crowns	Old jewelry	Ties
Dolls	Paper bags	Tools
Dress-up clothes	Paper plates	Water hose
Dresses	Paper towel tubes	Wigs
Drums	Pictures of animals	Wrapping paper
Funnels	Pipe cleaners	Yarn
Glasses or goggles	Poems	
Gloves	Pots and pans	

Representational pieces for animal play (tails, ears, noses)
Recordings of songs (especially those with a strong rhythm)

The Teaching Team's Role

The teacher has a pivotal role in determining the quantity and quality of the dramatic play of children in the classroom. The teacher sets up the environment, provides time and space, and sets the stage so that children's imaginations are stimulated. The teacher selects and arranges materials so that they offer the most opportunity for development. The teacher's response to children's play determines whether they feel free to express feelings. The teacher can enhance children's play through thoughtful observation and guidance.

Observation

Children should choose the dramatic play center freely and should select their own themes and roles (in cooperation with others in the same area). Their play sometimes follows what, to adults, seems a logical progression. At other times, it shifts and follows unexpected directions.

The teaching team usually remains outside of the play area, yet near enough to see, hear and learn what is on the children's minds. The teaching team acts primarily as a resource, deciding which props will enhance play, or which curricular activities to plan for furthering the children's developmental needs.

The teaching team must be careful not to interfere with, or direct, what goes on in dramatic play unless it is a matter of physical or emotional safety. Any intervention may inhibit free expression and the spontaneity of the dramatic play. Be aware that what may appear to be faulty understanding in the enactment of a role or a theme may, in fact, be fantasy play that even the children recognize as such.

Dealing with Problem Situations

What should a teaching team do if children play at the same theme over and over, day after day? No one answer is right for all such situations. The teacher must know the children in order to decide whether the play is constructive or not. On one hand, the repetition may indicate that the area no longer stimulates ideas. Perhaps the teaching team should introduce new props to trigger new ideas. Repetitive play might also be an indication that the children are limited in their experiences and that the curriculum should provide new opportunities to enrich their experiences so that they may expand their play. Finally, playing at the same theme over and over may indicate that the children are troubled because of a traumatic event in their lives or persistent problems. In this case, the playing and re-playing of the theme is emotionally therapeutic. Should this be the case, teachers must be aware that they are not trained psychotherapists. While teachers usually want to understand their children's needs, the school is not the place for psychotherapy.

What does the teaching team do when the play in the center becomes rambunctious and wild? Sometimes this happens because too many materials are out at the same time or that they are not well organized. Too many materials can be over-stimulating and disorganizing. If that is the case, the teacher should unobtrusively remove some materials, reorganize them, or put them back where they belong. Creating order in the environment is often enough to reestablish order in the play.

How does the teacher help a child who is shy and is afraid to join in the dramatic play center? The teacher may intervene by helping the child enter (for example, knocking at the "door" and saying something like, "Aunt Mary has come to visit you," or, "Your brother Tom is back from the country"). The teacher should move out as soon as the child has been accepted in the play.

If children are destructive or hurtful to others, teachers must intervene promptly and stop the behavior. It is important, however, to recognize that behavior has causes, some of which the teachers (and the destructive child) may not understand. Teachers must set limits to protect children and property. They must also protect destructive children from themselves, from getting out of control, and from the feelings of guilt that result from such behavior. It is important not to call such children "bad" or to reject them. There are any number of possible causes for these behaviors. Teachers must be accepting of children who are difficult to manage in a classroom. Teachers must be accepting of the emotions children express, but they must not permit the behavior. The teacher should be firm and calm, accepting the child's need and redirecting it to other activities that provide a positive outlet (for example, "You may pound the clay, but you may not hit children," or "You may hammer nails at the workbench, but you may not bang the chairs").

Recording Progress

Over the course of the school year, the teacher's records should reveal growth in ideas and information, language usage, self-confidence, cooperation, and control of personal behavior in, and as a result of, the children's dramatic play. Observations should focus on the following activities:

- Pretending to be someone else
- Using one object to stand for another
- Using gestures, sounds, and words to define an object, situation, or setting
- Sharing pretend play with others.
- Talking with others within the context of the role play situation

How to Nurture Dramatic Play

Books relating to themes in the children's play may be used in a number of ways. Once the children have shown interest in a theme, a book may expand that interest. If there has been evidence of anxiety or fear related to a theme (perhaps a visit to the doctor's office or a parent's hospitalization), a book may help children understand the situation and alleviate worry. If the play gives evidence of confusion or misconceptions, there may be a book to provide correct information. Books can also provide new experiences that may stimulate fantasy and make-believe play.

Brief trips within the community may stimulate dramatic play, provide information and concept development, and clear up misconceptions. Such trips might include a visit to a store, a bakery, a firehouse or police station, a dentist's office, a doctor's office, or a hospital.

Classroom visitors may be used as resource people if invited for a specific purpose. Almost any type of professional or community worker is of interest to children; the visitor may be a doctor, street cleaner, violinist, baker, or any other worker. If they tell the children about their job and bring related objects, the children will respond. Visits by parents or friends of parents and teachers whose work might be of interest to the children give children pleasure and pride as well as information and experience that may stimulate dramatic play.

Hang pictures illustrating aspects of the themes children choose for dramatic play. The pictures may also be used as the basis for discussion to enhance children's conceptual development. Pictures related to recent trips may add meaning to what has been experienced first-hand.

Activities and Projects

Rhythmic Play

Rhythmic play is a combination of fundamental movement and creative self-expression. It is an inseparable companion to music and dance.

The first stages of rhythmic play are bouncing up and down or swaying to music. From this, movement grows. At the preschool level, rhythmic experiences should emphasize the development of motor control and the expression of emotions and feelings. With time, self-assured, relaxed rhythms develop.

Early foundations can be established in such basic rhythmic activities as clapping, marching, skipping, galloping, and swaying to the regular beat of music.

Clapping

Activity One: Clap to the Beat

- Gather the children in a large group (sitting on the floor or standing in a circle).
- Tap and count a simple *one-two beat* out loud.
- Teach the children to clap on the second beat.
- Practice this with the children seated then as they walk in a circle.
- Allow one of the children to set the beat and have everyone else follow that child's lead.
- From this point, more elaborate rhythms can be tapped out with the children following the lead of the teacher.

Activity Two: Clap to the Rhythm of the Music

- Play a recording with a strong rhythmic beat.
- Clap out the rhythm.
- Have the children join in.
- Play a different recording and let the children discover the rhythm on their own. (Encouragement, questioning and perhaps demonstration may be needed.)

Activity Three: Clap to the Rhythm of a Story

- Read a familiar short story to the children that has both a strong rhythm and repeated words.
- Demonstrate clapping to replace the repeated word or the rhythm of the story.
- Have the children clap to replace the repeated word.

Marching

Marches, parades, and processions should be an everyday occurrence in your classroom. These marches serve as wonderful physical exercise for the preschool child. They assist in the development of motor coordination and the expression of feelings. Marches can be inside the classroom or outside on the playground. They can be helpful in transitions from one activity to another. Marches can to be the beat of recorded music, to tapped out rhythms from sticks or drum or to the rhythm of student-made instruments (see straw horns).

Children can try many different marches:

- March in step, march with a high step/low step
- March with left foot slam, with right foot slam
- March and turn left, march and turn right
- March forward, turn and march back
- March with a clap, a stomp, or a yell on moving
- March with arms and feet moving together, moving in opposition
- March in a circle, in lines, or in rows
- March high and low (for example, an obstacle course)

Skipping / Galloping

Skipping and galloping need not be taught to young children. Both movements emerge in the developing child naturally. Children will skip and gallop as they pretend to be animals. Both movements can be incorporated into creative drama and play. They are best done outdoors or in large, open indoor spaces, for freedom of movement and for safety.

Swaying

Very young children love to sway to the rhythms of music, the beat of a drum, the pattern of words in a familiar story, and, at times, to the natural rhythms of life. (Just watch a child as she sees the wind move the leaves of a large tree.)

The rhythmic whole-body kinds of movements should be constantly encouraged in young children. Encourage them to use their arms and hands, their heads and shoulders, and their hips and legs.

Finger Plays and Puppets

Finger Play

Finger puppets and walking puppets are fun for children and offer unlimited opportunities for creative expression. Children like to act the role of the puppet using the sounds, actions and dialogue associated with the figure.

Children may use finger figures in pretend plays, make-believes and fantasies, or to act out a favorite story or song.

Finger Puppets

Materials: Construction paper, scissors, crayons and paste

Procedure:

1) From construction paper, cut a head of a person or animal. At neck level, cut strips extending to each side.

2) Color any necessary features with crayons.

3) Paste the extended strips together to form a band which fits snugly around one finger tip.

4) Place the puppet on the finger , and wiggle the finger to make the puppet nod its had or move as desired (Platts, 1966).

Walking Puppets

Materials: Construction paper, scissors, crayons and paste

Procedure:

1) Cut the head and torso of the desired character from construction paper. Cut strips that extend to each side at the desired hip level.

2) Draw in a face and any other features or decorate with crayons.

3) Paste the strips together to form a band that fits snugly around the index and middle finger. The child's own fingers then become the puppet's legs, so the puppet can walk, run, and dance. (Platts, 1966).

Puppets

Puppets add life to the classroom. They are a natural vehicle for creativity, imitation, and self-expression. Puppets also make powerful teaching tools. Even though the word *puppet* comes from the Latin word for doll, puppets are more than dolls. They invite children to explore their imaginations and share their imaginings with others. Puppets are the perfect props for many forms of creative drama.

Creating their own puppets makes learning even more valuable for children. The puppets become their own as they focus on the creative process rather than on the product. When a child plays with a puppet, she has a chance to act out both sides of the conversation. She has a chance to play the part of a favorite character. She can act out for herself the things she has seen on television. She can play the part of parents or friends. Playing different roles gives a child many opportunities to use expressive language.

Occasionally the teacher has to demonstrate how a puppet can talk, move and act out a favorite story.

Suggestions for Class Work With Puppets

• Create a puppet center with a box of puppet-making materials and a place to store finished puppets.

• Provide opportunities for children to play with puppets before they create their own.

• Provide a mirror so that children can watch themselves as they use movements, voice, and gestures to bring puppets to life.

Easy to Make Puppets

Painted Hand and Scarf Puppets

1) Make a fist. The tip of your thumb should touch the second joint of the index finger.

2) Using lipstick and washable makeup, draw a simple face on the side of your hand.

3) Decorate the top of your hand with yarn for hair. Cover with a bit of cloth as a scarf.

4) Make the puppet talk and show feelings by moving your thumb.

Sock Puppets
Old white socks make wonderful puppets.

1) Split the seam of the sock foot and sew in an oval shaped piece of fabric to form a mouth.

2) Sew yarn for hair and add buttons for the eyes and a nose.

3) Embroider other details and stitch on cloth ears and yarn whiskers.

Paper Plate Puppet Masks
Masks can be made by decorating the curved side of a paper plate.

1) Draw or paint a face onto a paper plate.

2) Decorate the paper plate with construction paper, yarn, or fabric. Glue cut shapes on plate.

2) Attach a strong strip (preferably wood) to fit on the back of the decorated plate. This enables the child to hold and operate the puppet mask.

Folded Paper Plate Puppets

1) Fold a paper plate in half to form a puppet that resembles the upper and lower jaws of many animals.

2) Decorate by coloring and using construction paper.

3) Hold these puppets between fingers and thumb.

Foot Puppets

1) Paint a face on the ball of the child's foot. Let his toes be the hair.

2) Have the child prop his feet up on a chair.

3) Use a mirror so the child can watch his own "foot puppet."

Pantomimes

Pantomime is a type of spontaneous or informal drama. It is a good starting point for creative drama. In pantomime, children use only gestures and movements—never words or dialogue—to communicate ideas, feelings, and actions. For example, as a part of a unit on pets, some children might pantomime feeding their dogs and cats while others pretend to hold their animals.

Pantomime helps children feel comfortable with their bodies. Because it begins with a physical experience, it makes concepts more concrete.

Young children often need help to get started with pantomime. They need background and modeling to stimulate their imaginations before they can create their own interpretations. Good verbal cues are: "Show me with your body," or "Show me with your face."

Appropriate Mime Activities for Young Children

- Acting out nursery rhymes

- Being a character or an animal in a favorite song

- Modeling familiar everyday actions such as washing hands, brushing teeth, making cookies, or throwing balls

- Imagining that they are animals in the jungle, walking, stalking and hunting

---

Charades

Charades is a guessing game in which some children act out stories and others try to guess what they are acting. Children should be encouraged to act their favorite stories, complete with props and costumes. Try stopping the action at the high point so that the children can carry on with their play without narration (Isenberg, 1993). For example, if you are reading *Three Little Pigs*, stop whenever the big bad wolf "huffs" and "puffs" and let the children act out the part of the wolf, without words (Isenberg, 1993).

Mimetics

Mimetic exercises are physical movements that imitate well-known activities, without the equipment usually required for such activities. Through mimetics, children may imitate a movement that some other person, animal, or machine performs. The children must use their imaginations to provide the necessary props.

Mimetic exercises can be based on any of these following actions:

Being a jack-in-the-box	Riding a bicycle
Catching butterflies	Rowing a boat
Chopping wood	Shooting a basketball
Climbing a wall	Singing like a rock star
Crawling like a snake	Skating
Digging a ditch	Swimming like a fish
Flying like a bird	Sword fighting
Galloping like a horse	Waddling like a duck
Jumping like a frog	Walking like a bear
Jumping rope	Walking like a spider
Kneading bread	Washing clothes
Leaping like a deer	
Picking flowers	

Start mimetic activities with simple imitative physical movements, next add imitative sounds. Combine movements and sounds to form more complex combinations with added emotion. For example:

- Show the children pictures of a dog, a horse, a monkey, and a tiger.

- Ask the children how these animals move and ask them to demonstrate.
    (The dog trots down the street. The horse gallops. The monkey swings from the tree. The tiger stalks.)

- Talk about the sounds that these animals make. Ask the children to imitate the animal sounds.
    (The dog barks. The horse neighs. The monkey screeches. The tiger roars.)

- Ask the children how the animals are feeling.
    (The dog is happy. The horse is free. The monkey is excited. The tiger is hungry.)

- Ask the children to combine the movements, sounds, and feelings. (The happy dog trots down the street barking. The horse gallops freely over the open field. The excited monkey swings from the tree and screeches. The hungry tiger roars as he stalks his prey.)

The possible mimetics combinations are endless. With practice, children will soon begin to incorporate them into their play.

Other good subjects for mimetics include: bears, birds, frogs, deer, wolves, clowns, cowboys, cows, ducks, pigs, snakes, cats, carpenters, cooks, pilots, tightrope walkers, fishermen, models, bakers, and high jumpers.

Prop Boxes and Dramatic Kits

Children love to imitate adults. Through imitation, they learn about roles, jobs, and how it feels to be an important person with special tasks to perform. Although playing house is one of the most frequently engaged themes in dramatic play, many other themes often develop spontaneously according to the children's interests and recent experiences or worries. The dramatic play center may become a doctor's office, a hospital, a store, a school, a firehouse, or a police station. It is not necessary to convert the whole area. It may be preferable to convert only one part of the dramatic play center so that the children may go from the "home" to the "doctor's office" part of the area. If there is enough space available, it may be desirable to move the office, store or other play setting out of the dramatic play center and set it up nearby so that the children can go from "home" to the place of interest and back.

To encourage a broad range of dramatic play, "prop boxes" or "dramatic kits" should be available.

Each prop box or dramatic kit contains items that are related, such as a beach blanket, sunglasses, an empty tanning lotion container, and a beach ball. Real items can foster and extend children's dramatic play. The prop boxes and dramatic kits:

- promote experiences with real materials and tools related to a theme.
- extend interest so that children can sustain their theme play.
- provide opportunities to enact familiar roles.
- develop career awareness.

The teacher's role is to encourage the children to try out new roles and new activities. The teacher supplies the props. The children will do the pretending.

Children especially enjoy these kits:

Kitchen Kit

Pots, pans, bowls, egg beaters, spoons, measuring cups, measuring spoons, cookie sheets, cake pans, etc. A cardboard carton turned upside down can become a stove.

Market Kit

Toy cash register, play money, price tags, sales slip pad, unopened canned goods, empty food containers, empty cake mix boxes, wax fruits and vegetables

Restaurant Kit

Plastic or paper cups, saucers, plates, tableware, napkins, empty food containers, tablecloth, handmade menus

School Kit

Paper, pencils, crayons, chalk, small blackboard, books

Hospital Kit

Adhesive tape, gauze, assorted bandages, stethoscope, small plastic bottles, cotton balls, nurses hat

Disguise Kit

A pair of dark glasses, a hat, a false mustache, a false nose, makeup, a wig, a fake beard

Police Kit

Badge made from cardboard, a whistle, a magnifying glass, a two-way radio, pad of paper, pencil

Cleaning Kit

Several brooms, mops, sponges, dust cloths, paper towels

Young children need adequate props, space, and time to take part in dramatic play, even though their roles and themes shift frequently. Allowing the children to take an active role in the creation of these boxes and kits will make them more meaningful. Provide adequate background experiences such as reading stories and fairy tales, taking field trips, and getting to know the jobs of people in the community that will support their play with these materials (Isenberg, 1993).

Theme Corners

Theme corners are activity centers devoted to a particular topic. They should contain materials focused on a high- interest topic that is familiar to the children in your class. Theme corners encourage children's spontaneous interactions with a variety of roles (Woodward, 1985). Theme corners make study units more real to children and add to their interest.

In *Creative Expression and Play in the Early Childhood Curriculum* (1993), Isenberg and Jalongo suggest that teachers use theme corners to encourage dramatic play. They recommend that teachers:

- Provide a variety of background experiences through pictures, stories, and discussion centered on the theme. Children need to be familiar with roles in order to enact them.

- Create an attractive physical setting with posters, books, and materials. The physical setting conveys a powerful message that can invite or discourage children from entering the area.

- Provide simple, durable props. They help children enact desired roles and behaviors.

- Intervene only when necessary. When introducing a new theme corner, teachers and children should set limits jointly. For example, the number of children who can play there at any one time.

- Encourage children to suggest ideas for themes and periodically plan new theme corners. Children can make and collect the necessary props.

One suggestion for a theme corner is the Toy Shop. The theme corner would be set up to resemble a small toy store. It would be decorated with posters and pictures of all types of toys. Toys and stuffed animals would be tagged for sale, and children would play the roles of shopkeeper and customer. An old cash register and play money would add to the excitement.

Children's dramatic play in the toy shop would include pricing toys for sale, counting items on the shelves, sorting and classifying toys, counting money and making change, and wrapping toys after they are sold.

The possibilities for theme corners are endless:

Airport	Circus	Market
Bakery	Clothing Store	Post Office
Bank	Drugstore	Repair Shop
Barber Shop	Fire Station	Science Laboratory
Beauty Shop	Flower Shop	Theater
Birthday Party	Gas Station	Train Station
Bus	Hospital	Zoo
Camping	Library	

Summary

Creative drama nurtures children's expression from within. It contributes to every child's learning and is an important part of the early childhood curriculum. Dramatic play enhances the development of children's imaginative thinking, problem-solving, and communication.

LITERACY

XII. LITERACY

Children at Play: The Literacy Center

Children are curious, spontaneous, concrete thinkers who are anxious to gain access to the adult world. Literacy is one key to that world.

Before they can plan or implement a literacy program for young children, teachers must understand that language acquisition is a natural, biological process. It follows a predictable series of steps, just as learning to walk does. Teachers must understand the sequence and logic of the process. (See Cambourne's *Conditions for Natural Language Learning* at the end of this chapter.)

Literacy is defined as the acquisition of language-based skills that are socially transmitted within a culture. These skills, which are closely related, include reading, writing, and spelling. Research shows that literacy learning is ongoing from infancy (Heath and Taylor, 1983). For example, most children come to school knowing how to speak. They have been spoken to, listened to, encouraged to articulate correctly, and corrected in their social interactions with the important people in their lives. This interaction takes place regularly and develops over time as children work to become communicators in their societies. In school, children need to build on what they have already learned so that, regardless of culture, background experience, or language facility, they are helped to have a strong, positive feeling about themselves and to see themselves as speakers, readers, and writers (Harste, 1989).

Setting Up the Literacy Center

The physical setting for learning literacy must be carefully planned. A program that promotes literacy requires a literacy-rich environment, an

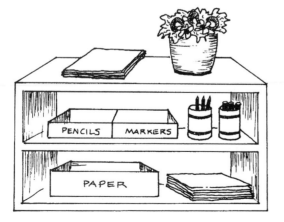

interdisciplinary approach, and a recognition of individual differences and levels of development (Morrow, 1989). According to Jean Piaget, children come to know the world through their physical interactions with objects and people. They learn by doing (Piaget and Inhelder, 1969). Therefore, classroom settings should reflect real situations. Materials should be familiar as well as appealing.

239

The literacy center should contain a writing area, library corner, book-making table, and listening center. These areas should be designed to be used daily by the children as they respond to experiences in class and choose to work in the literacy center. In the writing area, the child should have a variety of pens, pencils, markers, crayons, and paper (lined and unlined) from which to choose. Restock supplies regularly.

The Library Corner

The library corner should be inviting and cozy; ideally, it should have a rug, small chairs, pillows, and possibly a sofa. The books should be attractively displayed on racks. They should reflect a range of reading levels, from picture books for early pre-readers to more challenging books. Include picture books, storybooks, and information books, as well as poetry, biography, fairy tales, and resource books. The types and levels of books depend on the ages and interests of the children.

The Book-Making Center

This area encourages children to think of themselves as authors. Blank books in a variety of sizes elicit a wide range of written responses, from personal reflections and poetry to pages of dialogue, complete with illustrations. Extra paper, staplers, hole punchers, brads, and any other items helpful for self-made books should be available. A computer and printer are real assets at this center. As children write and make their own books, they not only acquire literacy skills but also feel increasingly competent and independent. The children's own books should be added to the library corner's collection.

The "author's chair," situated in the book-making area, is a formal setting from which a child can present her "published" book to the group before it is added to the library collection. Encourage discussions, questions, and comments to help the children understand that an author writes for an audience and has a particular voice and point of view.

The Listening Center

This area should be equipped with tape recorders, players, headphones, and audiotapes of stories and books. Children can choose to listen to a story on tape while reading along. The teacher should record the children as they recite favorite rhymes, poems, or stories. She can also record stories herself. A variety of tapes should be available including: songs, myths, and stories from other cultures. Ideally, a focused theme or particular interest of the children will -

determine the selections for the listening and library centers (for example, bones, Japan, or photography).

The Teaching Team's Role

An effective teacher of literacy focuses on learning. Learning proceeds from the known to the unknown. It is, therefore, the teacher's job to find out what the child knows and then to extend that knowledge. Teachers can learn from what parents tell them about their child's interests in books, letters, drawing, literature, music, and other social arts. Ideally, such information can be conveyed during a teacher-parent meeting before the school term begins. Opening remarks to help an easy exchange might be, "Tell me some of your child's favorite things to do. Does he have a favorite fairy tale, story, song? What are some of his favorite games? Is she interested in looking at books? Does she attempt to write?" Communication between parents and teacher is vital in establishing a shared focus on the child's learning.

The teacher is not only a communicator but also an architect who designs the classroom space and selects age-appropriate materials. Through thoughtful selection of a variety of literature and tools for literacy, the teacher sets the stage for active language use. Within the planned setting of the literacy center, the teacher is the child's partner in language exploration, the resource guide, and the caring adult who models enjoyment of literature. As she comes to know each child, the teacher guides his literacy growth. She helps them in making book choices, takes dictation for their stories, helps pair children to share books, and answers questions.

The teacher is also a record keeper. He observes and records each child's progress. He thinks and cares about each child as he works to know every member of his class individually.

Activities and Projects

Literacy is a social activity. Children learn best in low-risk environments where exploration is supported and accepted. The teacher creates the classroom climate that establishes such support. The social aspect of language is one of the things that determines growth. Becoming literate depends on interactions with others. A strong literacy program enables teachers and children to exchange ideas about the world in a secure, print-rich environment.

Continuous exposure to, and experience with, various forms of oral and written language will help children construct their own personal knowledge about what it means to be literate. Adults who read aloud and silently, write letters, open mail, take notes, make lists, and use computers to communicate are modeling the functional aspects of reading and writing. Communicating within the conventions of society, learning to use good grammar, and building vocabulary can be done easily when these activities are engaged naturally, as a result of spontaneous questions based on real needs.

To encourage discussion among all children, questions and story telling are vital. Paper and pencils should be in every activity center and easily accessible throughout the room. Visual information, in the form of pictures, labels, charts, and graphs can provide constant challenges. Access to scissors, crayons, paint, paste, paint, clay, and a varied choice of arts and crafts materials, as well as woodworking equipment, provides the opportunity for expression of thoughts, feelings, and ideas.

An effective literacy program respects the child's early efforts in reading, writing, spelling, and speaking. This respect and recognition is shown by encouraging meaningful and purposeful communication experiences. The young child's natural curiosity about print and language is the starting point of a literacy program. All children will eagerly imitate written language as they pretend to write. The early markings on paper by three and four year old children progress from drawings to more refined attempts to imitate letters. These early exercises are important as the child establishes the language conventions of her particular culture; for example, the direction that print is read on a page, how a book or paper is oriented, spacing between words, and the use of punctuation. In a classroom one might see children gathered at the writing center busily writing page after page, then moving about the room passing out the newly produced notices. These children are demonstrating their awareness of the functional aspect of writing. Another child may be copying the labels located in all the areas around the room. Still another may be looking at a picture book and sharing the "story" with his friend, while a visiting parent reads to a small group of children.

242

In another part of the room, one child may be performing a puppet show for two friends, repeating, in his own words, a story that the teacher had read earlier. Every day, stories are read aloud to the whole class as well as to small groups of children who request a book of particular interest. Rereading old favorites is important. Repetition helps the children come to know the regularity of language and the permanence of symbols.

Children gain communication or language skills when their classroom is immersed in language experiences — talking, dramatic play, and singing. As teachers talk with children about their interests and ask questions to expand their answers, children develop the capacity to share their personal experiences and thoughts.

Real-life adventures like games or visits to museums, libraries, shops, the zoo or a concert, provide common experiences to talk about in groups or one-to-one.

Play telephones, props that stimulate acting, puppets, and dramatic play encourage dynamic conversations between children.

Using large and small group opportunities for finger plays, music and singing, and rhyming games help children enjoy the fun and repetition in language.

Children can name objects or describe what they see in pictures and then teachers can remove the object or cover part of the picture and ask, "What is missing?"

Flannel boards equipped with pictures of the characters from favorite nursery rhymes and fairy tales should be available in the literacy center. They are important in helping children sequence a story line, develop characters, and use language for entertainment.

Having children work in groups to develop a list of visits the class might take, supplies that may be needed, or projects that the children might like to do gives them a practical understanding of one of the purposes of writing. Older children can write their own lists, while younger children can dictate the lists for the teacher to write.

Classroom tasks, such as jobs for classroom helpers, daily attendance charts, written notes, and special news, should be prominently displayed. Pictures and words help children of all ages begin to understand the importance of writing and reading. As children put ideas on paper, develop a sight vocabulary, and begin to associate sounds with letters, they are establishing the foundations of reading.

It is important to offer opportunities for letter matching and sorting, forming letters with clay, sand writing, and manipulating movable letters. These activities emphasize the basic sensory motor elements of reading. Surrounding children with a print-rich environment in which they are free to choose, to follow their interests, and to imitate the important adults in their world are some of the ways to create an effective literacy program.

Samples of Children's Work

Children develop skills and interests in literacy at different ages. The following are examples of writings done by children in the United States at four, five and six years of age. These samples demonstrate the children's developing awareness of the purposes of writing, the particular skills and conventions of writing, and the pleasure of literature.

This is an example of a dictated story in which a four-year-old child sequenced the events of a class trip.

We are going to the mill. 1

This is the house that was decorated. It has a wreath. 2

It is where you can look down and see the room below. 3

We are riding back to school. 4

Five-year-olds are frequently interested in words that rhyme. Below is a sample of a word-family book in which a five year old child used the "-an" word-family group to make rhyming words.

CAN

VAN

PAN

DAN

FAN

MAN

TAN

A six-year-old who was interested in elephants and had read a book about them wrote:

The elephant is the biggest four legged animal. Elephants can eat peanuts without breaking the shell. If you attack an elephant it will attack you.

If you be nice to an elephant, it will be nice to you. The elephant can take a shower by spraying itself with water.

The elephant is
the bigist for-lagide
anuml. Elephants can eat
peauts with owt braccKing
the shell. If you
attack an elephant
it will attack you.
If you be nise to
it, it will be nise to
you. The elephant
can taeck a
shawr by spraeing
itself with water.

Conditions for Natural Language Learning

Immersion
From the moment a child is born, meaningful, purposeful, "whole" spoken language washes over and surrounds the child. The child is immersed in a "language flood" for most of his waking hours.

Demonstration
As they learn to talk, children receive thousands of demonstrations (models or examples) of the spoken language being used in functional ways.

Expectation
Unless the infant is severely damaged, all parents expect the child to walk and talk. So strong is this expectation, that parents "give off" subtle forms of communication, to which learners respond, and "learn" to walk and talk.

Responsibility
When learning to talk, children take responsibility for what they learn about their language and when. Each child decides which set of conventions to master and by which route she will get there, yet all children eventually arrive at the same destination. This is natural learning.

Employment
Ample time and opportunity to use spoken language are provided when children are learning to talk.

Approximation
Children just beginning to talk are not expected to display complete adult competence. They are rewarded not for being "right," but for being "close."

Feedback
Adults and older siblings who teach young children give them a special kind of feedback (e.g., Toddler: "Dat cup." Adult: "Yes, that's a cup." The message is received ("yes"), and the conventional, adult response is given back in a nonthreatening, meaning-centered way. Furthermore, recognition is given to the fact that " baby" talk and other immature communication attempts will continue until the child decides to change, and the conventional adult form would not be expected the very next time the child uses it.

(Brian Cambourne, Workshop Handout)

MATHEMATICS/ MANIPULAYIVES

XIII. MATHEMATICS / MANIPULATIVES

Children at Play: Mathematics / Manipulatives

Mathematics, like language, pervades all of human experience. In every culture, mathematical concepts are used in ordinary life: in measuring and keeping track of the passage of time; in practical activities like farming, construction, and cooking; and in every sort of commerce, from food shopping to global finance. Mathematics has provided the foundation for the astonishing technological progress that has taken our world from the industrial revolution into the space age and onward into the age of telecommunication. As we approach the twenty-first century, our children will live and work in a world driven by the exchange of information through technology. The key to economic self-sufficiency may well be mathematical competence. We must instill in our children a mathematical literacy that will continue after they leave school. To be successful in the larger world, they must be able to communicate mathematically and conceptualize problems in a mathematical framework.

Mathematics is an abstract system for organizing and ordering experience. Young children, however, think very concretely. Concepts such as quantity and ordination mean nothing to them if they do not have concrete objects to count and put in order. Therefore, young children must have opportunities to experience mathematical relationships through the manipulation of concrete objects, that is, they must play with things that they can count and sort. Such play achieves meaning for children with the supportive intervention of an adult facilitator or teacher. Early childhood teachers help children construct and become aware of mathematical concepts operating in their everyday lives. The learning and mastery of mathematical concepts does not come from workbook pages or paper and pencil tasks; instead, children construct enduring, useful mathematical knowledge and develop mathematical competence through directly interacting with the world around them. They internalize and reconstruct this knowledge through hands-on experiences with real-life activities.

In the early conceptual development, the foundations of mathematics overlap with many other areas of knowledge, especially language and logic. For the sake of clarity and simplicity, the Step by Step Program defines early childhood math concepts as follows:

- **One-to-one correspondence** involves the distribution of related items in direct relation to each other, such as one cookie for each child, one pillow for each cot, or one chair for each child.

- **Seriation** involves the ability to put things in order, first by size (smallest to largest) and then by number. In order to do the latter, a child must recognize numerals and be able to assign a quantity to them.

- **Counting** involves the ability to demonstrate an understanding of number and amount. It involves the ability to answer the questions, "Which number is this?" and, "What comes next?"

- **Calculation** is the process of adding and subtracting, as it is experienced concretely.

- **Classification** involves the ability to sort objects by attribute (for example, color, shape, size). It involves the ability to answer the question, "Why do these belong together?"

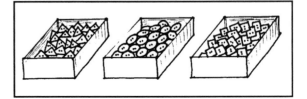

- **Measurement** is the process of finding the number of standard units in an object.

- **Comparison** involves the ability to determine that one object is greater than, less than, or equal to another through measurement.

- **Geometry** is the study of spatial relationships. For young children this involves the exploration of objects and their relationships, as well as the recognition of shape and pattern.

- **Pattern** is a theme that connects mathematical topics. It encourages children to see relationships, find connections and make generalizations and predictions. Understanding the concept of patterns guides children into recognizing the implied predictability and repetition of patterns. For example:

  — Patterns represent a basic unit: yellow-red, yellow-red
  — Patterns expand: snap-clap, snap-snap-clap
  — Patterns of nature: fall, winter, spring, summer

Young children should experience regularity and repetition in motion, color, sound, position, quantity, and time. Patterns describe, extend, transfer, translate, and create patterns.

Integrating Mathematics into the Daily Schedule

Daily classroom routines offer many occasions for concrete mathematical experiences. For example:

- At **arrival time**, hanging up coats can offer an experience in one-to-one correspondence: one hook or cubby for each coat.

- Taking **daily attendance** offers practice at counting and calculation (How many are here? How many are absent? How many are there in all? There are ten of us here, but there should be fourteen; How many are absent? Using photographs of the children present and absent makes the counting and calculating a concrete experience).

- **Breakfast time** provides children with another chance to experience one-to-one-correspondence: one placemat, one plate, one cup, and one napkin for each child.

- **Circle time** offers the opportunity to read number stories and sing many number songs, recite nursery rhymes and sing chants for pattern recognition and a sense of rhythm. It also offers chances for counting children and classifying them by attribute: How many girls are there? How many people are wearing red? How many boys have white socks?

- **Outdoor time** features physical activity, which is an excellent way to give children concrete experiences in math. Any activity that involves rhythmic movement of the body can be used for counting: climbing or descending steps, when one number is said for each step; swinging, and counting each swing out loud; jumping or hopping; or bouncing a ball. In such activities, the child's whole body reinforces the meaning of the number. Rote counting and identification of numerals are meaningless without such concrete experiences.

- Even **toileting** can be a time for mathematical conversation. The teacher can introduce calculation, for example, by saying, "We have three sinks and four children. How many children are waiting?" Distributing towels for drying hands can be another opportunity for one-to-one correspondence.

The daily schedule offers a concrete experience in measuring the passage of time. Digital clocks that show the passage of minutes can be used to call children's attention to time periods. Standard clocks that show minutes and have a second hand are also useful. Other, more concrete time measuring devices can give more vivid experiences in measuring time. For example, a sand-filled three-minute egg timer can be used to alert children to prepare for transition from one activity to another. A kitchen timer that measures seconds, signaling the passage of time in both movement of the dial and the corresponding "tick" sound, adds similar drama to the passage of short intervals of time and can help impatient four-year-olds learn to increase their ability to wait.

Calendars and weather are popular topics at circle time in many early childhood classrooms. Standard calendars, however, are not very meaningful to young children, and rote repetition of the number of the day of the month and the year does not have much potential for helping children grasp the concept of time. A month is too long; the numeral for the day of the month and for the year far too abstract. On the other hand, most young children can grasp days of the week. Three- and four-year-olds can understand a calendar of weeks better than a calendar of months. Teachers can make a simple week-by-week calendar with each page showing seven days. Each day should be a different color, with all Mondays the same color, all Tuesdays a second color, etc. Label the days and differentiate the days that children are in school from the days they are not in school.

This calendar can be used to record the weather each day. The number of sunny days versus cloudy days can be calculated. The teacher can use pictures to indicate special events that are to take place during the week, and help the children count the days to that event. When a child is sick and must stay at home, her absence can be noted on the calendar, and the teacher can help the children count the number of days of her absence. This is particularly helpful when a child must be out of school for a hospital stay. Marking the day when he will return helps the children understand, within the concept of time appropriate to their developmental level, how long their friend will be out of school.

Field trips offer many opportunities for mathematical experiences. Marking trips on the calendar several days in advance gives children the experience of measuring time by counting days. The length of time to get from school to the destination can be noted and discussed. There should be one adult for every two children on any field trip; children can calculate how many adults are needed. Any time children climb stairs, they can be counted.

Trips to stores are particularly rich sources of math experiences. For example, a shopping trip can precede a cooking activity. Planning can include calculation of how many of each item are needed, and a picture list can be developed. Actual purchase can involve counting and calculating with currency.

Integrating Mathematics with the Other Activity Centers

All the learning centers in an early childhood classroom offer opportunities for mathematical learning:

- **Dramatic Play Area** One-to-one correspondence can be reinforced in playing house, for example, dolls to beds or coffee cups to "mommies." Playing "store" offers opportunities to use play currency for simple calculation.

- **Literacy Corner** There should be a good stock of picture-number books with clear, simple numerals and interesting pictures to count.

- **Sand and Water Table (or Rice and Bean Table)** Filling and emptying a variety of containers gives children experience with the concepts of measurement and comparison.

- **Art Area** Art activities offer other opportunities for reinforcing one-to-one correspondence, for example, brushes to colors of paint or papers to children working in that area. Simple calculation can be introduced. For example, each child is using three crayons: How many crayons are we all using? Designing projects can involve geometry through the use of shapes and patterns.

- **Manipulative/Table Toys** Manipulatives are small materials that most often are used at a table. These materials require children to use their eyes and hands to do or make something. Among the many examples of such materials are puzzles, pegs, Lotto, and Legos. Manipulatives are usually used by children individually rather than in pairs or in groups.

Everyday items such as dried beans, buttons, bottle caps, shells, and pebbles are ideal for counting and classification. Muffin tins or egg cartons make excellent containers for this activity. Peg boards and rubber bands offer both counting and geometric possibilities. Construction sets based on a unit and regular multiples of that unit give experience in all the math concepts (except time) emphasized in this activity center. Such sets are much more useful in helping children develop math concepts than materials that present numerals out of context, such as games and puzzles involving numeral identification.

Block Area If only one commercial item can be purchased for a new early childhood classroom, it should be a set of wooden unit blocks. Working with such a set to make their own structures, children experience mathematical and geometric relationships at an intuitive level which provides the basis on which the abstract concepts of algebra and plane geometry will build.

Cooking Area Teachers can copy recipes onto chart-size paper, with measurements represented in pictures, for example, if the recipe calls for three cups of flour, there would be a picture of three cups and a bag of flour. *Although European recipes call for metric measurements, and dry ingredients are usually specified in grams, the early childhood teacher might consider converting to cups, since a measuring cup is far less abstract than grams measured on a scale.* Children can count ingredients as they are added to the mix, count how many times it is stirred, time the cooking process, use geometric shapes to form cookies and sandwiches, and calculate how many each child may eat.

Setting Up a Mathematics / Manipulatives Area

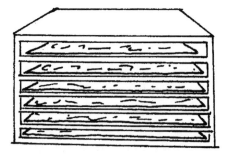

A spacious area in the classroom, separate from the more active play areas like the Dramatic Play Center, should be set up for use of manipulative materials. Well-organized, open shelves should be used to display the materials. The materials should be clean and intact (puzzles should have all their pieces, pegboards should be shelved with containers of pegs, and Lotto cards should have all their tiles). Puzzle racks should be used to keep puzzles complete and separate.

The area should have tables and chairs and provide enough space for several children to use their materials comfortably and simultaneously without interfering with each other.

Materials from everyday life have as much potential for revealing mathematical concepts to young children as learning tools that are specifically designed for teaching mathematics. However, several items that offer systematic, concrete experiences in counting, ordination, calculation, and comparison can have a profound impact on children's grasp of mathematical concepts. These items include:

- **Inch Cubes**, such as Unifix Cubes, for counting and measuring activities.

- **Floor Numbers** Nonskid squares with the numbers 1 - 10 printed on them. These are valuable for gross motor games in which motor activity reinforces the experience of counting. These can be made with carpet or paper or taped on the floor. They also can be used for games involving ordination and numeral recognition.

- **Measuring Equipment** Concrete experiences with measurement do not require standard measuring devices; teacher-made or child discovered units can be used. Nonetheless, standard equipment can be helpful. Liquid and dry metric measuring cups in graduated sizes, measuring spoons, rulers, tape measures, scales, and thermometers should be available for use by the children or for demonstration. Simple balance scales are more meaningful than metered scales (such as bathroom or kitchen scales), because they give children the opportunity to see the comparison of two items and offer the possibility of comparing diverse items against a standard weight.

- **Number Lines** are helpful as children begin to understand the concepts of counting and ordination and to move toward performing simple calculations. A number line on the floor that is large enough to walk along offers the physical reinforcement of stepping out a calculation.

- **Parquetry Blocks** offer experiences in geometric patterning and sequencing. Blocks can be matched for color and shape, and designs can be created with them.

- **Attribute Blocks** These plastic blocks can be very helpful in helping children discover mathematical concepts. The blocks are in three shapes, three thicknesses, three colors, and three sizes. One block might be a small, thick, red triangle; another might be a large, thin, blue circle; a third might be a large, thin, yellow square. Children can sort them by one, two, or three attributes. Their simplest use is in concrete experience with geometric shapes. At the next level of sophistication, they offer children the experience of classifying by one attribute: size, shape, color, or thickness. At the next level, a child can classify by two attributes simultaneously. Moving from one attribute (all the thin ones or all the red ones) to two attributes (which ones are both thin and red?) introduces the child to symbolic logic. Symbolic thinking does not occur until children are between five and seven years old.

- **Coins** "Play money" and real coins in small denominations offer experiences in classification and calculation.

- **Learning Clock** The best clocks for learning to tell time have a large face with second, minute, and hour hands connected by visible gears. Numbers for the hours and marks for the minute and seconds are clearly indicated. By manipulating the hands, children discover the relationship between seconds, minutes, and hours.

- **Puzzles** Puzzles help children focus on size and shape as well as on the relationship of parts to a whole. These are necessary concepts for both math and reading. Using puzzles, children become aware of clues (science). They classify ideas as they figure out where the green grass goes, where the blue sky is, and where the head, arms, and legs of the child in a puzzle picture fit. Classification is important in math, science, and reading.

  Working on puzzles also requires analyzing and testing ideas, another aspect of science. Some puzzles have pictures of vehicles, some of community workers, and some of animals. Analyzing the nature and environment of these scenes can contribute to concepts used in science and social studies. Puzzles with letters of the alphabet can contribute to reading readiness; puzzles with numerals can contribute to math concepts. This learning can be done at simple or more complex levels, as puzzles vary in complexity, depending upon the number and size of the pieces.

- **Pegboards and Pegs** Pegboards and pegs of different colors are also good for sorting and classifying. Math concepts are developed as children count pegs by cardinal numbers (one, two, three) or by ordinal numbers (first, second, third). By adding and subtracting pegs, they develop concepts such as "more than," "less than," and "the same as."

  Children may also develop patterns with pegs. Recognizing patterns is important in learning math and science, in reading readiness, and in developing creative artistic expression.

- **Lotto Games** These games come in varying types and degrees of difficulty. They may involve identification of colors, numerals, or pictures. All require observation, comparison, and matching skills, which are necessary in the development of science concepts and reading readiness. Lotto games that feature pictures of community workers contribute to the development of social studies concepts.

- **Lego or Duplo Blocks** These blocks offer endless possibilities for creating structures: buildings, towers, vehicles, and other objects. They also offer opportunities for children to experiment without needing to create anything objectively identifiable. Accessories for these small building blocks include wheels, people (family members and community workers), vehicles, and animals. Play with these materials contributes to the development of concepts related to math (patterning, cardinal and ordinal counting, understanding area, and dealing with comparative sizes).

  When turned into ramps, bridges, and tunnels, these blocks contribute to the development of concepts of balance, strength, and stability. They provide an introduction to understanding of architecture, patterns, symmetry, and design.

- **Dominos** Dominos come in many forms. With some, children have to match geometric shapes. With others, children work with pictures or colors. Still others require that children match numbers of dots or numerals. (Some dominos have a numeral on one side and the corresponding number of dots on the other.) As with Lotto games, dominos require children to observe, compare, identify, and match. All of these skills are important in the study of science and in reading readiness.

- **Colored Beads** When children put beads of different colors on a string, 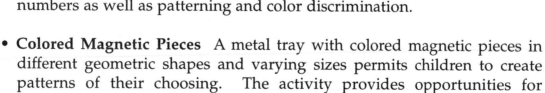 they learn cardinal and ordinal numbers as well as patterning and color discrimination.

- **Colored Magnetic Pieces** A metal tray with colored magnetic pieces in different geometric shapes and varying sizes permits children to create patterns of their choosing. The activity provides opportunities for developing number theories and geometric concepts, increasing a child's understanding of colors, creative expression, and dealing with the scientific concept of magnetism.

The Teaching Team's Role

The first role of the teaching team is to ensure that the classroom environment is full of materials that offer a variety of opportunities for developing mathematical thinking skills. In conjunction with this, the teacher must practice his skills at catching the "teachable moment." Rather than imposing math lessons on children, teachers should observe child-initiated play and take advantage of opportunities to introduce or discuss a math concept. Thus, the teacher acts as facilitator to the children.

This approach is particularly successful when the teacher helps children arrive at a mathematical solution to a problem that a child has presented. A child may have a problem, for example, with a building she was trying to construct with blocks. The teacher can act as an adviser, suggesting various sizes and arrangements of blocks to achieve what the child wants. Even a social problem can have a mathematical solution. If, for example, two children have a dispute over the use of a building set, the teacher can ask them to divide the pieces of the set between them so that each child has the same number of pieces. Too few tricycles for all the children who want to ride may lead to the use of a timer to solve a social problem.

The teacher helps the child expand concrete experience by modeling mathematical language. For example, in an activity involving comparison, he can introduce the phrases, "greater than," "less than," and "equal to." All of the opportunities for meaningful counting described above illustrate this math-language role modeling. To reinforce a particular mathematical experience, the teacher can frame mathematical questions. In setting the table, for example, she can ask, "How many napkins do we need?" or, "How many more spoons do we need?"

The more the teacher observes what the children have chosen to do, the more she can use their chosen activities to introduce or reinforce mathematical concepts.

Mathematical Activities and Projects

Children can gain an understanding of the basic concepts of one-to-one correspondence, counting, ordination, calculation, classification, measurement, comparison, geometry, and time, as they manipulate objects in their environment.

- **Counting** Counting is meaningful only when it applies to concrete objects and is most meaningful when it solves a problem that interests a child. However, simple teacher-made card games that involve counting cards out and matching designs and teacher-made board games that involve counting "moves" on a board, counting dots on dice, or using a number spinner, are enjoyable activities that reinforce the concepts of number and amount.

- **Ordination** Stairs present an excellent opportunity to help children learn to put things in order by number. Nonskid number squares can be placed in order going up the stairs ("1" on the first step, "2" on the second, and so forth). The teacher can then scramble the number squares and ask the children to reorder them, on the stairs. Each child can choose a number and place it on the appropriate stair. To avoid falls, this activity should involve only two or three children at a time and must be carefully supervised. Another activity for introducing ordination uses a teacher-made set of cardboard tubes in graduated lengths. Children can work in pairs to stand them in order from the shortest to the longest. Number the tubes to reinforce the concept of ordination.

- **Calculation** Simple addition and subtraction can be introduced in dozens of routine activities. Computation can often solve a concrete problem presented by the children ("How many more cookies do we need so that everyone has one?"). Any sorting activity can be made into a computational activity involving addition or subtraction: for example, "Take all the small buttons out of the cup of red ones. How many are left?" or, "Put the white buttons with the black buttons. How many do you have?"

- **Classification** Sorting is most meaningful as a problem-solving technique in a child-initiated activity. However, teacher-made classification activities can reinforce the concept. For example, a box of buttons can be sorted into groups by shape, color, size. Children can then be encouraged to describe the criteria for classification, naming how the buttons are alike and different. ("These buttons are red; those are blue.") Helping the child to reclassify the buttons by a different attribute introduces the child to logical relationships. ("These red buttons are square; those red buttons are round.")

- **Measurement** Cooking activities provide a natural context for the introduction of measurement. Other measurement activities include comparing children's heights with marks on the wall and comparing weights using a balance scale. Floor tiles can be used as a measuring unit for all kinds of things, from children's height to the length and width of furniture to the length of ribbon streamers for a dance activity.

• **Comparison** Graphing is a way to combine counting and measurement to make concrete mathematical comparisons. A week calendar could be transformed into a weather graph, with sunny days compared with cloudy days. Another graph could compare the number of boys to the number of girls in the class. On any given day, numbers of children wearing certain colors could be graphed. Other topics include favorite foods, pets, lost teeth, birthdays, and shoe sizes.

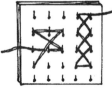

•**Time** Children can construct simple time-measuring devices such as a drip clock. A clear plastic bottle (such as a soda bottle) works well for this project. The teacher makes a small hole in the bottom, and suspends the bottle over a container to catch the drips. At regular intervals (preferably short, like one minute), she and the children note and mark how much water has dripped out. The bottle then can be used to time such regular classroom activities as transition time, or time how long each child may play with a coveted toy.

•**Geometry** An excellent activity for discovering the properties of geometric shapes is a teacher-made nail board. Small nails are pounded part-way into a square board to form a grid. Using rubber bands stretched from nail to nail, children can experiment with the construction of various shapes. Different colors of rubber bands allow overlap and comparison of shapes.

Summary

Early experiences with math concepts build the foundation for higher-level mathematical thinking. Using mathematical thinking to solve concrete, everyday problems will give children confidence in their mathematical skills. A strong foundation in math ensures that, as adults, they will be able to apply mathematical knowledge in practical situations as well as to use it to participate successfully in the technologically complex global community.

XIV. MUSIC

Children at Play: Music in the Classroom

People in all times, all places, and all cultures have made music. For example, the cultures of Eastern Europe have given the world some of the greatest musicians of all times: Tchaikovsky, Mussorgsky, and Stravinsky (Russia); Liszt and Bartók (Hungary); Smêtana and Dvorâk (the Czech Republic); Mahler (Moravia); and Chopin (Poland) to name only a few. Music is a universal means of communication.

Music has always been used to soothe, comfort, entertain, and enlighten children. Children are natural music makers. Two Eastern European musicians, Carl Orff and Zoltan Koldaly, gave considerable thought to the place of music in child development. Orff formulated some basic principles about music in childhood. He believed that speech, movement, play, and song are one. He urged that the natural speech and movement of children be used as springboards for musical experiences, and that children be active participants in music making. He even believed that the natural chants of childhood were the building block for all melody. Koldaly used Orff's theories to build a system for teaching older children musical symbols and, ultimately, musical notation and sight reading. The thinking of these two composers has influenced the way in which music is used in early childhood education worldwide.

Impact on Developmental Areas

Emotional Development

Music is a rich resource for fostering the development of children. Its most obvious role is in emotional development. Parents use lullabies to comfort their children, and children who have been sung to sleep will sing to their dolls. Comforting music need not even be a song. Mothers of all times and all places have hummed to their babies in a repeated falling two-note sing-song. Every culture has simple songs of celebration and love that children can learn and that can help them express these feelings. Marches can help children express pride. Songs of anger and sorrow may help children understand and cope with these more difficult feelings. Since music is such a strong vehicle of emotion for adults, listening to music with children and talking about the feelings it evokes can be a way of fostering communication about our emotional life. Children are natural dancers and do not need to be taught formal "steps." If given the chance to respond to joyous music, they will invent their own dances to express exuberance and joy.

Social Development

Music is a powerful tool for fostering social development. A group of children can share in singing or dancing and have a marvelous time together, without having to wait their turn or share scarce equipment. Children can also engage in call-and-response songs, practicing turn-taking by waiting for their chance to respond. (There are, for example, many versions of a song that asks each child to answer to his or her name by singing, "Here I am," or simple words to that effect.) Children who are reserved and reluctant to speak up in a group activity will often join in a song or dance. Many children's songs have accompanying gestures. These songs, where all children do the same thing at the same time, are a particularly effective way of involving children who otherwise might just watch.

Language Development

Music can also enhance language development. All spoken language is both rhythmic and melodic. Children naturally play with words in rhythmic and melodic ways. A teacher can use this natural play to help children pay attention to the sound of language. For example, she may help children learn the names of their classmates by clapping the rhythm of each child's name and using its repetition as the basis for a dance. Music can help children expand the complexity of their language. Melody aids memory; therefore, a child may remember phrases from a song that are slightly more complex than his natural speech and use them later in talking. Music can increase vocabulary. There are many songs of labeling and listing that can introduce children to new words. Children may want to make up their own songs, using known or invented melodies to tell their own stories or express their personal feelings.

Intellectual Development

Music can be used to enhance the development of concepts in children. Ideas of "same" and "different" can be introduced through changes in the volume or pitch of music. Every culture has counting songs for children. When coupled with gestures, especially those that involve the whole body, counting songs provide kinesthetic meaning to the exercise. Songs that recite the letters of the alphabet, however, probably do not help in concept development except to help a child remember a particular sequence.

Motor Development

Motor skills are enhanced through the use of music. Finger plays encourage the child to move each of the fingers independently in response to a certain song, and thereby increase eye-hand coordination. Simple homemade instruments increase fine-motor skills, both in the making and in the playing. Spontaneous dancing and movement to music encourage the development of coordination. Although dances of the child's own invention have the most to offer for their development, it may be appropriate to teach a few simple steps of folk dances that children can perform as a group.

Children can also be encouraged toward self-help skills through music. Songs about bathing are particularly effective, but there can be songs about dressing, eating, and cleaning up as well.

The potential of music for early childhood development cannot be complete without a discussion of the science of sound. Children can witness the vibration of a wire or rubber band as they hear the tone that it makes when plucked. They can stop the sound by stilling the vibration. Although young children will not grasp the abstract concepts involved, they can gain intuitive understanding from demonstrations of the differences in tone and pitch from different sources of sound. Some examples are air blown over bottles with various levels of liquid in them, vibration of strings of various length and textures, and the quality of sound from various drums and rattles.

Integrating Music into the Classroom Schedule

If it is not possible to have a music activity center, music can be integrated in many activities throughout the classroom and the day. A word of caution about background music. When music is used, it generally should be the primary focus for the children. Background music, which may be pleasing to adults, may be distracting to children.

Music can help establish the comfortable routine of the daily schedule. Songs can be learned or invented to help children through the day. There can be greeting songs when children arrive. Songs also are an excellent activity at group times. Songs can be used as a guide for transition from one activity to the next or as a "holding" activity while waiting for lunch or toileting. Songs are a wonderful way to soothe children during their rest time. As children leave school, a familiar song of parting is a fitting way to close the day.

When designing the art and science areas of the classroom, consider the possibilities for music activities. Many art and science materials have music-making potential. For example:

- **Rattles**   Empty plastic containers with lids; aluminum soda cans; boxes that contain rice, dried beans, or buttons; natural rattles, such as seeds and gourds

- **Plucked instruments**   Rubber bands, boxes, tubes, wire

- **Percussion instruments**   Blocks, sand paper, anything that clangs

- **Wind instruments**   Plastic bottles, tubes, pipes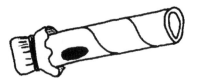

If commercially made instruments are used, it is probably wise to store them in a closed cabinet and make them available only at specific times. The sound of rhythm instruments is likely to distract children from other activities, so you may want to offer instruments only when music is the focal point for the entire group. Carefully supervise children when they are using adult instruments.

Every culture has folk instruments that are easy to make, inexpensive, and easily used by children. You may want to add local versions of kazoos, mouth harps, whistles, and rattles to the classroom rhythm instrument collection. In each case, be sure to check the instrument with child safety in mind. Is it free of sharp edges? Does it pose any danger of choking? Is it made from nontoxic materials?

To help children appreciate the different sounds and possibilities for each instrument, introduce them to only one type at a time. Let each child experiment with the newly introduced instrument. Rhythm instruments can be used spontaneously, with children making music as they wish. They can be used to reproduce a rhythmic pattern established by a child or the teacher. They also can be used to accompany the rhythm of a song or dance.

The Teaching Team's Role

Teachers should sing! A teacher of young children does not need to worry about perfect pitch or operatic tone; children will enjoy all lively and warm-hearted efforts. Singing is a wonderful activity for speeding work, expressing feeling, and telling stories. Teachers can model this for children by singing their way through the day, using songs of greeting, transition, work songs, story songs, lullabies, and good-bye songs.

If a teacher is able to play an instrument, this is another way she can provide musical leadership. In classrooms where record players and tape recorders are available, commercially prepared children's songs can be used; however, they should not substitute for teachers and children joining together in song.

Teachers can also follow the children's lead in musical experiences. Use tapes or records of folk and classical music to encourage children to invent dances. Young children also enjoy creating their own dances to popular music. Generally, children respond enthusiastically to music with a good beat and interesting melodies and harmonies.

Once the idea of creating musical instruments is introduced, children may discover the possibilities of making music with objects designed for other uses, such as the pots and pans in the cooking area. Although teachers may want to redirect this activity if it interferes with other activities going on at the time, they can also call attention to its musicality.

Music Activities and Projects

Making and Using Rattles

Making musical rattles is a worthwhile and fun activity for a large or small group of children. The materials required are simple: empty, clean aluminum soda cans (at least one per child); several handfuls each of dried beans, rice, sand, or pebbles; and masking tape.

The teaching objectives or rationale for this activity are many. The children can

- Make rattles for each child to use in musical activities

- Practice fine-motor skills by putting small objects into small holes (for example, beans into soda-can hole)

- Increase short-term memory by practicing repetition of a rhythmic sequence

- Practice matching sounds by finding which rattles sound alike

- Experience the music of other cultures

Making the Rattles

Set out one can for each child (or two, if you have enough). Put the filler materials (beans, rice, sand, or pebbles) in trays or bowls in the middle of the table so that each child has access to each. If you want the children to make pairs of matching rattles, you may want to limit each table to only one kind of filler. (For example, all the children at one table will make only bean rattles while those at another table will make pebble rattles.) If the children are very young or have difficulty sharing materials, you may want to have one container of filler for each child. In this case, divide the filler materials into individual portions ahead of time.

Show the children how to put one object (a bean or pebble) into the opening of the can, and then shake it to demonstrate the sound. Ask them to do the same.

They will have fun shaking the cans as they go along and listening to how the sound changes as the can gets fuller. When the can is full enough to make a satisfying rattle, help the children tape the top closed. You may want to cut the tape in advance so that children do not have to wait for you to cut it. Younger children may need your help with taping.

Using the Rattles

- Have each child take a turn establishing a rhythm, which the group then follows. To start, you might use the rhythm of each child's name.

- Establish various rhythms for the children to follow.

- Sing a song, using the rattles to keep time.

- Have a parade using the rattles to establish the beat of a march.

- If you have made pairs of rattles, mix them up and ask the children to rematch the pairs.

- Play music on a record or tape and use the rattles to keep time.

Science and Music Using Bottles of Water

Science and music activities can be combined. For example, one such activity gives the children an intuitive experience of the relationship between length and pitch in a vibrating column of air and provides practice in pouring.

Have these materials available:

- Heavy, glass bottles (preferably one for each child)
- Water
- Water containers
- Metal spoons or forks

Preparing the Bottles

Place a bottle and a fork or spoon at each child's place. A water table is an ideal spot for this activity. Set the bottles up in the empty water table, and you won't have to worry about spills. (You may also want to do this activity outdoors.) If you do this activity indoors, spread newspaper on the floor and have sponges or rags available for spills. Trays with low sides, like cookie sheets, may also be used to contain spills. Depending on the children's social skills, you may want to have a cup or pitcher of water for each child or have one pitcher for every three children, to encourage sharing and taking turns.

Using the Bottles

Begin by tapping on an empty bottle to demonstrate the sound. Next, blow across the top of the bottle. Ask the children to experiment by tapping and blowing across their bottles. Now, add a little water to your bottle and repeat the sound-making activities. Let the children add water to their bottles. Once they get the idea that the sound changes, they will want to experiment by adding water and pouring it out. Ask them to describe what happens. Reproduce the note by singing it and have them do the same. You may want to talk about "lower" and "higher" notes.

Younger children can tap their bottles in rhythmic patterns that you demonstrate, or they can create their own patterns, or even tap an accompaniment to a song.

With your help, older children may be able to arrange bottles in an order that roughly represents a scale. They may need your help in making the necessary discriminations, telling you which bottles are higher and which are lower, and whether water must be added or poured out to get the notes. You may be able to play a simple tune for them, either by tapping or by blowing, or both!

A Visit to a Pipe Organ

A pipe organ and a willing organist. Some towns and cities have old churches with wonderful pipe organs. Pipe organs are fascinating creations for people of all ages, but especially for young children. On such a visit, children have the experience of seeing, hearing, and playing a magnificent musical instrument.

If you can locate a church in your community with a pipe organ, contact the organist (probably through the priest or pastor), and ask if you can arrange for a class visit. You will need to explain that you are not asking for a concert, but for a tour of the organ. Explain that the children will want to see and touch the parts of the organ, and be certain that he is agreeable to that. Explain that they probably will not be interested in hearing long pieces, but that they might enjoy a short tune, especially variations on a tune that they know. (Many organists can take a simple tune and improvise variations on the spot.) Ask how many children you can bring at one time. You may need to divide your group and go on more than one day. Find out how you get into the building, who will greet you, how you get to the organ loft, and where the children can sit or stand during the demonstrations.

The bottle activity described above would be a good preparation for the children, since the sound of an organ depends on variations in the length of columns of air. Children will not understand the abstract physics of the relationship between the bottle activity and the organ, but they will get the idea of a connection between air, pipes (bottles), and sound.

It is important to prepare for the trip. At least a week in advance, get written permission from each child's parent(s), and ask for family volunteers to accompany you on the trip. Parents help by shepherding small groups of children, and by participating in the activities when you arrive at the organ. A few days in advance, explain the trip to the children. Tell them where you are going, how you will get there, how long it will take, and what they will see and hear. If there are pictures of the church and the organ, show these to the children. If you have recordings of organ music, play them for the children. Allow them to draw, paint, or dance while the music is playing to express the feelings the music arouses in them.

The Trip

When you arrive, ask the organist to show the children the keyboard and foot pedals. Ask him to demonstrate each one, and, if possible, let the children try themselves. Also ask him also to demonstrate the different "voices" of the various stops on the organ. He may be able to play a simple tune that the children know in several different voices. He may let the children pull the stops. A very old organ may have mechanical bellows. Ask the organist to demonstrate how this works. Ask him to remove some of the smaller pipes (they can be easily lifted out) and to blow on them to demonstrate their different sounds. (Children should not blow on the pipes, since they may contain lead.) Relate this to the children's experiences with the bottles.

Ask the organist if you can visit the organ case. This is where the big pipes are housed. (If the organ is large, your whole class may be able to fit inside the case!) Many in old organ cases in Eastern Europe are works of art.

Before you leave, the organist may play a short piece, perhaps, (as was suggested above) one that contains a tune the children know. If you have recording equipment, record this "performance," along with a greeting from the organist.

After the Trip

When you return to the classroom, have the children share their impressions and feelings. Write these down on large chart paper as "experience stories," to be read again and again to remind the class of the trip. Have the children make drawings of the organ. If you were able to make a recording or have recordings of organ music, play them, again allowing the children to draw, paint, or dance to the music.

Summary

Music is one of the richest resources for teaching young children. It is a natural part of their play and provides many positive and nurturing interactions with adults. Music does not require expensive and technologically advanced equipment; the most valuable instrument for early childhood education is the human voice. There are intimate connections between music and the emotions and music and language. Music should be an integral part of every day in the early childhood classroom.

OUTDOORS

XV. THE OUTDOORS

Children at Play: The Outdoors

The outdoor environment includes not just play areas but also parks, neighborhoods, lakes, and small gardens. It is an exciting place where children can learn and grow.

Children show a natural enthusiasm and curiosity when they play outside. Things are always changing in space that is not enclosed by four walls. Here, children can learn in all the developmental areas, and teachers can enhance their growth through observation, interaction, and planned activities.

Children enjoy the changes in weather and seasons. Young people love to be outside in the rain or during a snowstorm (it is often the adults who are skeptical about going out in harsh weather).

Any outdoor area can be exciting for children. Rolling in grass, smelling the air after a spring rain, watching baby birds leave their nest, and watching the snow melt are fascinating outdoor experiences. Even indoor activities can be brought outside and experienced in a different way. Hearing a story about a windy day while sitting under a tree when the wind is blowing is different from hearing that same story indoors. The outdoor environment adds textures, colors, smells, and sounds to indoor activities. Being outdoors links children to nature and awakens their senses.

The outdoor environment also adds balance to the day. It is healthy for both children and their teachers to breathe fresh air, feel the weather, enjoy the freedom of open space, and use muscles in a new ways. Movement and a change of atmosphere reduce stress.

Using both the outdoors and indoors as a classroom bridges the two environments. An empty bird's nest brought indoors offers children the chance to touch it, study how it is built, and learn more about birds through books. Taking paint, crayons, trucks, or water outside enables children to have different experiences. The difference between drawing with crayons on paper at a table and doing the same activity while sitting on the sidewalk is exciting to children; it also offers teachers a chance to teach new concepts and expand children's language. Teachers are often surprised at the skills children use outdoors, skills that children have not used in the classroom.

Impact on Developmental Areas

All areas of a child's development are enhanced through outdoor play and exploration. This includes physical development, social skills and cultural knowledge, and emotional and intellectual development.

Physical Development

The outdoors can be the site of many exciting activities and learning opportunities for children; however, for a majority of children, its most important role is to stimulate physical growth and development. Physical education activities also give children the opportunity to be social, learn rules, learn interdependence, develop self-confidence, grow intellectually, and solve problems. A planned program for physical exercise is an important part of the early childhood program.

The outside environment invites large muscle development. The freedom of space offers children a natural opportunity to run, skip, jump, and move their entire bodies in uninhibited ways. Basic playground equipment encourages climbing, balance, coordination, and the development of upper- and lower-body strength.

Small motor skills are also developed as children dig in sand and dirt, pour water, pick up and collect stones, leaves, or other small objects, and play outdoor games like marbles.

Outdoors, children become aware of how their bodies operate in different spaces by feeling what it's like to be on top of a climber, to swing high on the swings, to crawl through a tunnel, or to roll in autumn leaves.

Physical strength, coordination, balance, and endurance are slowly developed with daily practice. The outdoor environment offers a special place for children to build these skills.

The physical skills that older children need for sports and physical activities can be learned and practiced in the early years. It is important that these skills be learned in an enjoyable, noncompetitive setting so the children learn to enjoy sports and feel comfortable participating. Avoid games where one person or group wins and one loses. Children who continually lose at games or competitions often do not feel good about their abilities and will soon stop participating. The goal of physical education for young children is to develop skills and a life-long interest in being physically active.

Physical development occurs at a different pace in each individual. Some four-year-olds can skip easily, while others may not skip until they are five or six. Some may be able to jump and catch a ball easily while others may only be able to catch a very large ball or to roll a ball back and forth. Teachers must observe children's developmental levels and plan activities appropriately.

The Development of Social Skills and Cultural Knowledge

The outdoor environment naturally encourages interactions among children as well as between adults and children. "Outside voices" are allowed, and singing and shouting provide different ways of interacting. Some children who are quiet when they are indoors may be more gregarious when they are outdoors. Because the atmosphere changes between the outside and inside, teachers are able to observe children in different social situations and to learn more about them.

Children build their social skills as they negotiate with others for tricycles or for a turn on the swing and as they play outdoor games. Negotiation skills are learned when trading the tricycle for the wagon. Children learn to compromise when they have to take turns, "It's my turn to fly the kite; you've been playing with it a long time." Cooperation is learned as children push each other on the swings, fill a pail with sand, pull a wagon, and play on the climbing equipment. Through these activities, children make friends and enjoy each other in a relaxed atmosphere.

Children learn about their community by taking walks, visiting a fire house, asking about a dump truck, seeing a person in a wheelchair, or talking to the mail carrier.

Emotional Development

Mastering the many challenges offered in the outdoor environment enables children to develop positive self-esteem. Children feel good about themselves when they reach the top of a slide, see a plant grow from the seed they planted, or build a wooden structure with some friends.

Children gain confidence as they realize what their bodies can do and how to control their movements. They come to feel good about themselves as their confidence in their new physical skills grows.

Trust in self and others is fostered through real-life experiences. A child who needs help getting down from the swing has to learn to ask for it and then to trust it when it is offered.

279

The dramatic play that takes place outdoors helps children reenact life experiences much as it does inside. However, because outdoor space is less restrictive, dramatic play can be on a broader, more expansive scale: for example, they can pretend to travel using roads, tricycles, signs, boats, planes, trucks, spaceships—and their imaginations!

For many children, talking about feelings happens naturally in the outdoor environment. For some children, sitting on a swing with a teacher makes it easier to talk about why he feels bad (or good). Joy, anger, and competition are sometimes more easily expressed outdoors.

The outside environment fosters an appreciation of beauty. Children learn through all of their senses: they enjoy the smell of flowers, the feel of dirt, the sound of crickets, and the comfort of sun on their faces. This appreciation leads to environmental awareness.

Intellectual Development

Children learn through direct interaction with objects and ideas. The outdoor environment offers teachers the opportunity to reinforce concepts such as colors, numbers, shapes, and sizes. There are many natural colors outdoors for children to observe (leaves, flowers, sky, buildings). There are objects to count and categorize (the number of flowers that have bloomed since yesterday, the number of pieces of litter that need to be picked up in the playground, and how many times the swings go back and forth).

Some concepts are taught more naturally outdoors than indoors. The wonders of science can be observed directly. The changing of the seasons can be document-ed every day. Clouds moving in to produce a rainstorm can be observed, as can squirrels burying nuts. Planting, watering, and weeding a garden throughout the summer teach the concepts of cause and effect, principles of growth, names of new tools, plants, colors, and shapes.

Children learn to observe and analyze outdoor situations. The interactions of nature are questioned and basic intellectual skills are challenged. When children ask, "Why is the snowman smaller today?" they learn about temperature changes and evaporation.

Language development is expanded in the outdoor environment. There are so many things to look at, touch, smell, and be curious about that children naturally want to talk and hear about them.

The outdoor environment enables children to expand their imaginations and creativity. They engage in dramatic play, as a way of helping them understand the world. While swinging, a child may pretend she is flying. While riding a tricycle, another child may act out driving a truck. These opportunities to stretch, move, touch, feel, smell, and experience the outdoor environment help children develop.

By thinking of the outdoor environment as another classroom, teachers can provide opportunities for children to grow in all the developmental areas.

Setting Up the Outdoor Environment

Ensuring Children's Safety

Safety should be the primary concern in looking at the play area that already exists or in designing a new one. Below are some things to consider when analyzing play spaces for safety:

- Is the area laid out so that a teacher or volunteer can see the children at all times?

- Is there an area where children can be by themselves and engage in quiet activities?

- Is there soft ground cover under swings, climbing toys, and slides?

- Are the boundaries of the play area well-defined?

- Is there enough equipment so that children don't have to wait for a place to play?

- Are all drainage areas, electrical wires, and other hazardous equipment covered, or otherwise inaccessible to children?

- Is a water fountain and a bathroom available?

- Is a first-aid kit available to handle minor scratches and cuts?

Need for Supervision

The best way to guarantee children's safety while they play outdoors is to supervise them carefully.

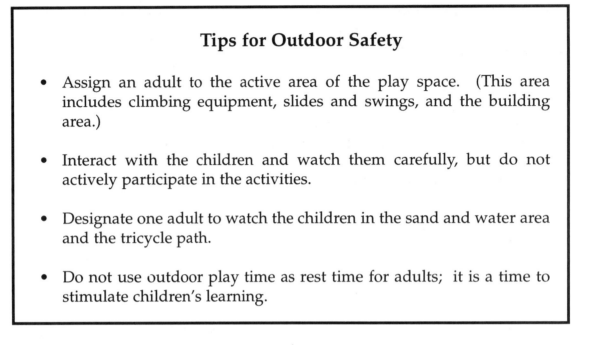

Tips for Outdoor Safety

- Assign an adult to the active area of the play space. (This area includes climbing equipment, slides and swings, and the building area.)

- Interact with the children and watch them carefully, but do not actively participate in the activities.

- Designate one adult to watch the children in the sand and water area and the tricycle path.

- Do not use outdoor play time as rest time for adults; it is a time to stimulate children's learning.

Teach children about safety both in the classroom and while they are outdoors. Encourage them to think about safety and to take personal responsibility for it.

Playing Areas

The outdoor environment, like the indoor environment, requires careful planning. An ideal outdoor play area has several different types of play spaces that are inviting to children and that stimulate them to learn in a variety of ways.

Be sure that the traffic patterns among the outdoor areas are easy to follow and safe, so that children are not running into each other. If areas are not clear, put up signs, rope the areas off with string, or have adults give instructions. Having clearly designated areas will help avoid accidents, confusion, and hurt feelings.

Climbing Area

Most playgrounds have some type of climbing equipment. Children of all ages love this area. Younger children may climb only a little way off the ground, while older children may climb to the top and swing "like a monkey."

It is important to allow children to learn at their own pace and not force them to go beyond their ability. Most accidents occur in this area, so it must be well-supervised and have a soft ground cover.

The climbing area usually includes the following:

Hanging bars   Slides
Jungle gyms   Swings
Logs   Teeter-totters/seesaws
Obstacle courses   Tire structures
Over/under platforms and   Trees
 bridges   Tunnels
Ramps   Wooden climbing structures

Digging, Water Play, and Mud Area

This part of the playground should be large enough so several children can comfortably play alone or together. Ideally, this area should be close to a water supply. If you have no outside faucets or water fountains, haul water in plastic jugs. Putting the jugs in a wagon and letting the children help to pull them is an entertaining and educational way to transport water.

Cleanliness is an important consideration for the sandbox. If possible, have a locking top over the box. This will stop cats and other animals from using it as a litter box. If the sandbox does not have a cover, rake it each day before the children use it and discard any garbage.

Basic sand, water, and mud toys include the following:

- Plastic and metal buckets, bowls, and pails with handles
- Shovels, spoons, and scoops of all sizes
- Old toy trucks, cars, fire engines, trains

- Funnels, sifters
- Pans and molds
- A wheelbarrow
- Small cardboard boxes
- Old wooden or plastic blocks
- Natural objects like shells, sticks, stones, or leaves

Transportation Area

This is the only area in the outdoor environment that should have a hard surface. It is easier and safer for children to balance, pedal, negotiate turns, start, and stop on a hard surface.

As they ride and pull, children build large-motor strength and practice balance. Be sure to include riding toys for children of all ages. Wagons, tricycles, and pull toys are appropriate for younger children, while bicycles, scooters, and skates are suitable for older children.

The transportation area is also a place that is used for dramatic play. Encourage this by adding hats, signs, or dress-up clothes. If the children are interested in hospitals, put red crosses on a tricycle or wagon and bring out hospital props. Encourage them to act out their feelings and think about adult roles.

Children may also use the transportation area for other activities: bouncing and throwing balls, jumping ropes, playing hopscotch, or music and art. These activities should not take place while wheel toys are being used.

The major hazard in this area is falling. (Have a first-aid kit on hand.) Some accidents can be avoided if the area is well marked. Use chalk, moveable signs, "one way" arrows, and adult monitors to help children avoid running into each other.

Quiet Area

Every outdoor area needs a quiet space, preferably in the shade, so children can cool off. Use blankets or ground covers for children to sit and lie on.

This area can be used for many different quiet activities. Some, like relaxation or imagery, require no props or materials. Others may require teacher preparation and planning: coloring, reading books, collecting objects, and listening to music. Quiet group games can also be played in this area.

Recommended basic materials for the quiet area include the following:

A blanket (or towels) to sit on   Books
Chalk   Crayons
Measuring sticks and games   Paints and easels
Paper   Picnic and snack foods
Science equipment (e.g., magnifying
   glasses)

Woodworking Area

A woodworking activity center can be set up indoors or outdoors. In either case, it should be in an out-of-the-way place so the children and materials will not be disturbed.

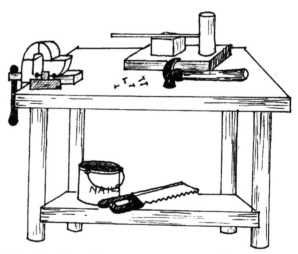

Children often spend all of their outdoor time in this area. This area needs careful supervision, since children will use tools. Careful instruction, rules for using tools, and supervision by adults will help avoid accidents.

This area challenges children's creativity. It gives them an opportunity to use large and small muscles and to develop language skills.

Materials that are recommended for the woodworking area include the following:

Blocks   Boards
Cross-cut saws   Hammers and large-headed nails
Packing and other cardboard boxes   Packing boxes
Saber saws   Scrap pieces of soft wood
Short ladders   Steering wheels
Wire spools   Wood sawhorses

Garden Area

Planting seeds and watching things grow is a wonderful learning experience. Look around the available outdoor space for a small, sunny area where the children can plant a garden or grow flowers.

Recommended garden materials include the following:

- Several sets of child-sized garden tools
- A wheelbarrow
- Seeds or plants
- Bags of dirt and fertilizer
- Access to water
- Watering cans and hoses
- String and wood to mark off the rows

Storage

If outdoor storage is not available, teachers may have to transport some materials daily from the inside to the outside area. The ideal situation is to have a storage shed. Assembling a shed can be a wonderful activity for the children to be involved in. Volunteers, parents, and grandparents can build sheds. If the shed is built of wood, the children can "paint" it with large paint brushes and buckets of water.

Summary

All programs may not have enough room or enough resources for every one of the play areas described. In that case, alternate some of the outdoor activities from day to day. For example, you can use the riding area for woodworking and the quiet area for group games.

The Teaching Team's Role

Playing outdoors should be part of each day's schedule. Teachers should plan for outdoor experiences just as they do for indoor experiences. Schedule outdoor time for the same time each day so that it becomes a routine.

This can be accomplished by carefully planning the transition times as well as the outdoor activities. Plan approximately forty five minutes for the whole process. This allows enough time for children to get ready, walk to the outdoor play space, get involved in several activities, and return to the classroom. As the children become familiar with the routine of getting ready to go out, the transition will go more smoothly.

Be flexible so that you can take advantage of outdoor opportunities. It is wonderful and magical to take a walk during the first snowfall. On a hot summer day, it's fun to go out and play in the sprinkler for the afternoon or surprise the children with a picnic under the trees.

When scheduling outdoor activities, several factors should be considered. If classrooms are divided by age, three-year-olds should go outside later in the morning if possible; it is warmer outside, and they will be more comfortable. Consideration also has to be given to the number of other classrooms using the outdoor space. Schedules may have to be staggered; another option is to join two classes.

It is important for teachers to discuss scheduling with other teachers ahead of time to ensure children's safety as well as optimum use of the outdoor space. The teaching team can also plan with other teachers how to transport materials.

Special Considerations for Outdoor Activity

Weather

Unlike the indoor environment, the outdoors is constantly changing and weather influences outdoor activities. The basic rules regarding the weather are to be flexible and to use common sense.

Children need to experience all types of weather. Some programs cancel outside time completely when the weather is not "perfect." However, a walk in a warm spring rain shower is the time to listen to raindrops on an umbrella, smell the fresh air, and learn about flowers. Outside time can be extended on a warm, sunny day or shortened on a blustery day. Be reasonable, but daring. All weather can be enjoyed.

287

Clothes

If children and adults are going to enjoy the outdoors in all seasons, they must be appropriately dressed. When you explain the program to families, tell them that the children will go outdoors each day unless the weather conditions do not permit. Newsletters or parent conferences can be used to emphasize the importance of outside play. It is important for parents to know about outdoor play ahead of time, so they are not surprised when a child comes home talking about walking in the rain.

Each child should have a set of clothes for each season. Occasions on which children bring in the new season's clothes and take home the old season's clothes can be good teaching tools. As the season begins to change, talk about the next season's weather, and have children make a list of what they will need and why they can take some clothes home. Send a list home with the children requesting the next season's set of clothes. Children may need jackets, sweaters, hats, mittens, boots, swimming suits, towels, raincoats, rubbers, and umbrellas. Each program should have extras, in case someone doesn't have something.

Teacher should have extra clothes for outside play, too. Teachers often get cold before the children do because they are less active. Finally, when inviting parents or other adults to participate in an outdoor activity, be sure to inform them of what type of clothes to wear.

Other Considerations

Some children may be afraid to go outside; others may be incapable of becoming fully involved in outdoor activities because of illness or a disability.

Children who are fearful of the outdoors should be encouraged to join the others outside while receiving the special support of an adult. Never force them to go out. Allow them to stay inside and play if they want to. Eventually, most children who have fears of the outdoors will feel comfortable enough to join the others.

Often, children with health conditions can go outside, but may not be able to do all the outdoor activities. Teachers have to make sure they have planned a variety of activities. It is also important to talk to the child's parents to find out exactly what they allow the child to do. Careful planning ensures that children with a range of abilities can enjoy the outdoors. Children who have health conditions that absolutely prohibit them from going outside should be given an opportunity to engage in indoor activities of interest to them. It is best if some other children also stay in so the child does not feel so different.

Expanding Children's Outdoor Learning

Teachers can do several things to expand children's outdoor learning:

- Observe what interests the children

- Watch for and use the teachable moment

- Ask open-ended questions

- Use a varied vocabulary to describe new things

- Be curious about things yourself

The outdoor environment offers many opportunities for "teachable moments." "Why," "how," and "where" questions encourage children to think about what they see, to answer your questions, and to ask questions themselves. Children often lack the vocabulary to describe what they see. The teacher can provide the words to use. For example, as they plant the garden the children may wonder about the different sizes of seeds and how large they will grow. Their questions offer the teacher a whole range of teaching responses from learning the names of the flowers and vegetables, to measuring the seeds, to designing a chart so they can follow the growth of the plants and compare them with the original size of the seeds.

Teachers do not always know the answers to children's questions. Finding the answers to those questions is part of the challenge of teaching. When a teacher says that she does not know the answer but will find it, children learn two things. They learn that no one, including teachers, knows everything and, more important, they learn how to find answers to questions. A trip to the library or looking through science books can be an enjoyable learning experience for everyone.

Intervening in Children's Outdoor Play

The outdoor area is a busy place. Children are often intensely engaged in building a space shuttle in the woodworking area, creating a gas station in the riding area, and weeding the garden. It is easy for the teacher to intervene and say such things as, "Ivan, be careful with the hammer" or "Eva, don't you think you've climbed high enough?"

It is instinctive to be protective of children as they try new skills and take risks. This is particularly true outdoors, where there is so much activity and children are moving from one area to the next. Teachers should trust children and let them explore. Children know when they need help and will usually ask for it.

The basic rule of intervening in children's outdoor play is, therefore, *not* to intervene, unless it is necessary for safety reasons. Children have to concentrate, think, and problem solve, especially when they are playing on outdoor equipment, and any interruption disturbs their concentration.

When you do intervene for a reason of safety, be sure to give clear specific directions. Yelling, "Klara, watch out!" will not help Klara understand she is in danger of being hit. Saying, "Klara, move back, Tibor is coming on his bike!" will help her understand and move out of the way of the bike.

Many adults are overprotective because of fears that carry over from their own childhoods. If you believe that this is a problem for you, make a note of each time you intervene in the children's play for "their own safety." Then look at your record and determine whether it was appropriate or not. If watching children climb on the jungle gym makes you uncomfortable, maybe you should supervise a less active area.

Helping Children Share and Take Turns

Children often argue about whose turn it is to ride the bike, use the hammer, or go down the slide. Even when there are enough toys for everyone, someone may be upset. It is best to let children solve these problems themselves. If they cannot, a good solution is to use a kitchen timer. Set the time for a specified period (usually not more than five minutes.) When the timer goes off, the next child can use the toy. This method offers a concrete explanation of time. Children can understand it, watch it, and hear it.

Having Fun with Children Outdoors

The outdoors and fun go together. Outdoors is less formal than indoors. It's fun to be outside with children and listen to their explanations of the world. It's enjoyable to teach them new things and answer their questions about nature. Children love to play games with teachers.

Because of the informality, children feel comfortable talking about themselves or asking questions while they sit under a tree or set the picnic table. Children are curious about their teachers and welcome the opportunity to ask them questions about where they live and what their kitty's name is. Children and teachers can giggle together or make up jokes or songs as they walk to the park. This informal time makes children feel special and important.

Activities and Projects

The activities that children engage in and learn from in the outdoors are limitless. Many can be expanded and changed as the seasons and children's interests evolve.

Dramatic Play

The climbing area encourages language development, social interactions, and dramatic play. Some children pretend that they are mountain climbers or explorers. Others will pretend to be monkeys. They will make up and act out stories, and will describe what they are doing.

Imaginations are alive outside. There are places to be active and places to sit and watch others. Few materials are usually needed to encourage dramatic play: a blanket, a hat, or a board can transform climbing equipment into a jungle or a space craft.

Digging and Water and Mud Play

The sandbox area is a wonderful space for children explore. Cities, castles, rivers, towers, and even gourmet meals, can be made (and destroyed) in one play period. Small children can sit and watch sand sift through their fingers. Walking on sand, with or without shoes, is a challenge in balance and footing. Young children love to shovel sand into buckets. (Be sure the buckets have handles so they can be carried easily.)

Adding toy cars, dump trucks, trains, boats, and other vehicles to the sandbox encourages children to design highways, buildings, fishing villages, and construction areas. They can use bowls, sticks, and plates for igloos, fishing poles, or flying saucers. Any child-safe object that is big enough to find in the sand can be brought to the area.

If the sand is very dry, add some water. The water makes the sand stick together and lets the children build more elaborate roads and structures. If it has rained recently, you may not have to add water. During or after a rain, children can observe the rain patterns in the sand, see how far down the rain was absorbed, make rivers, and watch the water flow.

In the winter, snow adds to the fun. Tunnels, bridges, and igloos can be made with snow and sand. Sand and snow structures can be watered down and frozen. In autumn, the sand area will be cluttered with leaves and other objects that the wind sweeps in each day. They can be collected and used for building, left in place for the next day, or taken inside to the science table. All these objects are starting points for teachers to encourage children to watch and observe their environment and nature.

A word about mud. Its texture is very different from that of sand, and children should have the opportunity to feel it and play in it. Mud is plentiful after a warm spring rain. If you have a garden space that hasn't been planted, let children walk in it. They love to feel and watch the mud squish between their toes and cover their feet. Mud pies and cakes are fun, too. Making them is messy, and you may want to save this activity for a summer day when the children are wearing their bathing suits.

Don't avoid mud because it's messy! It is fun and uses several senses.

Art

Creative art projects can be done outdoors. For example, foot and toe painting are great fun. You can either use long paper for the children to walk, run, skip, or draw on with their toes, or let them use the sidewalk or asphalt. Mix the paint with liquid soap and it will wash off easily. Finger and brush painting are fun to do outside. The texture of the pavement, grass, or sand adds a new dimension to the activity. Use brushes and paper of many sizes. The size of the outdoor space easily enables children to work together on large projects. On a warm day it is fun to use large house-painting brushes and water to "paint" the building or trees. Bring old paint cans and painter's hats. In the winter, use brushes and water with food coloring to paint pictures on the snow, or decorate the children's snow and ice sculptures.

Children can paint their creations in the building area with real paint and brushes. The children should wear "paint clothes" or coveralls and use latex, not oil-based, paint. (Latex paint cleans up with soap and water, oil-based paint does not.)

Another outdoor art activity is water play. It can be done in the quiet area or the riding area, when it is not being used. A hose and sprinkler will add laughter and coolness to a hot summer day. Water and bubbles are a winning combination with children. Drinking straws and pans of soapy water provide lots of fun. Other things to take outside for art experiences include the following:

- Glue and paper for natural collages
- Clay
- Large and small colored and white chalk
- Easels and paint
- Crayons and paper
- Materials to make kites

- Sponges to use with paint and water
- String and wire to make wind chimes
- Water to turn snow sculptures into ice sculptures

Science

Everything in the outdoors is science. Take time to look at water running in the gutter after the rain. Throw a stone and a leaf in the water and watch what happens. Show children the new growth on tree branches or the effect of sun and water on the siding of a house.

When planning the outdoor environment, include things that encourage scientific exploration: for example, measuring tapes, yardsticks, magnifying glasses, collection cups, binoculars, string, and science books.

Physical Activities

Physical activities that help young children develop fundamental motor skills include the following:

- **Moving** Encourage children to move their bodies in many ways. They can move like animals, move fast, move on one foot, stretch, move with a partner, move to music or rhymes, move slowly, move like a truck—let their imagination go!

- **Running** Children can simply run like children, run like animals, run to a target, or run in pairs.

- **Jumping** Jumping is a wonderful outdoor activity — teachers should follow the children's lead. Children can jump over boards on the ground, jump from one circle to another, follow footsteps, turn as they jump to the rhythm of music, jump like animals, jump off low objects (sturdy boxes), jump on two feet, jump on one foot, or jump with a partner.

- **Throwing a Ball** Young children should practice throwing and catching large (5 inch or 13 centimeter diameter), soft balls. Older children can use smaller balls. Kicking a ball is fun and children can practice kicking at a target. Children can toss balls as high as they can, catch them with two hands or one hand, or play catch with a partner. Bouncing a ball of any size improves eye-hand coordination; tossing bean bags at small targets does the same. Rolling balls within a circle can be an enjoyable activity.

- **Obstacle Courses**   Children enjoy the varied challenges offered in obstacle courses. Adults and/or children can design obstacle courses together. These can be constructed either indoors or outdoors, as space and equipment permit. Teachers must be present to assist children and to monitor safety. Obstacle courses can be simple or complex, depending on the interests and developmental levels of the children. Obstacles that provide opportunities to climb through, climb over, hop over, or roll through are fun.

- **Games** Young children like games, and the best games are those in which all the children are actively involved. Circle games where only one child is "it" can be frustrating for young children, because they have to wait for a turn.   Games that include the whole group are preferable. Experienced teachers modify traditional games to make them more participatory. For example, a game of tag may have several people who are "it" so that more children are involved.

Quiet Activities

Have a quiet place for children to cool off, or be by themselves. Children and adults can sit and talk. Teachers can lead activities like yoga, reading, and role-playing. Children can count branches, watch ants, or feel the wind. Singing and listening to music are pleasant, quiet activities. Teachers and children can make up songs or sing the old favorites together. Children will choose to come in and out of the quiet area. The quiet area is a good place to gather the children for a quiet activity to calm them down before returning to the classroom.

Eating Outdoors

Both children and adults enjoy a picnic in the park or a surprise snack outside. Make sure foods are easy to prepare and carry. Children will enjoy helping to prepare the picnic foods. If you are growing a garden, have children pull the carrots, wash them, and put them in a salad. It is a thrill for children to prepare and serve what they have grown. Invite families and other site staff to join in the fun.

Woodworking

Children think, design, experiment, and work with others to construct art forms, buildings, obstacle courses, and moon rockets in the building area. Some children may spend all of the outdoor time in this area and return to it day after day. Some children may build

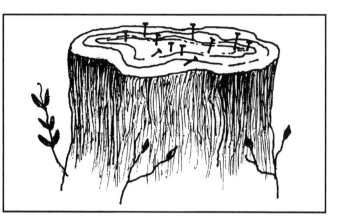

alone and make a structure to take home. Others may build a large structure as a group and decide that it is a hospital, dungeon, farm, or an imaginary palace where only children are allowed.

Children who have highly developed eye-hand coordination and upper-arm strength, and feel comfortable creating something out of nothing need no special assistance in this area. Other children need encouragement and instructions. All children who are using saws, hammers and nails, screwdrivers, and other tools need close supervision at all times. They must know and follow the safety rules so no one is injured.

Many of the materials from the other outdoor play areas are used in the building area. If children are building a town, they may borrow trucks and cars from the sand area. If they are designing something big enough to ride through, tricycles and a wagon may be needed. If they build a perch to sit on, they may borrow a book or stuffed animal from the quiet area. If they want to decorate a structure, they can take paints from the art area. The areas are not distinct, and materials can be shared among areas, as long as there are enough for everyone.

Gardening

Children dig, plant, nourish, water, pick, eat, and enjoy the wonders of their garden. They watch nature first hand and ask questions about the "whys" of the earth. They learn where food comes from and get the joy of giving their parents something they have grown.

A successful garden takes some planning. First, find a flat place in the outdoor space that has at least five hours of sun each day. An 8 foot by 8 foot (or 2.5 by 2.5 meter) area will allow space for several different plants, but, a smaller space will do. Make sure the soil is good, and add fertilizer or compost.

The following are guidelines for successful gardening. Involve the children in all the steps.

- Use good-quality seeds and plants. Plant sturdy plants that young gardeners are less likely to damage.

- Plant a variety of plants and flowers. Some, like radishes and tomatoes, come up quickly; squash can be harvested later.

- Plant for all the senses. Think about brightly colored geraniums, fragrant mint, and silky pansies.

- Plant for more than one season, so that spring bulbs will come up through the snow.

Many things can be taught in the garden. Use graphs and measuring tapes to chart the growth of plants, compare sizes and shapes, learn colors, and discover the facts of nature (for example, what happens when there is too much sun or not enough water). Children learn about taking responsibility and enjoy the rewards of a job well done. They learn to work and plan together. They learn how seasons affect the garden, as they watch it during each season and discover the differences. They can bring some plants in for the winter and compare them to the ones left outside. Gardens are wonderful learning tools. Use whatever space you have to create one.

Community Trips

Trips within the community can expand the children's world and provide exciting learning opportunities. As the trip is being planned, think about its goals. What do you want the children to learn and experience? How can goals be accomplished? What activities can be planned before and after the trip to enhance the experience?

Be sure the trip is carefully planned. Have a staff planning meeting to discuss all the details. Supervision and safety are the key elements to a pleasant trip. Community trips should not be too far away or in a place that is crowded and noisy. Visit the place ahead of time to discuss your expectations with staff. Be sure that there are things that children can touch, explore, and try. Ask families to join you. Think about the details of transportation, parent permission, food, bathrooms, and correct clothes.

Below are a few ideas for community trips:

Art store or gallery	Hardware store or repair shop
Beauty or barber shop	Hospital
Bookstore	Lumber yard
Florist shop, greenhouse, or	Museum
nursery	Nature center or bird sanctuary
Gravel pit or construction site	Theater

Walks

Walks are a wonderful way to explore the outside environment with children. They are easy to plan and do not take as much preparation time as a community trip. The class can take walks in response to beautiful weather (for example, the first snowfall); the teaching team can also incorporate them into the weekly schedule. Children can learn many things on walks when teachers are observant of the environment and talk to the children about what they see. The teaching team can focus the children's attention by asking them about certain animals, flowers, buildings, colors, shapes, textures, smells, shadows, and community workers. This increases the children's attention to details and helps them concentrate.

Children can also collect interesting items as they walk. Many of the objects can be brought back to the classroom and placed in the natural science area or other interest areas. As you plan walks, look for books, songs, poems, and finger plays that reinforce a theme. If you can't find any, create them and have the children help.

Involving Families in Outdoor Play

Although most parents appreciate the value of letting their children go outside to play, some do not realize the learning value of the outside environment.

It is part of the teaching team's responsibility to explain outdoor learning opportunities to parents. Most parents already spend some time with their children outside, and when they learn the value of the experience, they will have more fun themselves.

From the very beginning of the year, families should know that their children will spend time outside every day. As a reminder of the importance of outdoor activity, periodically send a note home explaining some things the child has learned outside.

The outdoors is an important learning environment. Looking at the outdoors from this perspective will help teachers to find creative ways to promote and guide children's learning.

SAND AND WATER

XVI. SAND AND WATER

Children at Play: The Sand and Water Activity Center

From the time they are toddlers, most children enjoy the sensations of playing with sand and water. In water, they love to splash, fill containers, pour from them, and float and sink objects. In sand, they enjoy digging, sifting, and burying. Combining sand and water allows children to mold, build, and tunnel.

In the classroom, young children should be able to explore the sensation of touching sand and water. At first, they can do this without many accessories. Slowly, they can make their play more complex by using a few tools, such as two measuring cups and an eggbeater, or two dolls, washcloths, and a bar of soap. Older children who are more familiar with the tactile sensations of sand and water may use more complicated accessories, such as corks, sponges, soap, boats, and stones to explore the ideas of floating and sinking.

Regardless of their age, all children may choose to spend some time just feeling sand flow through their fingers or enjoying the touch of water as they move their hands in warm bubbles.

Impact on Developmental Areas

Sand and water play promotes growth and understanding in all developmental domains. For example:

Mathematical Development

- Pouring similar amounts of sand or water into various containers and comparing which container holds more material (conservation of matter)

- Estimating how many bowls of snow it will take to fill a water table

- Comparing the weight of wet sand with that of dry sand

Scientific Development

- Using experimental inquiry and observation: "What will happen if I put bubbles in this water?"

- Making things change by adding water to dry sand, colors to water, or ice cubes to warm water

- Classifying objects that sink and float

Physical Development

- Using eye-hand coordination when copying designs, writing names, or drawing symbolic pictures in wet sand

- Mastering coordination of fingers and hands while pouring from one container to another or picking up slippery bars of soap

- Building small muscle control using eye droppers to fill jars with different colors and adding water from a pitcher

Development of Social and Cultural Skills

- Working cooperatively in a small group to plan joint activities and to play together

- Negotiating who uses the favorite pitcher

- Sharing materials that are added to the sand and water table

- Acting out social roles, such as being the captain of the boat or washing the dishes in the family center

- Building what they see in their own world or in books, such as bridges, tunnels, castles, and roads

Emotional Development

- Helping comfort a child who is sad

- Providing opportunities for success, such as filling the ice cube trays or washing the doll clothes and hanging them up to dry

- Solving problems through categorizing corks as "floaters" and rocks as "sinkers"

Setting Up the Sand and Water Activity Center

Each classroom should have a table with a large container built into it that can be filled with either sand or water. Although this table can be used outside, it will generally be used inside the classroom. It should be placed in an area of the room where messy, and probably loud play, is appropriate and where the floor can be easily cleaned. Since the floor tends to get slippery from sand and water, pick a space that is not in the middle of traffic patterns so that children will not slip as they walk by. Also, as children take on social roles like mommy or construction worker, they often speak loudly, so it is best to keep the table away from the literacy center.

The tub should be filled with enough sand or water to encourage a variety of play activities. For young children, the water should be low enough for splashing and pouring. For older children, the water table can be filled to a depth of three to four inches in order to encourage more complicated play. The sand should be deep enough for digging and tunneling, but not so deep that it spills over the sides.

The sand and water table should be at waist height — a height that allows children to work comfortably. Some young children may need to stand on sturdy stools or on large wooden blocks in order to reach the table. If these are needed, place them on a surface that is not slippery and supervise the children carefully.

Water should be changed every two or three days to discourage the growth of bacteria. The table should not be covered at night. Sand should be clean and, if possible, fine-grained. The floor should be mopped after play and kept dry so children do not slip. Towels and a mop should be nearby to wipe up accidental spills.

The sand and water table can hold other materials that encourage touch and exploration. These include sawdust, snow, leaves, acorns, large wood shavings, and ice cubes. Children can gather some of these materials outdoors, or the teachers can obtain them from lumber yards and construction sites.

Most of the play materials and accessories that you can add to the sand and water table can be found at home or be made by the teachers or by the children's family members. Suggested accessories include the following:

Boats	Empty cans	Small toys (trucks,
Brushes	Eye droppers	cars, animals)
Buckets	Food coloring	Soap
Cookie cutters	Funnels	Sponges
Corks	Measuring cups	Spoons
Cups	Molds	Sticks
Dishes & pots (from	Muffin and cake tins	Stones
the family center)	Rocks	Strainers, sieves, or
Doll clothes	Scales	colanders
Dolls	Shovels	Whisks
Egg beaters	Sifters	

All materials should be displayed and accessible, so the children can choose the props they want to work with. Plastic tubs can hold some of the materials; others can be displayed on pegboards or nearby shelves. Materials can also be stored in bins or trays under the sand and water table; the bins or trays can be placed on an adjacent table each morning.

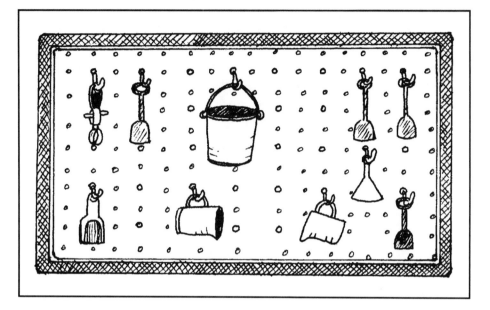

When children finish playing, they should place wet materials on a towel to dry. Sandy materials can be put on paper for the next children to play with. At the end of the day, the teacher should dry, clean, and put away materials.

The Teaching Team's Role

Teachers introduce materials and props into the sand and water area gradually. The teacher varies the materials, and observes which ones are being used by the children, and removes those that are no longer interesting.

The teaching team introduces materials to complement a theme or project that the class is exploring. For instance, if children are interested in bridges, the teacher helps the children collect rocks or branches to build bridges above the water. She brings in boats that float under the bridges. A sailboat that is too tall to fit under the bridge might start a conversation about drawbridges.

As teachers observe the children's play, they encourage the children to think about what they are doing and explore the attributes of the materials they are using. For instance, asking two children who are pouring to estimate how many tea cups filled with water will fill a pitcher may promote a discussion of the difference between size and volume. Teachers help expand dramatic play by asking a child to describe what she is planning to make for dinner with the delicious sand she is playing with. Teachers' questions will prompt children to solve problems and generate hypotheses. For instance, a teacher can ask, "What will happen if you add red coloring to the water?" The next questions could be, "What did happen?" and, "Why do you think that happened?" This sequence models the scientific process. Children will begin to do this on their own and in small groups.

Children should feel free to explore sand and water without worrying about making a mess. Teachers should have plastic smocks available for the children and should watch for spills. If a mop and towel are handy, a child can help clean up without feeling bad about spilling.

Activities and Projects

Outdoor Activities

- **Giant Bubbles** Save this activity for a warm day when you can take the water table outside. Use one cup dish washing detergent to one gallon (3.8 liters) of water. Let the children dip rounded coat hangers or string tied into circles into the bubble solution, and carefully lift their circles out of the tub. A large bubble will cling to the shape. It can be blown or shaken free.

- **Invisible Painting** Children love to use water and large brushes to paint bricks, wood, buildings, floors, and paper. When the water dries, it becomes invisible.

- **Mud Pies** Filling molds, buckets, muffin tins, and other containers with very wet sand and unmolding them onto newspaper or plastic is messy but fun to do outdoors. Children enjoy cooking pretend mud meals that they can serve at a dinner party on the playground.

- **Dams, Tunnels, and Bridges** Children can use a piece of hose or plastic tubing as a siphon to let water flow from the water table to the ground. As the water nears bridges or rock dams that they built, children can anticipate what will happen. They will see the water being stopped by the dam (temporarily) and will see it pass under the bridge.

- **Rain** Build a terrarium and have the children observe the water cycle. Discuss processes such as condensation and evaporation.

Indoor Activities

- ***Washing Art Materials*** Children will see that cleaning art materials can be fun. They can use soap and a scrubber in the water table to wash brushes, rolling pins, cookie cutters, and other equipment.

- ***Learning Geography*** Sand and water can be used to make land forms. Older children marvel as a sand mountain disappears when water is poured on it. They find it leaves only the peak, which becomes an island or a peninsula. Using water, sand, shells, coral, and toy fish, they can create underwater worlds that duplicate the floor of the sea.

- ***Sand Paintings*** Using glue, children can draw a design, letter, or name on a piece of cardboard. While the glue is still wet, the child can sprinkle it with sand. When this dries, the sand adheres to the glue, making a rough-textured drawing.

- ***Regatta*** Children can build boats with twigs and sails from string and paper or cloth. They can then take turns blowing their boats across the water table.

- ***Sink and Float*** Provide a box of materials, including paper clips, rocks, marbles, cork, sticks, and sponges. Let the children guess which objects will sink and which will float. Let them try all the objects. They will discover that heavy objects sink while lighter ones float.

- ***Dissolving Substances*** Compare salt, sugar, flour, tapioca, rocks, sticks, screws, soda, and gelatin. Have the children make a graph that depicts which materials dissolve and which do not.

Making Paper: A Project For The Water Table

Making paper can be a joyful activity for young children. A water table works nicely for this activity. You will also need a handmade mold made from window screening.

Directions for Making Paper

- Tear up old paper into small pieces. Old newspapers and scraps of construction or white paper work well. Do not use treated paper, such as waxed paper.

- Place the torn fragments of paper (very small pieces) in a pail or bucket of water. Cover the bucket and soak the pieces for about three days.

- Rinse the wet paper in clear water. The wet paper is called "pulp" or "slurry." (If the classroom has a blender, place the wet paper into the blender to make it even more mushy.)

- Put the paper pulp in the water table. Dip a screened mold or frame into the pulp and water mixture. When the children lift up the frame, they should have a surface of wet paper pulp on top of the frame.

- Allow the water to drain through the screening into the water table.

- When the water is drained, have children carry the frame to a table and blot the pulp down onto a towel. Let the pulp dry for a day. The children will then have their own paper piece to decorate or draw on.

- To make textured paper, the children can add threads, small seeds and broken leaves to the pulp in the water table.

Directions for Making the Screened Frame

1. Buy square wooden molding; 3/4 inch (two centimeter) will do very well.

2. Cut wood into lengths that will make a 6 or 7 inch (18 centimeter) frame. Nail or staple the frame together.

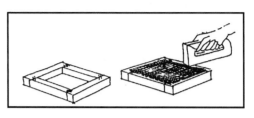

3. Staple screening over the top of the wooden frame For smoother and safer edges, cover each edge with tape.

4. As an alternative, staple tongue depressors together to make a simple frame. Follow the directions described in numbers 2 and 3.

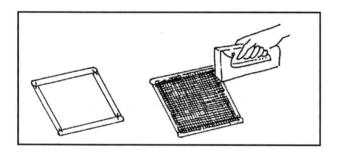

Ideas For Paper Art

Press thread, glitter, or strings into wet paper.

Press leaves and small sticks into wet paper.

Press cutouts made from paper into wet paper.

Place another piece of paper on top of the wet paper. This is called "couching." It works well if you want to put a raised object in between.

For color, add food coloring to the pulp in the blender (1/2 teaspoon coloring to 1 cup water) or add acrylic paint (1/4 teaspoon to 1 cup water).

Mix paint and water and put into squeeze bottles. Decorate wet paper as you would a cake.

SCIENCE

XVII. SCIENCE

Children at Play: The Science Activity Center

Children are natural scientists who actively seek information about their surroundings. They try to understand their world through observation and experimentation. The natural curiosity shown by children leads to learning.

Rachel Carson captured the essence of children's interaction with their world in her book, *A Sense of Wonder* (1956).

> *A child's world is fresh and new and beautiful, full of wonder and excitement. It is our misfortune that for most of us that clear–eyed vision, that true instinct for what is beautiful and awe–inspiring, is dimmed and even lost before we reach adulthood. If I had influence with the good fairy who is supposed to preside over the christening of all children, I should ask that her gift to each child in the world be a sense of wonder so indestructible that it would last throughout life, as an unfailing antidote against the boredom and disenchantments of later years, the sterile pre-occupation with things that are artificial, the alienation from the sources of our strength. (pp. 42–43).*

Science is both a product and a process. As a product, science is an organized body of knowledge about the physical and natural world. As a process, science entails exploring, observing, and experimenting. It is especially important that young children participate in the process of science, because the skills they develop will carry over to other curricular areas and be useful for the rest of their lives. These skills include observing, comparing, describing, predicting, communicating, classifying, and measuring.

Science should not be treated as an isolated discipline. Consider how the study of trees can be integrated with other discipline areas. The number of seeds produced in a particular seed pod can be calculated. Seeds from trees can be collected and compared. Leaves and bark can be used in art activities, such as crayon rubbings. In the autumn, leaves can be raked into a big pile; children can jump into the pile and, using their senses, describe how leaves look, sound, feel, and smell. The children can create a "tree diary" that includes their observations of the tree through the seasons. Pieces of wood can be used for various construction projects, such as building bird feeders. Tree cross-sections can be used to count and compare tree rings and used to estimate the age of the tree. Children can visit the local park or forest. Fruit from apple or cherry trees can be used in a classroom cooking activity.

Before planning any science activity, the teacher must evaluate it in order to ensure the children's safety. For example, before permitting children to jump into a pile of leaves, the teacher should determine that it contains no broken glass or other dangerous materials that would make the activity unsafe for children.

Setting Up a Science Program

Scientific inquiry fits readily into the rationale of the Step by Step Program and its emphasis on activity centers that are stocked with different materials for children to explore. Activities to foster the development of science skills should be integrated into all curriculum areas. An important way to individualize and extend learning is to set up science stations in the room.

Science Areas

The science activity center should include the following:

- **A place for displaying science-related items** This area can become a "mini-museum" where children can share collections or objects or place cages for classroom animals. A small table, pedestal, or pretty box may be used to display sea shells, crystals, a bird's feather, or a butterfly's wing. The teacher, children, and parents can supply the objects.

- **A place for storing frequently used science materials** Magnets, magnifying glasses, color wheels, and prisms can be kept in clearly labeled boxes. The boxes should be stored on shelves labeled with pictures and words so children can remove and return materials to their original place. Children will begin to take responsibility for the proper care of these materials.

- **A sunny windowsill**, where children can water and care for a variety of plants and seedlings

To keep the science activity center dynamic and interesting to children, the materials, displays, and themes should be rotated and changed whenever the children begin to lose interest in them.

Active exploration should form the core of the preschool science curriculum. Science experiences lead to the development of lifelong skills. Examples of skills and how they may be applied include the following:

- *Observing* Temperature, wind, clouds, colors, shapes, textures, smells.

- *Questioning* What will sink? What will float? Where can I find a bird's nest? How fast will the snow melt?

- *Comparing* Which container will hold the most? Which seeds grow the tallest?

- *Classifying* Gather a collection of leaves. Then put all the smooth leaves in one bag and the rough leaves in another bag.

- *Communicating* Tell us a story about a snake. Draw a picture of our garden. Tell us how to keep the blocks from falling off the truck.

Science Materials

Collecting appropriate materials for the science activity center is a continual process that should involve children, parents, teachers, and community members. Letters to parents and local businesses can include lists of materials needed, and monthly newsletters can acknowledge contributions. Recyclable materials, such as Styrofoam trays, plastic cups, empty soda bottles of all sizes, assorted bottle caps, cardboard pieces, wood scraps, and fabric squares are all useful materials for creative technological challenges.

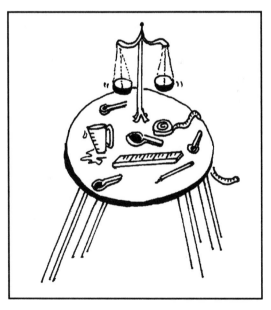

A master list of needed science supplies can be posted in the classroom. When something is donated, cross it off the list. Parents can keep up with classroom needs by looking at the list on a regular basis.

The following is a partial list of useful materials for a preschool science activity center:

Aquarium	Glue	Rubber bands
Baking soda	Hammers	Rubber tubing
Balance	Hand lenses	Sand paper
Barometer	Hourglass	Scales
Batteries	Kites	Screw drivers
Beans and seeds	Liquid soap	Screws
Bolts and nuts	Locks and keys	Shoe boxes
Bones	Magnets	Small cages
Buckets	Measuring cups	Sponges
Candles	Nails	Spoons
Clocks	Old magazines	Stethoscope
Coffee cans	Plastic bags	String
Compass	Plastic cups	Sugar
Dry soap	Pliers	Sundial
Egg cartons	Popsicle sticks	Thermometer
Food coloring	Potting soil	Toy boats
Funnels	Prism	Watering can
Fur	Pulleys	Wood
Gardening tools	Rocks	Yarn

Integrating Science Skills with Activity Centers

The Step by Step Program organizes classroom equipment and materials into activity centers that encourage children's play and work. Science skills can be integrated into each activity center. For example:

The **Literacy Activity Center** provides opportunities to use children's observations of a classroom pet to compose a story, create picture books about clouds and weather, or compose a song about the feeling of sunshine on a cold day. Books on animals, plants, machines, weather, and other science topics should be displayed.

The **Block Activity Center** provides opportunities to compare how many small blocks are needed to balance four large blocks, to place a group of blocks in order from smallest to largest, or to design a building as tall as the children. Planks and boards can be used as ramps for small balls or vehicles to roll down. The block center could become an insect colony, an ant city, or a beehive.

The **Dramatic Play Activity Center** provides opportunities to experiment with different situations, observe how adults behave and to imitate them in play, and test ideas and consider change. Games can be encouraged such as, "What Would Happen If. . .?" This game allows children to act out different scenes such as, "What would happen if the mouse got loose?" "What would happen if the lights went out?" "What would happen if the snow was so deep that it came over the top of our boots?" or, "What would happen if you became an ant? . . . a bee? . . . a caterpillar?"

The **Outdoor Activity Center** provides a wealth of opportunities to integrate science skills. Drawing tree shadows, comparing the color of leaves, turning over a rotting log, looking for footprints in the mud, listening to birds, observing ants and other insects, and growing a garden are a few examples.

The Teaching Team's Role

In *A Sense of Wonder* (1956) Rachel Carson wrote about the role of the preschool science teacher:

> *I sincerely believe that for the child, and or the parent seeking to guide him, it is not half so important to know as to feel. If the facts are the seeds that later produce knowledge and wisdom, then the emotions and the impressions of the senses are the fertile soil in which the seeds must grow. The years of early childhood are the time to prepare the soil. Once the emotions have been aroused — a sense of the beautiful, the excitement of the new and the unknown, a feeling of sympathy, pity, admiration or love — then we wish for knowledge about the object of our emotional response. Once found, it has lasting meaning. It is more important to pave the way for the child to want to know than to put him on a diet of facts he is not ready to assimilate (p. 45).*

An effective science teacher knows that young children quickly perceive the teacher's attitude about science. If the teacher is excited about exploration, asks questions, and demonstrates the "let's find out" attitude basic to science learning, children absorb and model that enthusiasm.

In the beginning, the science teacher's role is to help the children observe common objects and events. Once the children have fully investigated these objects and events, additional materials are presented. The role of the teacher is to provide interesting materials work and play — to encourage children to question as they manipulate the materials and to begin to find ways to find answers to their questions. As children feel the textures of different soils in an activity center, they may begin to question why they are so varied. The responsive teacher would then provide magnifiers, assorted rocks, containers of water, and other materials that children might use to experiment. Providing materials and time to experiment and guiding activities will encourage children to discover answers to their questions.

When confronted with new materials, children pass through three predictable stages:

- The first is a **period of experimentation**. The duration of the experiment period will vary, depending on age, ability, and previous experience. The child will explore the materials using all senses — sight, touch, smell, and, with the teacher's or adult's consent, even taste.

- The second stage is the **introduction of necessary vocabulary** related to the new materials. The vocabulary is best introduced while the new materials are actually being used. The teacher might ask open-ended, probing questions such as: "What can you tell me about this?" or, "How are you going to do that?" or, "What are some different things you could try?" During these exchanges, it is important for teachers to value children's views of the world and listen carefully to their inventive meanings for words and ideas. The teacher provides new language, helps the child by writing about the material, encourages the child to draw pictures, and reads stories about the materials.

- The third stage involves **identifying a problem**, often a question that the child has posed during the discussion. After the problem has been identified, the teacher encourages the child to search for solutions or answers.

Using soil exploration as an example, the new materials might include buckets of different types of soil (rich organic garden soil, hard–packed clay, and sandy soil), spoons and trowels, plastic containers, a source of light, wooden shelving, radish seeds, and a watering can. The vocabulary encompasses soil characteristics, including color, texture, smell, and plant nutrients. The teacher might ask, "What will happen if the three soils get wet?" or, "What is the best way to plant radish seeds?" He might encourage the exploration of a question raised by a child that leads to experimentation with the materials. The teacher supports this process by providing and organizing the materials, observing the children at work with the materials, and asking questions to encourage the children to explore the materials as deeply as they are able. Teachers can use their observations to modify and extend the children's thoughts and help them grow toward a better understanding of the phenomenon.

Science Activities and Projects

The Classroom Museum

A classroom museum gives children the opportunity to see and handle interesting materials. Collect rocks, feathers, leaves, teeth, seeds, shells, bark, fur, fabric,

insects, and other objects. Use boxes of various sizes, egg cartons, and plastic containers to arrange and store the collection. It is essential that the children have opportunities for interactions with the objects: observe, compare, classify, predict, and communicating. This interaction can be encouraged through guided discovery. For example, the teacher can suggest: "Let's find out which rocks will make a mark on tile or cement."

Introducing live animals into the preschool classroom offers many excellent opportunities to develop science skills. Most children are fascinated by living things. Setting up a small aquarium with a secure top to hold beetles, crickets, or caterpillars and butterflies can enrich the preschool science curriculum. A collection of live animals in the classroom offers children the experience of caring for the animals, determining their food, water, and shelter needs, and comparing the classroom habitat to the animal's natural habitat. The teacher can keep a classroom journal of children's observations of the behavior of classroom animals. She must stress the need to care for and respect animals. Insects and animals from nature should be returned to their natural habitats after a short period of classroom observation.

The class may create a seed museum that features a favorite seed or seed pod chosen by each child. Children can classify seeds by size, color, texture, or shape. They can put seeds with a rough texture on a piece of sand paper and place smooth seeds on a piece of typing paper. Different colors of construction paper could be used to classify seeds according to color. Children can use pictures of flowers to try to match seeds with the plants they come from.

Outdoor Science

The experiences of young children's day-to-day lives provides the content for the early childhood science curriculum. Children take an active interest in exploring objects and phenomena that they encounter in their surroundings. Children need time to tell others what they see, what they think, and what it makes them wonder about. As teachers provide materials for guided discovery they should set aside time for students to talk about what they are observing and for comparing observations. Teachers are encouraged to have children work in small groups, in teams, and individually. Teachers should take care to model respect for living things.

The school grounds or a local park provide year–round opportunities for children to develop science skills. Special planning is required to canvass the community to determine what sites are available, how the children will work in the outdoor classroom, and whether parents are available to help. Sending a note to parents informs them of the objectives and gives them an opportunity to be involved.

Themes are used to focus the activities in the outdoor classroom. For example, the neighborhood plant study could include walking around the school or community and observing different types of plants — where they grow, how they are shaped, how they are similar, and how they are different. The teacher can make a list of children's questions about plants, reframing their comments as questions to extend their ideas. The teacher can also model how to begin to find answers. For example, she can ask, "Is the plant growth on the north side of the building different from that on the south side?"

Exploring local trees might be a theme. Children can gather leaves from each different tree and, with the help of the teacher or parent, create a book of mounted leaves on clear plastic wrap or waxed paper. Children can do bark rubbings with paper and crayons to compare texture from tree to tree. Winter buds can be examined and seasonal changes in a particular tree observed. Collect stories about the activities of animals observed on or near a tree.

Weather observations and comparisons can be a regular feature of the outdoor classroom. What can the children see that is affected by the wind? Where do the leaves go in the wind? Where does the water go when it rains? Who has left tracks next to the mud puddle? Which materials in the playground feel hot after they have been in the sun? Which feel cool?

Children can observe ants. Where are they going? What kind of food do they like? Will they be attracted to a piece of apple or a piece of bread? Can children follow the ants' path on a sidewalk with a piece of colored chalk? Can children move and communicate like the ants?

Water

Most young children like to explore water. They bathe in water, drink water, and like to play with it. After a rain shower, young children, and even older children and adults, take pleasure in stepping into every puddle they can find. Exploration with water includes the concepts of sinking, floating, and absorbing. Children begin to understand that water is a necessary element for living things.

Some concepts about water that are useful for teachers as they plan a water activity center for young children include the following:

- **Water evaporates.** Guide the children's observations of water in a container on the radiator, not on the radiator, in direct sunlight, and in complete shade. Paint a sidewalk or chalkboard with water and observe the drying process. Which surface will dry faster? What happens if you add salt to the water or use hot water?

- **Water is needed to maintain most plant life.** Observe the differences between two plants, one watered and one not watered. Start some seeds in two similar containers with similar soils. Provide water for only one of the containers.

- **Water can mix with some liquids and not mix with others.** Mix water with milk, juice, salad oil, honey, or other liquids. (Clear plastic containers with lids provide good mixing and observing vessels.) Which other liquids would the children want to mix with water?

- **Water soaks into some materials.** Put water on different types of fabric, different types of paper, and other materials to observe the rate of absorption.

- **Rain and water from melted snow flow in streams and rivers.** Walk around the school or neighborhood to observe where the rain water goes. Observe a local stream and write a story about what you see. Is there evidence of birds or fish? Is the stream polluted?

Water can be used to investigate and manipulate physical properties. Provide children with opportunities to explore the physical properties of water by gradually introducing containers, funnels, spoons, tubing, sieves, sponges, and floating materials. A sink, plastic dishpan, children's pool, or metal tub can be used. Additional materials include food coloring, soap, and materials to do sinking and floating experiments.

Magnets

The concept of magnetism — that magnets create a magnetic field or force of attraction or repulsion — can provide young children with many opportunities to develop numerous science skills. Experimenting with magnets, iron filings, and other metal objects helps to develop observation, comparison, predicting, and communication skills.

One good way to manage the iron filings is to create magnet boxes. Magnet boxes are small boxes made of cardboard or clear plastic. (The latter is more effective for seeing results.) Place iron filings in the box and cover it with heavy plastic wrap. Seal the box completely with clear tape. The sturdy, escape–proof box can be used by children to move a magnet along the outside of the box and observe the reaction of the iron filings to the magnetic pull. Magnet boxes allow children to work independently with magnets and iron filings. A team of parents can help assemble enough magnet boxes for a small group or the whole class.

A related idea is to have the children draw a city, including the network of streets, on a paper plate. Small model cars, made of metal or with metal glued to the bottom, can be directed along the road network by moving a magnet along the back of the paper plate.

Magnetic attractions can also be part of an art activity. Use small boxes to confine this activity. Cut paper to fit inside the bottom of the box. Drip several drops of paint on the paper. Put a small metal object, such as a paper clip, on the paint drops. By sliding the magnet underneath the bottom of the box a design is created. For variety, change objects or add another color of paint.

By testing classroom objects and objects brought from home, children can create a classroom list of the characteristics of magnetic objects — which are attracted, or not attracted. Predicting whether an object is magnetic or not can lead to further discussion and experimentation.

References

Almy, M. (1986). Spontaneous play: An avenue for intellectual development. In *Early childhood play: Selected readings related to cognition and motivation.* New York: Associated Educational Services.

Bredekamp, S., & Rosegrant,T. (1992). *Reaching potentials: Appropriate curriculum and assessment for young children.* Washington, DC: National Association for the Education of Young Children.

Bredekamp, S. (1987). *Developmentally appropriate practice in early childhood programs serving children from birth through age eight.* Washington, DC: National Association for the Education of Young Children.

Beaty, J. (1996). *Skills for preschool teachers.* Englewood Cliffs, NJ: Prentice-Hall, Inc.

Brooks, J., & M. (1993). *In search of understanding: The case for constructivist classrooms.* Alexandria, VA: Association for Supervision and Curriculum Development.

Bronfenbrenner, U. (1975). "Is early intervention effective?" In B. Friedlander, G. Sterrit, & G. Kirk (Eds.), *Exceptional Infant: Vol.33 Assessment and Intervention.* (pp.449–475). New York: Brunner/Mazel.

Caney, S. (1972). *Toy book.* New York: Workman Publishing Company, Inc.

Carson, R. (1956). *A sense of wonder.* New York: Harper and Row.

Charney, R. (1992). *Teaching children to care.* Greenfield, MA: Northeast Foundation for Children.

Cohen, D., & Rudolph, M. (1977). *Kindergarten and early schooling.* Englewood Cliffs, NJ: Hall, Inc.

Cohen, D., & Stern, V. (1974). *Observing and recording the behavior of young children.* NY: Teachers College Press.

Cooking in the Head Start Classroom — An everyday affair. (1979, March). Parkersburg, West Virginia Head Start Training Office Newsletter. p. 2–10.

Dewey, J. (1938). *Experienced education.* New York: Macmillan.

Dodge, D.T., & Colker, L.J. (1991). *The creative curriculum for family day care.* Washington, DC: Teaching Strategies.

Dodge, D.T., & Colker L.J. (1988). *The creative curriculum for early childhood.* Washington, DC: Teaching Strategies.

Fortson, R.L., & Reiff, C.J. (1995). *Early childhood curriculum: Open structures for integrated learning.* Needham, MA: Allyn and Bacon.

Frost, J. & Jacobs, P. (1995). 'Play deprivation: A factor in juvenile violence." *Dimensions of Early Childhood*, 23 (3), 14–39.

Galambos, J.W. (1974). *A Guide to Discipline.* Washington, DC: National Association for the Education of Young Children.

Glassman, M. (1994). "All things being equal: The two roads of Piaget and Vygotsky." *Developmental Review, 14, 186–214.*

Goodwin, M, & Pollin, G. (1974). *Creative food experiences for children.* Center for Science in the Public Interest. Washington: DC.

Greenspan, S., & Greenspan, N. T. (1989). *The essential partnership.* New York: Penguin Books.

Hansen, K., Kaufmann, R. & Saifer, S. (1996). *Education and the culture of democracy: Early childhood practice.* Washington, DC: Children's Resources International.

Hansen, K.A. (1987). *Mental health in Head Start: It's everybody's business.* Department of Health and Human Services, Head Start Bureau. Washington, DC: Government Printing Office.

Hansen, K.A. (1987). *Join in: Play is free and fun.* Lubbock, TX: Institute for Child and Family Studies, Texas Tech University.

Harste, J. (1989). *Creating classrooms for authors: The reading-writing connection.* Portsmouth, NH: Heinemann.

Hartley, R. (1964). *Understanding children's play.* New York: NY.

Heath, S.B., & Taylor. (1983). *Ways with words: Language, life and work in communities and classrooms.* Cambridge, England: Cambridge University Press.

Hobbs, N. (1984). *Strengthening families*. San Francisco: Jossey-Bass.

Isenberg, J., & Jalongo, M. (1993). *Creative expression and play in the early childhood curriculum*. New York: Macmillian Publishing Company.

Johnston, M. (1982). "Strategies for a successful parental involvement program." In *How to involve parents in early childhood education*. Provo, Utah: Brigham Young University Press.

Lowery, F. (1979). *The everyday science sourcebook*. Boston, MA: Allyn and Bacon, Inc.

McIntyre, M. (1984). *Early childhood and science*. Washington, DC: National Science Teachers Association.

Marrow, L.M., (1989). *Literacy development in the early years: Helping children read and write*. Englewood Cliffs, NJ: Prentice Hall.

Marzollo, J. & Lloyd, J. (1972). *Learning through play*. New York: Harper & Row.

Montessori, M. (1965). *Spontaneous activity in education*. New York: Schocken Books.

Murphy, L. B., & Leeper, E.M. (1972). *Preparing for change*. Washington, DC: U.S. Department of Health, Education and Welfare

National Council of Teachers of Mathematics Curriculum and Evaluation Standards for School Mathematics Addenda Series Grades K–6 (Kindergarten Book).

Piaget, J., & Inhelder, B. (1969). *The psychology of the child*. New York: Basic Books.

Platts, M. (1966). *Create a handbook for teachers of elementary art*. Benton Harbor, MI: Educational Services, Inc.

Prelutsky, J. (1990). *Something big has been here*. New York: Scholastic Inc.

Restak, R.M. (1984). *The brain*. New York: Bantam Books.

Saifer, S. (1990). *Practical solutions to practically every problem*. St. Paul, MN: Redleaf Press.

Seefeldt, C., & Barbour, N. (1994). *Early childhood education: An introduction*. New York: Macmillan College Publishing.

"Setting up for cooking". (October 1994). *Early Childhood Today*. New York: Scholastic, vol. 9, 2.

Sheehy, E. D. (1974). *The fives and sixes go to school*. New York: Henry Holt & Co.

Southern Iowa Economic Development Association. (1986). *Parent handbook*. Ottumwa, IA: Author.

Taylor, T. D. (1996). *Promoting cultural diversity and cultural competency checklist*. Washington, DC: Georgetown University Child Development Center (UAP).

U.S. Department of Health and Human Services, Head Start Bureau (1992). *A guide for providing social services in Head Start*. (DHHS Publication No. (ACF) 91-31188). Washington, DC: Government Printing Office.

U.S. Department of Health and Human Services, Head Start Bureau (1991). *A handbook for involving parents in Head Start*. (DHHS Publication No. (ACF) 91-31187).

U.S. Department of Health and Human Services, ACYF, Region VII (1991). Program instruction PI-92-03: Client confidentiality for Head Start programs. Kansas City, MO: Author.

U.S. Department of Health and Human Services, ACYF, Head Start Bureau (1986). *A guide for education coordinators*. Washington, DC: Government Printing Office.

U.S. Department of Health and Human Services, ACYF, Head Start Bureau (1986). Mainstreaming preschoolers series. (DHHS Publication No. (OHDS) 86-31115). Washington, DC: Government Printing Office.

Wadsworth, B.J. (1979). *Piaget's theory of cognitive development*. New York: Longman, Inc.

Williams, R.A., Rockwell, Robert E., & Sherwood, E.A. (1989). *Mudpies to magnets*. Mt. Rainier, MD: Gryphon House, Inc.

Wolfe, B. (1986). Motivating parents: Workshop materials. Portage, WI: Cooperative Service Agency #5 (Unpublished material).

Wolfe, B., Griffin, H., Zeger, J., & Herwig, J. (1982). *Training guide: Development and implementation of the individual service plan in Head Start*. Portage, WI: Cooperative Service Agency.

York, S. (1991). *Roots and wings*. St. Paul, MN: Redleaf Press.

PUBLICATIONS BY
CHILDREN'S RESOURCES INTERNATIONAL

Creating Child-Centered Classrooms: 3–5 Year Olds — curriculum and methods for teachers of children ages three to five

Creating Child-Centered Classrooms: 6–7 Year Olds — curriculum and methods for teachers of children ages six and seven

Creating Child-Centered Classrooms: 8-10 Year Olds — curriculum and methods for teachers of children ages eight to ten

Education and the Culture of Democracy: Early Childhood Practice — a book explaining the link between democracy and early childhood teaching

Early Childhood Faculty Seminar: Individualized Teaching — a university-level course designed for use by early childhood education faculty

Early Childhood Faculty Seminar: Learning Through Play — a university-level course outline designed for use by early childhood education faculty

Early Childhood Faculty Seminar: School and Family Partnerships — a university-level course outline designed for use by early childhood education faculty

Early Childhood Faculty Seminar: Child-Centered Curriculum — a university-level course designed for use by early childhood education faculty

Early Childhood Faculty Seminar: The Study of Children Through Observation and Recording — a university-level course outline designed for use by early childhood education faculty

CHILDREN'S RESOURCES INTERNATIONAL
2262 Hall Place, NW
Suite 205
Washington, DC 20007

(202) 625-2508
(202) 625-2509 fax

email: CRIInc@aol.com